The West Bank—Is It Viable?

The West Bank-Is It Viable?

Vivian A. Bull
Drew University

Lexington Books
D.C. Heath and Company
Lexington, Massachusetts
Toronto   London

Library of Congress Cataloging in Publication Data

Bull, Vivian A
   The West Bank—Is it viable?

   Bibliography: p.
   Includes index.
   1. Jordan (Territory under Israeli occupation, 1967-   )
2. Israel-Arab War, 1967—Occupied territories. I. Title.
DS127.6.03B84   956.95'04   74-33978
ISBN 0-669-99143-0

Published simultaneously in Canada

Printed in the United States of America

International Standard Book Number: 0-669-99143-0

Library of Congress Catalog Card Number: 74-33978

To my parents
Lydia and Russell Johnson,
with love and appreciation

Contents

List of Figures

List of Tables

Preface

For some years, prior to the establishment of the State of Israel in 1948, the tensions between Arab and Jew in the area of British Mandate Palestine foretold what was to be a long period of attack, counterattack, and a continuing state of war. Between 1948 and 1967, Israel accomplished something of an economic miracle in setting up and operating a state that was totally cut off from all her neighbors and almost completely dependent upon the rest of the world—particularly the Jewish diaspora—for economic support and sustenance.

During this same time period, the Arab world and particularly the Hashemite Kingdom of Jordan was also advancing in both economic and social terms, but the rate of growth and the level of development lagged far behind that of Israel. In the early years of nationhood, Israel depended upon Western immigration to provide job skills, high levels of technological knowledge, and academic training; the Arab world had to "buy" all such advancement. Israel learned and benefited from the experience in both agricultural and industrial development of the Western world while the Arab world seemed to have to learn by trial and error.

In Jordan, aid from foreign countries was encouraged and readily accepted, but frequently projects became bogged down in governmental red tape or because there was the necessity of training and teaching job skills before work could be undertaken. Also, greater emphasis was placed on industrial development of the territory east of the Jordan River, which, until 1928, did not even have any governmental structure. The Arabs in the territory west of the Jordan, known as the West Bank Territory, had known a different way of life. These inhabitants were not of the Bedouin tribes, but were indigenous Palestinians, many of whom were refugees from the 1948 war. They had long been settled in urban contexts, had learned the way of government, and were more highly educated and trained than their East Bank counterparts, but they were treated as a minority and a "conquered people" by the ruling authorities—the Turks, the British, and the Jordanians—of various periods.

In June 1967, at the end of the Six Day War, the West Bank found itself in the hands of yet another occupier: Israel. This time, the occupier found it desirable and necessary to improve the economic conditions—particularly in the agricultural sector—of the occupied people, which was an extremely expensive undertaking in both economic and social terms for the occupier. However, no matter how benevolent an occupier, there will still be suffering, discontent, and hope for self-determination on the part of the occupied.

It was only a matter of months after the June war when it became obvious that there was to be no early settlement or, for that matter, even attempts towards negotiations. The world began to consider alternative solutions to the problem of the West Bank Territory. Why not establish the West Bank as an independent state, to serve as a buffer between Israel and Jordan and the rest of the Arab world? Some in Israel thought that this might also be an opening to the Arab world for possible trade and might lead to eventual Arab recognition of the State of Israel. The response to this suggestion, both within Israel and the Arab world, was a highly emotional and usually a politically oriented response. Some months later, however, after a long period in which no direct negotiations were undertaken, King Hussein of Jordan proposed a federation in which the West Bank would become an independent state. Responses again were more emotionally charged than rationally oriented. People were concerned with the societal implications, the political realizations, the religious aspects of the problem, but few raised the important question of whether or not the West Bank would have economic viability.

In October 1974, the Rabat conference and subsequent events refocused attention upon the West Bank. By this time, another party—the Palestine Liberation Organization (PLO)—had entered the scene. Political independence is meaningless without economic independence. Could such a territory ever be economically independent? It was this aspect of the problem that arrested my attention.

My first trip to the Middle East was in the summer of 1957, when I spent some six weeks in various Arab countries and in Israel. In 1960, I returned as a staff member of the Drew-McCormick Archaeological Expedition, which was working at the site of ancient Shechem, just east of present day Nablus. Over the next fifteen years, during ten different trips to the area that varied in length from three months to fifteen months, I had the rare opportunity of observing a society move from perhaps a seventeenth- or eighteenth-century way of life in terms of European industrial development into that of the twentieth century. The rural areas were going through a period of adjustment which had been experienced in the Western world over several generations but had occurred in only a few years in the Eastern world.

Were the people of the Territory ready for independence? It would be, of course, most difficult to gauge the sociological and psychological readiness of a people, but surely there would be the possibility of investigating the economic aspects of independence—or so I thought. The original hypothesis to be evaluated was that the West Bank Territory can become an economically viable independent state. I was immediately faced with two problems. First, what is meant by economic viability? Economists tend to talk about states becoming economically viable and then remaining so. It would be necessary to examine various concepts and measures of economic viability and to determine whether any would be relevant for evaluating the potential of the Territory. The second problem was more formidable: the gathering of economic data needed for a reasonable evaluation.

In Chapter 1, we examine the question of viability and see that it is not a measure that is important in our considerations, but rather the constraints upon the nation itself. The size of a nation may place constraints upon viability. The West Bank Territory, which is smaller than the state of Delaware, is approximately 2,350 square miles. Trading relations with neighboring states may place constraints upon viability. The economies of Israel and the West Bank Territory are becoming integrated, particularly in the agricultural sector. At the same time, the West Bank is trading with Jordan, and via Jordan, with other Arab states. To maintain these relations would require some form of political settlement between Jordan and Israel, with some form of accommodation for the Palestinians of the Territory. The role that will be played by the PLO requires further definition.

In preparation for this project, I read a considerable number of general works on the economics of growth and development as well as a variety of studies on particular areas mostly classified as underdeveloped or developing nations. With few exceptions, the works dealt mainly with the economic problems and relegated discussions of various social, psychological, and religious problems to footnotes or referred to them only in a casual way. It seems that in the Middle East and perhaps in the West Bank Territory, in particular, these problems are of great importance and frequently may be of more significance than many of the economic data. For this reason I have attempted to weave considerations of sociological and cultural factors into the overall design of the project. The desire for growth is a precondition for the promotion and achievement of growth and development, and the willingness of a people to undertake the implicit and explicit costs of development is closely related to their social, cultural, and religious environment. The last of these is of crucial importance for the Middle East. I believe that there is a predisposition towards development on the part of the West Bankers. There are, however, many obstacles to be overcome.

Chapters 1 and 2 examine theoretical considerations relevant to viability and the history of the Territory and introduce some of the more important non-economic problems which condition development. Chapter 3 deals with general economic conditions. Subsequent chapters deal with explicit economic sectors: agriculture, industry, and human resources and labor. Chapter 7 considers some particular sociopolitical problems of the area including the future of Jerusalem, the fate of the refugees, and Israeli settlements in the Territory. Chapter 8 presents the conclusions.

This study was originally prepared as a dissertation and submitted to the faculty of New York University Graduate School of Business Administration. I would like to express my appreciation to the members of my dissertation committee and particularly to Dr. Robert G. Hawkins and Dr. Gearhard Bry who not only continually encouraged me to persevere but provided direction; to Dr. Don Patinkin and Dr. David Amiran of Hebrew University who gave me new insights to the problems and who directed me to sources of information and data; to members of the Research Department of the Bank of Israel for discussions and data; and to my many Palestinian and West Bank friends who, over the years, have contributed immeasurably to these analyses. I assume, however, full responsibility for any errors of omission or commission, as well as for the interpretation of the material.

I would like to express my appreciation to those who assisted in the preparation of the manuscript: David Palmer of Drew University and Shibley Kharman of Jerusalem for drawing the maps and figures; Paul and Yasuko Grosjean of Drew University who assisted at various stages; the typists of Drew University and Dan Bleicher of Jerusalem for hours of typing.

And finally, my appreciation to Alice Glock whose loving care of the children gave me free hours for work; and to the family, my husband Robert and the boys, Camper and Carlson, who bore up nobly under the pressures of my study.

1
Some Concepts of Development Theory and Their Bearing on the Economic Prospects of the West Bank Territory

In recent years, a vast literature has been written on the problems of economic development and growth. Much of this literature reflects, for social as well as economic reasons, a strong concern for the glaring disparities in income and wealth between developed and less developed nations. There are two main motivations for the study of underdeveloped countries. The first, influenced by the pressure of postwar international tensions, deals with the need to alleviate poverty in underdeveloped nations. The second—of a more academic nature—is concerned with attempting to understand the differences that exist among nations, and how these affect growth and development.[1]

It is beyond the scope of this study to examine the literature of development theory in general, but it is necessary to describe and examine some concepts that are of relevance to any consideration of the economic prospects of the West Bank Territory. Let us therefore consider some aspects of developmental theory that are important to the general topic. We shall discuss measures of comparative national income and growth, classification of developmental stages, economic and social conditions of development, alternative paths of development, and related governmental policies. We shall also deal with some specific problems, such as the importance of the size of a nation for its development options and the concept of economic viability.

Measures of Development: Levels and Changes

One traditional way of gauging the economic development of a nation is to compare its per capita national income with some standard, such as the corresponding income level of a developed country or of a group of developed countries. The per capita income measure is subject to a variety of qualifications. Many underdeveloped or developing nations have a large degree of barter in their economic activity. Much agricultural effort is undertaken by family units for self-consumption or barter, and this output is not included in the measures of per capita income. Specifically, in the West Bank Territory, many farms are tended by women and children while the men seek employment elsewhere. Even the smallest of children are often at work in the fields. No wages are paid and no statistics collected. Furthermore, foodstuffs have been exchanged between vil-

1

lages under barter arrangements. Although the terms of barter are established by current market prices, the barter is nowhere recorded as a market transaction. There are other reasons related to statistical compilation problems–why many of the per capita income figures for underdeveloped countries are very crude and subject to wide margins of error. Furthermore, low income per capita is only one aspect of the complex problem of underdevelopment.

Income measures the output available for use by the community but does not necessarily reflect standard of living. Any measure of standard of living falls short of an income measure insofar as the former refers not only to the part of income that is allocated to current consumption, but also refers to certain extra dimensions such as life expectancy, availability of doctors per capita, conditions of employment and similar indicators of the way in which human existence is conditioned and enriched.[2]

Stages of Development

Some authors have attempted to describe the development of countries within the framework of so-called "stage" theories, which suggest that, historically, the growth of most economies follows fairly uniform patterns. The German historical school stressed the stage theory, with different theoreticians emphasizing transition along different lines of development. More recent theories have been developed by W.W. Rostow and A. Gerschenkron.

Rostow's system[3] has five stages: (1) traditional society, (2) preconditions, (3) take-off, (4) the drive to maturity, and (5) high mass consumption. There are certain difficulties in attempting to use Rostow's theory, however. While it may not be difficult to define the periods using historical data, it is far more difficult to decide where a country is currently in the sequence of periods. Also, at an early point in the process, it may be difficult to predict how far any one stage will carry, or whether there may be slowdowns and spurts within a period. Rostow's facts are questioned by some historians, and the inevitability of the transitions from one stage to the next is questioned by historians and economists alike.[4] But his emphasis on the discontinuity between the static equilibrium of the traditional society and the dynamics of growth–that is, on "take-off"–has attracted widespread attention.

In attempting to apply Rostow's theory to the West Bank Territory, we find that the multi-dimensionality of the stage definitions makes application of the theory to a specific area difficult. Even so, the classification is suggestive. It is possible to identify each of the first three stages in the Territory's development (see Chapter 5, The Industrial Sector). Simon Kuznets points out this problem when he says that Rostow's stages are considerably blurred.[5] Much of what Rostow would attribute to the take-off, Kuznets argues, has already occurred in the preconditions stage. The traditional stage presumably does not see a rise in the investment ratio from 5 to 10 percent; yet both the agricultural revolution, which Rostow assigns to the preconditions stage, and the building up of the infrastructure, which is also assigned to the preconditions stage, in themselves would involve substantial increases in investment.

Alexander Gerschenkron[6] developed a stage theory which may be more applicable to the developing nations in general, and to the Territory in particular. Gerschenkron's theory differs in two ways from Rostow's. First of all, a fixed set of preconditions is neither necessary nor sufficient. Also, conditions can substitute for each other. As one production factor can substitute for another in neoclassical growth models, so can conditions facilitating growth in actual development. If there is a lack of entrepreneurship, for instance, government can provide the necessary organizational leadership.

Another difference between the two theories is very important. According to Gerschenkron, growth need not trace the same set of stages in each country. The more backward a country, the more it will rely on governmental, as against private, decision making, and the more readily it may short-cut the slow growth path of the more developed nations. This approach extends a greater degree of hope for the developing nations, for the time span for growth can be shortened. The West Bank Territory, for instance, is very dependent upon Israel for technology, know-how, and general planning. Particularly in the agricultural sector has the time span for growth been shortened because of the expertise of the Israel Department of Agriculture and the willing cooperation of the Territory's farmers.

Conditions of Development

To understand the quantitative and qualitative differences in levels and modes of production and the conditions of change, we must examine the underlying factors of production. Hence, we will discuss some developmental conditions with regard to labor force characteristics, entrepreneurship, capital requirements, and social overhead.

The labor force of underdeveloped countries is distinguished by characteristics with respect to birth rates, skills, education, and attitudes of workers. Typically, skills are low, education is lacking, and factory discipline unknown. To achieve rapid growth, not only technological knowledge and capital are necessary, but a large highly trained and responsible labor force is needed. A great deal of time and money is required to create a trained workforce and to develop attitudes conducive to large-scale industrial production. This condition becomes particularly important when we deal with the Middle Eastern Muslim population, which is steeped in religious traditions that conflict with the desired characteristics.

A developing country needs not only skilled laborers, technicians and researchers, but management personnel and Schumperterian entrepreneurs who are willing to innovate and to assume risks. There must be a desire for growth in order for growth to occur. Some countries which are poor in natural resources have been able to develop with judicious use of capital, labor, and technology—though most resource-poor developing countries must rely on help from outside their own borders. Lack of resources can be overcome.

The need for capital is an omnipresent problem for developing countries. If it cannot be generated internally (as is done by the oil-rich countries), then a country must rely upon the international community, with capital being supplied either by individual countries or by one or more of the international financial institutions. There is a desperate need for capital in the West Bank Territory but because of political uncertainty and instability, more than for any other single reason, this need is not being met. Apart from factor characteristics there are other conditions of growth, but these may vary with the specific circumstances of each country.[7]

Limits of a Purely Economic
Approach to Development

The subject of economic development goes far beyond the usual confines of economic analysis. The economic historian knows that any account of a nation's economic development efforts embodies its entire cultural history. Traditional economics is usually concerned with the immediate determinants of an economy's potential output: the state of technology and knowledge, the quantity and quality of the labor force, the quantity and composition of the capital stock, and the nature of natural resource conditions. Within this framework, the rate of development depends upon the degree of utilization and the rate of increase of these various productive means. But even within this relatively narrow approach, many difficulties arise. It is impossible to express quantitatively many significant characteristics of these productive factors, such as the role of motivation in the productivity of the workforce. When one attempts to trace the causes of changes among the productive factors, one becomes involved in a myriad of social, political, and economic forces. These forces can not be arranged in any neat hierarchy of cause and effect, for all of them are interrelated.[8]

Although there is much discussion about providing the underdeveloped countries with the material infrastructure such as transportation systems and power stations, there has been less concern with the problem of the social and institutional infrastructure as a necessary precondition to growth. "The developmental process is by no means solely or even predominantly an economic affair, but has profound psychological, political, social and cultural as well as economic implications."[9] One cannot change one feature of society without affecting others. So, to discuss development, it is necessary to attempt to achieve an over-all view of the process.

Theories of broad cultural change in which attempts are made to analyze both economic and noneconomic factors do exist. Consider, for example, the works of Marx and Schumpeter. Max Weber was concerned with sociological, political, and religious problems as they affected the economy.[10] Sombart, who emphasizes "the spirit of capitalism" as the creative force in the evolution of modern capitalism, Pareto, who develops a general cyclical theory of social change, as well as Parsons are all sociologists or economists who study development within a general socioeconomic framework.[11]

In the 1950s, a project known as the "Inter-university Study of Labor Problems in Economic Development", was organized by four economists: Clark Kerr, John T. Dunlop, Frederick H. Harbison, and Charles A. Myers.[12] A variety of separate studies was undertaken by the four organizers, as well as by a number of scholars from both American and foreign universities. The various projects were concerned with the complex problems of labor and management in economic growth. The studies found, among other things, that man appeared to be more readily adaptable to the industrial system than had been anticipated and that pre-existing cultures were not serious impediments to economic development.[13] Family and religion, the two immutables, were able to make adaptations. This is very important in our consideration of the West Bank Territory, for there appear to be certain tribal relationships and certain aspects of the Islamic religion that tend to mitigate against adaptation to a society in transition as a result of economic development. The Israeli agronomists found to their surprise and delight that the West Bank farmers were eager to learn new methods and adopt new technologies. Adaptation has been more successful in the agricultural sector than in the industrial sector. This is curious since, characteristically, moral beliefs and habits are more deeply ingrained. It may be that the results of modern agricultural methods are more highly visible in the country-side. Also decision making is easier when done by relatively small rural production units.

The Inter-university Study examined the economic aspects of labor and management within the general sociocultural structure. The most crucial determining factors for the formation of the labor force and the development of management appeared to be the population situation, the starting point of industrialization, the pace of economic growth, and the strategies of the industrializing elite. Along with development came the rise of the nation-state and the importance of nationalism as a very real force.[14]

The foregoing discussion underlines the need to consider a variety of problems that must be foremost in any analysis concerning the development of the West Bank Territory. Because of the social, cultural, religious, and political problems in the Territory, purely economic factors are of less relative importance than they would be in most other development discussions.

Industrialization as a Condition for Development: Balanced versus Unbalanced Growth

It is widely assumed that in order to become economically viable, a developing nation must become industrialized. There are other alternatives, and Kindleberger proposes the possibility of meaningful balanced growth, where growth takes place in both the agricultural and industrial sectors.[15] The problem with this version of balanced growth is that most underdeveloped countries cannot manage simultaneously an investment program in industry and the needed investment in agricultural improvements. A.O. Hirschman has argued that deliberate unbalancing of the economy, in accordance with a predesigned strategy, is the best way to achieve economic growth.[16] Hirschman does not deny the need for the big push, but he argues that the ability to invest is the one serious bottleneck in underdeveloped countries, and this is partly true as there has been no tradition of investing. The application of the balanced growth theory requires large amounts of precisely those abilities which are most likely to be very limited in supply in underdeveloped countries. So Hirschman develops a plan for unbalanced growth by placing emphasis on selected pacesetting industries which could in turn stimulate allied industries.[17]

The West Bank Territory is following a pattern of unbalanced growth which is atypical, for it is in the agricultural sector where there has been significant growth, rather than in any part of the industrial sector. We shall examine the implications of this in later chapters.

Problems of Industrialization: Capital Requirements and Entrepreneurship

The problems of industrialization that a developing nation faces are many. "Economists recognize that an investment of the order of 12–15 percent of the net national income is necessary if it is intended to diversify and advance a backward economy by the development of secondary and tertiary opportunities."[18] But capital investment, as we have already discussed, is only one part of industrialization, or as Simon Kuznets notes: "The major capital stock of an industrially advanced country is not in its physical equipment; it is the body of knowledge amassed from tested findings and the capacity and training of the population to use this knowledge effectively."[19]

Many developing countries have small enterprises which are of a workshop type rather than of a factory character. This implies a lack of modern, low-cost methods of production and distribution, a lack of economies of scale, and operations which are labor intensive rather than capital intensive. Industrial development seems to be characterized by the propagation of such plants; they play an important part in the economy, but they do not, in themselves constitute industrialization. In developed countries, a distinctive feature of growth has been entrepreneurship: the emergence of a relatively small body of persons who are quick to discern opportunities and willing to promote and advance industrial undertakings despite the attendant risks. Underdeveloped countries lack such individuals as they have no tradition of entrepreneurship and hence no training in the development of such a quality. Therefore, the use of foreign knowledge and entrepreneurial ability, as well as of foreign capital, is a characteristic of the spread of industrialization. We shall discuss these problems further in Chapter 5, The Industrial Sector.

The Form of Industrialization:
Industrial Composition
and Infrastructure

The selection of industries, the nature and scope of their operations, and the order of their introduction are influenced by limitations including scarcities of skilled labor, of capital, of markets, and of foreign exchange. Transportation facilities and transportation costs are also important factors. The Territory is land-locked and without an airport (the Kalandia airport has now been included in the extended boundaries of Jerusalem) and is therefore without access to the export market, except through either Israel or Jordan via the open bridges.

The development of some industries may encourage the development of related industries, and there appears to be a pattern of industrial growth in most countries, especially those not well endowed with fuel and ore supplies: first comes the development of food processing industries based on local agricultural raw materials and the proximity to market.

The next industries to develop are typically based on wood products such as furniture making, and industries connected with construction and derived from local mineral resources: cement, prestressed concrete, bricks and tiles, sanitary ware, glass, pottery and crockery. Assembly industries follow, made possible by cheaper transport costs of importing component parts to be assembled locally to make, for instance, bicycles or motor vehicles. And then other industries appear with less substantial bases and more hazardous lives: consumer goods industries making textiles, clothing, footwear, soap, and cigarettes. All of these are established in Rostow's pre-take-off period and all are generally restricted in character and scale by limited labor, capital, skills, and public utilities.

The development of an adequate industrial infrastructure should be the responsibility of the government: increased transportation facilities at minimum costs, adequate electrical grids and water supplies, a communications system,

and adequate arrangements for marketing and export relations. The government
should adjust tariffs so as to aid developing industries, supply loan funds at low
interest rates, subsidize goods seeking export markets, grant exemptions from
certain taxes in order to stimulate new investment, and offer preferential treat-
ment by special government orders.

Rosenstein-Rodan argues that if the government supplies the necessary
social overhead capital for an underdeveloped country, then this will provide the
basis on which private enterprise can proceed with directly productive investment.[20] Chapter 5 considers further problems related to development of the
infrastructure, with particular reference to the West Bank Territory.

Social Aspects of Industrialization
in the Middle East

In a study done by the United Nations on Middle East development problems, it was found that many of the difficulties of industrialization in this area
stem from the average worker's comparatively recent rural or Bedouin origin.[21]
The conflict between traditional values and new values of industrialized society,
between old loyalties and a new way of life creates anxieties and tensions in the
worker and tends to make him an unstable and sometimes an untrainable member of the labor force. Many of the workers of recent rural origin are ill prepared,
educationally, socially, and technically for industry. These conditions tend to
hamper productivity growth.

These workers have ingrained attitudes of distaste for manual labor, even if
it is of a technical nature, and they prefer classical educations and white-collar
employment. This deprives the labor market of many potentially trainable and
highly productive elements.

There are also other socioeconomic and cultural factors which weaken a
worker's commitment to industry and further lower his productivity: poor
housing conditions, substandard health and medical facilities, lack of adequate
management, and small workshop-type industries run by familial interests. To
raise potential productivity and enhance development, massive attempts by
government must be made to raise the professional, social, educational, and
health standards of the worker. The principal efforts must be aimed at providing
education and vocational training, including out-of-school training programs,
establishing schemes of social insurance and social services, and adopting pro-
gressive labor legislation and employment policies. There are few comprehensive
social policies related to the existing industrial development programs for the
West Bank. Israel has, however, extended many of the social benefits which
Israelis enjoy to the West Bankers who work in Israel. She has established some
regulations for the health, safety, and general working conditions of laborers,

developed vocational training centers and services, extended social welfare benefits to those residents working in Israel, and in the refugee camps, has made some attempts at improving housing. There has been a complete lack of planning for industrial development, and this is part of a larger political problem discussed below.

On the other hand, industries must provide basic health and safety measures in industrial plants, provide insurance for workers against industrial hazards, provide apprenticeships, on-the-job and accelerated training, and perhaps even share in the provision of transportation, housing, recreational, and cultural services. Industry in the West Bank has not responded to any of these responsibilities, with the exception of apprenticeships and training. But the nature of the industrial installations, small workshop-type establishments, employing only a few laborers, would mitigate against the possibility of fulfilling many of these responsibilities. In the near future, these provisions will therefore have to be supplied or augmented by the government.

Workers' organizations such as trade unions need to play a larger role in planning for the development of industry and related social services and must provide direct services to the workers. Some members of the Territory's labor force are unionized, but most of the workers receive their representation through the Labor Exchange offices.

The Size of Nations

There is yet another factor that differentiates developing countries: the size of the nation. Much theorizing about growth either explicitly or implicitly assumes a large closed economy model. It is, however, important to differentiate sharply between the growth process in a large, closed economy and that in a small, open economy.

Early interest in this problem developed in the 1950s and was associated with the debates on European economic integration. The problem continued to be of importance with the emergence of a number of small independent sovereign nations in the Caribbean, in South East Asia, and in West and Equatorial Africa. Particular works to be cited are the Symposium of the International Economic Association on the Economic Consequences of the Size of Nations[22] and the work of Demas on economics of development in small countries.[23]

The definition of size purely in terms of population and land area omits two important dimensions of the problem. The first dimension is per capita income, which when combined with numbers of population, gives aggregate purchasing power. The second dimension of size is access to foreign markets.[24] Aggregate income is more relevant to a wide range of development problems than per capita income and becomes increasingly important when we discuss

potential sources of investment. Access to foreign markets is of utmost importance to the West Bank Territory and will be a basic consideration in evaluating
the future status of the Territory.

Small countries, however defined, are prevented from highly diversifying
their economies and hence must rely heavily upon imports. Domestic markets
provide insufficient outlets, so they must also rely upon exports. The size of the
country does impose certain constraints on the pattern of growth and hence on
the character and degree to which such growth can be self-sustaining. The pattern
of growth in a very small country is different from that in a large continental
country. Resources in a small country are likely to be highly concentrated while
the composition of domestic demand for goods and services will be highly diversified. Most small countries, therefore, will have a concentrated composition of
exports and a diversified structure of imports. Economies of scale reinforce
these tendencies and make it necessary to produce for a market wider than the
domestic market.

Small countries must deal with the implications of size and the associated
economies of scale. First, though it may be desirable to have research carried
out on adapting technology to the requirements of small markets, such research
will pay off only in the long term, and perhaps no successful adaptation will be
possible. Second, plants of either sub-optimum size or plants operating below
the most efficient level involve extensive investment in terms of resources and
manpower and imply high costs. Furthermore, tariffs and trade restrictions may
limit the markets for production that the domestic market cannot absorb. Third,
there may well be significant economies of scale in basic governmental administration for countries above a certain size. This may also apply to other utilities,
such as telephone, water, and electrical systems.[25]

It has been suggested that in order for a small nation to benefit from economies of scale, which are generally only available to large nations, a small nation
could participate in a free trade area, customs union, or economic union. There
are two kinds of economies of scale to consider: (1) internal economies due to
an increase in the size of a firm and (2) external economies due to a more favorable geographical concentration of firms.[26] An increase in the size of firms
should lean to cost reductions, since better internal division of labor is possible,
as well as the use of more modern technology. Large firms seem to be more
capable of improvement and are more likely to have better access to capital required for development and modernization. Tibor Scitovsky in analyzing this
aspect of the problem has especially stressed the concepts of optimal and sub-
optimal investment. Many small firms use sub-optimal equipment and so are
usually not able to operate with the least costly method of production and
hence do not realize economies of scale. Scitovsky also argues that sub-optimal
equipment is not only a current handicap for the firms but endangers their future position, for it is feared that when demand increases new investment will
also be sub-optimal since existing entrepreneurs, for various reasons (including

lack of a spirit of competition), may not be anxious to try to expand their markets to the detriment of other firms.[27] Under these circumstances, an expansion of the small nations' markets by complete trade liberalization within a sufficiently large area and a return to the competitive spirit should enable small nations to realize economies of scale. A firm that can maintain its position under competitive conditions will be able to sell more cheaply due to economies of scale and lower costs may lead to increased demand and thus to increased production.

It is also possible that external economies of scale can be realized with a larger geographical area for distribution. Certain other improvements may be achieved as a result of a free trade area, customs union, or an economic union: development of service and supply industries, improvement of transport facilities and lower transport costs, an ample supply of labor—both skilled and unskilled—and possibly a better distribution of investment. The benefits of economies of scale might be available to small nations, depending upon the small nation's relations with its neighboring states. If a small nation were able to enter into some type of trade agreement, then it might be able to realize some of the benefits enjoyed by large nations. The problem, of course, is that this decision is not within the unilateral powers of any given small nation.

If a formal free trade area, customs union, or economic union is not feasible because of political considerations, as may be the case in the West Bank Territory, then some of the benefits discussed above may also be achieved through economic integration—a policy which Israel is carrying out in the administered areas. "Progress towards freer trade involves essentially the acceptance of specific limitations on the interference of political power in economic life, as a way to defend the interests of the group subject to that political power."[28] Triffin argues that contrary to general opinion, free trade can exist within areas that are not subject to the same political sovereignty. Various countries may be able to accept a partial pooling of their economic sovereignty sufficient to reduce—or even eliminate—national barriers to their mutual trade. "The economic significance of national boundaries may change as a result of economic integration as well as of political integration among the participating countries."[29] Triffin argues that regional cooperation may be a possible solution to the economic problems faced by small nations. This cooperation, if successful, may gradually evolve towards the actual merging of areas too small and too interdependent on one another to preserve national welfare. This idea will take on added significance in our discussion of the West Bank Territory.

Another problem that the development of regional areas poses is the establishment of an operative monetary system. The theory of optimum currency areas defines the optimal region as one within which there is factor and trade mobility and from which there is factor immobility. It argues that each such region should have a separate currency and monetary system, independent from the currencies of other areas.[30] However, a currency domain is usually an expression of national sovereignty, and thus regions are usually not economic units and the currency area is not an optimal one.

Even though Israeli banks have branched into the West Bank Territory, they still have a relatively small share of total monetary activity. There are two currencies in circulation, but with the Jordanian dinar being the preferred currency, there is little financial market integration with Israel. If the development of the infrastructure, for instance, will depend upon capital from Israel, it will require an inter-currency transfer which may inhibit capital flows from the region with which the labor and commodity markets are most closely integrated. There are certain political constraints which might preclude an extension of integration with the Israeli financial system. If there were one monetary system with equivalent bank coverage, West Bank borrowers might be discriminated against by Israeli banks. Yet the growing involvement of Israel in the West Bank's activities may require a relatively greater acceptance of the Israeli currency and banking services.

Economic Viability

In the literature of growth and development, little concern has been paid to the determination of economic viability. Bhagwati in *The Economics of Underdeveloped Countries* states that "historically, nations seem to have a tendency to become economically viable and to remain so."[31] But how does one measure viability, or determine when that state has been attained? Eliyahu Kanovsky, in an extensive study of *The Economic Impact of the Six Day War*, attempts to deal with this problem in relationship to those countries most directly affected by the war.[32]

The term "economic viability" is widely used though poorly defined. Kanovsky offers a variety of definitions.[33] If economic viability refers to a basic independence of foreign aid, then few developing nations would be considered to be economically viable. If the term implies a reduction in the balance-of-payments deficit, again few countries would be viable. Viability might be measured by the development effort of a country: this would involve measuring the ratio of investment to GNP or the ratio of investment to total available resources. It would seem that most frequently writers imply that economic viability involves rapid growth of production and income accompanied by a reduction in unemployment—that is, a period in which a country strives to reach a point at which balance of payments and budgetary deficits begin to decline thereby reducing dependence on foreign aid.

All of these considerations enter the broad concept of viability as it will be used in this book. A country will be regarded as economically viable if its economic characteristics permit it to experience sustained economic growth and rising welfare per capita and if its economic processes function well enough to permit a modicum of social and political stability; conversely, economic viability requires political and economic conditions that permit growth and development.

It is possible that an area such as the West Bank Territory could become economically viable, though it would not necessarily be economically independent. Viability for the West Bank Territory may be wholly dependent upon the relationship between the Territory and the neighboring states, Israel and Jordan. As the process of economic integration between Israel and the administered areas continues, this element of close economic ties with neighboring states takes on added significance. Economic viability must encompass not only consideration of resource development, but also some consideration of the effects of international trading relationships.

Methodology

It would have been most desirable if this study of the West Bank Territory could have followed the format used by J.E. Meade in his evaluation of the Island of Mauritius.[34] Meade examined the economy of Mauritius in great detail through an adequate quantity of data on agricultural products and productivity, precise data on industry, and growth trends in population, labor, and emigration. He was able to evaluate the financial sector and make estimates of the potential for development and growth of the economy.

Unfortunately, this method was not possible for our study because of the lack of data. Economic data prior to 1967 are not readily available for the West Bank Territory. It was not until the 1950s that the Hashmite Kingdom of Jordan began a systematic collection of data for the country as a whole. *The First Census of Population and Housing*[35] was not published until 1961. In 1967, the Food and Agriculture Organization Mediterranean Development Project published a report on Jordan[36] with data on the country, but all of the data were for the nation as a whole, and it was almost impossible to obtain data for the West Bank Territory or for the areas of Judea and Samaria. It was possible for one to make rough estimates of agricultural product, contribution to gross national product, and so forth if one had knowledge of land under cultivation, or the number of industrial establishments, and so forth. However, the reliability of these estimates is dubious.

Data for the Territory are available from 1968 on. Within weeks of the June war, the Central Bureau of Statistics of the State of Israel began preparations for a demographic survey of the administered areas. It was undertaken with all the expertise of the Bureau, but discussions with representatives of the department raised questions as to the reliability of the data. In January 1971, the Central Bureau of Statistics began issuing a publication, *Monthly Statistics of the Administered Territories.* It was published through 1972 and then it was issued as a quarterly publication. *The Israel Economist*, a monthly economic review, includes a section of "Business Notes on the Administered Area" in each issue and occasionally publishes special review articles on the areas. These are usually based upon government data that are not readily available elsewhere. The Bank of Israel publishes an annual review, *The Economy of the Administered Areas*. The June 1974 publication for the calendar year 1972 contains the following comment in the Introduction: "As the economic ties between the administered areas and Israel grow stronger, the statistical reliability of annual data decreases, making it more difficult tó analyze each economy separately."[37]

There have been some econometric models developed in recent years for various Middle Eastern countries, and early in the study of the problem these models were consulted.[38] Again, however, because of the lack of data and the lack of continuity in the data, it was not possible for us to make any use of these models, or to construct a model based on the conditions in the Territory. The fluctuations evident in our limited data are short run, not long-run fluctuations, and growth models cannot be developed on such information. Even informal models would be affected by the dominance of these short-run variations. Furthermore, the rapid and unpredictable changes in the Territory's conditions would defy any assumptions of structural stability or orderly progression. Finally, no model would be able to handle the most serious constraint in our study –the sociopolitical elements and their effects upon the future of the West Bank Territory.

It was therefore necessary to use analytical description, in the Mitchellian sense, as the major approach to the study of the Territory. Though this approach may not be the most desirable for formulating forecasts or predictions, it was the only possible approach, given the existing conditions.

The course of this study will be to examine in depth that area known as the West Bank Territory. Within the context of growth, the major sectors of economic activity will be investigated while bearing in mind the importance of the particular sociopolitical and cultural influences that exist in the Territory. An attempt will be made to evaluate the question of whether an area so constituted could be considered economically viable.

Notes

1. H. Myint, *The Economics of the Developing Countries* (London: Hutchinson University, 1967), pp. 9ff.
2. Jagdish Bhagwati, *The Economics of Underdeveloped Countries* (London: World University Press, 1966), pp. 11ff.
3. W.W. Rostow, *The Stages of Economic Growth* (Cambridge, England: Cambridge University Press, 1961).
4. Charles P. Kindelberger, *Economic Development,* 2nd ed. (New York: McGraw-Hill Book Company, Inc., 1958), p. 57.

5. Simon Kuznets, "Notes on the Take-Off", in W.W. Rostow, ed., *The Economics of Take-Off into Sustained Growth* (New York: St. Martin's Press, Inc., 1963).

6. Alexander Gerschenkron, *Economic Backwardness in Historical Perspective* (Cambridge, Mass.: Harvard University Press, 1962).

7. See also W. Arthur Lewis in *The Theory of Economic Growth* (London: Allen and Unwin, 1959) on the attitude of the people of a developing nation towards growth: a strong desire for growth is a major precondition for growth.

8. Gerald M. Meier and Robert E. Baldwin, *Economic Development* (New York: John Wiley and Sons, Inc., 1962), Chapter 6.

9. William L. Polk, *Developmental Revolution* (Washington, D.C.: The Middle East Institute, 1963), p. 3.

10. See the three-volume study *Economy and Society,* edited by Guenther Roth and Claus Wittich (New York: Bedminster Press, 1968).

11. Meier and Baldwin, *Economic Development,* p. 123.

12. See Clark Kerr, John T. Dunlop, Frederick H. Harbison, and Charles A. Myers, *Industrialism and Industrial Man* (Cambridge, Mass.: Harvard University Press, 1960), which reports on the approach and general findings and includes a bibliography of the work published.

13. Ibid., pp. 8–9.

14. See also Gunnar Myrdal in *Asian Drama, An Inquiry into the Poverty of Nations* (New York: The Twentieth Century Fund, 1968). Myrdal is consciously concerned with value premises and valuations as preconditions for shaping concepts and forming the framework for research.

15. Kindelberger, *Economic Development.* See also Alan B. Mountjoy who stresses that simultaneous emphases must be placed on the development of both industry and agriculture: *Industrialization and Underdeveloped Countries* (Chicago: Aldine Publishing Co., 1967).

16. A.O. Hirschman, *The Strategy of Economic Development* (New Haven, Conn.: Yale University Press, 1958).

17. Myrdal has discounted the propagative effects of such pacesetters and believes that they are apt to remain industrial islands surrounded by stagnation.

18. Mountjoy, *Industrialization and Underdeveloped Countries,* p. 87.

19. Simon Kuznets as quoted in *Processes and Problems of Industrialization of Underdeveloped Countries* (New York: United Nations Press, 1955), p. 5.

20. P.N. Rosenstein-Rodan, "Problems of Industrialization of Eastern and Southeastern Europe," *The Economic Journal,* June-September, 1943.

21. *Studies in Selected Development Problems in Various Countries in the Middle East* (New York: The United Nations, 1968). The countries included in the study are Iran, Jordan, Kuwait, Lebanon, Saudi Arabia and Syria.

22. E.A.G. Robinson, ed., *Economic Consequences of the Size of Nations* (New York: St. Martin's Press, Inc., 1960).

23. William G. Demas, *The Economics of Development in Small Countries with*

Special Reference to the Caribbean (Montreal: McGill University Press, 1965).

24. Ibid., p. 42.
25. Ibid., passim.
26. G. Marcy, "How Far Can Foreign Trade and Customs Agreements Confer Upon Small Nations the Advantages of Large Nations?" in Robinson, *Economic Consequences of the Size of Nations,* p. 276.
27. Ibid., passim. See also Tibor Scitovsky, "International Trade and Economic Integration as a Means of Overcoming the Disadvantages of a Small Nation," in Robinson, *Economic Consequences of the Size of Nations,* pp. 282ff.
28. R. Triffin, "The Size of the Nation and Its Vulnerability to Economic Nationalism," in Robinson, *Economic Consequences of the Size of Nations,* p. 263.
29. Ibid.
30. Robert A. Mundell, *International Economics* (New York: The Macmillan Company, 1968), p. 185.
31. Bhagwati, *The Economics of the Developing Countries,* p. 9.
32. Eliyahu Kanovsky, *The Economic Impact of the Six Day War* (New York: Praeger Publishers, 1970), pp. 422ff.
33. Ibid., p. 422.
34. James E. Meade, *The Economic and Social Structure of Mauritius* (London: Methuen Press, 1961).
35. *The First Census of Population and Housing* (Amman: The Government Press, 1961).
36. *FAO Mediterranean Development Project: Jordan Country Report* (Rome: FAO, 1967).
37. *The Economy of the Administered Areas 1972* (Jerusalem: Bank of Israel, 1974), Introduction, p. 3.
38. M.A. Cook, ed., *Studies in the Economic History of the Middle East* (London: Oxford University Press, 1970); and Khaled A. Shair, *Planning for a Middle Eastern Economy* (London: Chapman & Hall, 1965).

2

The West Bank Territory: History, Geography, and Cultural Development

History of the Territory

In order to understand the current political situation in Jordan and Israel it is necessary to examine, at least briefly, some of the history of that part of the world.[1]

Man first appeared in the area that today forms the territory of Israel and the Hashemite Kingdom of Jordan at least 200,000 years ago. This is the estimated age of the oldest stone artifacts found in Palestine. Archaeological evidence attests to the racial intermingling of Neanderthal man and a more advanced Cro-Magnon man—the ancestor of modern man. As man progressed from the Old Stone Age to the New Stone Age some 8,000 years ago, building concentrations began to appear, the earliest of which have been excavated at Jericho.

In the Neolithic period (about 6,000 to 4,500 B.C.) man produced great stone structures of monumental dimensions. Copper appeared as a basic material and a great advancement in tools and weapons took place. This marked the beginning of the Bronze Age, which saw the development of cities and city states, of agricultural and pastoral skills, of arts and crafts, of a complex mythology and religion, and of a syllabic script. The language was a predecessor of South Canaanite, to which Biblical Hebrew is closely related.

The second pre-Christian millennium was the period during which Abraham and his family roamed the Palestinian uplands (nineteenth to eighteenth centuries B.C.) and during which the Egyptians expelled the Hyksos from Palestine (sixteenth century B.C.). In the thirteenth century B.C. several Semitic speaking peoples occupied the area and established settlements in the Kingdoms of Moab, Edom, Ammon, Samaria, Judea, and others. The Hebrew tribes settled a century later along the banks of the Jordan and ruled the area from 970 B.C. until they were defeated by the Assyrians in 722 B.C. and by the Babylonians in 586 B.C. After the decline of Assyria, the Nabateans (a desert people) built up an empire centered in magnificent Petra, a city carved from living rock. They built their empire by taxing travelers on the major caravan routes north and south and east and west. For years they resisted the Greeks and the early Romans but finally surrendered in A.D. 106. It was more than 1,800 years before the peoples east of the Jordan River knew another indigenous independent government.

It is interesting to note the influence of these earlier periods on the Jordanian Arab today. The almost legendary period of the Hebrew prophets, all of whom are honored as prophets by the Muslim tradition, left an indelible impression on Jordanian Arab folklore and folk belief, whereas the Greek and Roman periods have left few traces in the memory of the people.[2] The ruins of the great Hellenistic and Roman cities still testify to their artistic, technological, and religious civilization, but their way of life and way of thinking have never become a part of the Arab consciousness. The Nabatean culture, a mixture of Arab and Greco-Roman elements, and the influence of the alliance of the Hellenistic Decapolis have all passed and have left only spectacular ruins as a testimony to what they had been.

While the Nabateans ruled the south, the northern areas were disputed over by the Selucids, the Ptolomies, the Maccabeans, and the Romans. For the Western world the most important event in the area was the coming of Jesus and the Christian era. After Rome fell in A.D. 476, the area remained under Byzantine control and was extensively Christianized. The decisive historical event that more than anything else molded the character of Jordan as it appears today was the Arab Conquest of 636 that brought the entire region south of Aleppo into the Islamic faith.

The Arab Conquest marked a turning point in the history of the Levant, and its impact was so strongly embedded that future non-Arab and non-Muslim conquerors were able to introduce no significant modification in their way of life, their thinking, or their attitudes and values. Even the century-long rule of the Crusaders left little lasting imprint on the society. Islamic thought and the Arab language have remained though rulers have come and gone.

The Ottoman Turks ruled the area for 400 years (1517 to 1918), and though the Turks were also Muslim, they too left little impression. Except for the last 75 years of rule, they did little more than collect taxes or dispense subsidies to the Bedouin for safe conduct through their territories.

It is impossible in so short a space to discuss the historical experience of the people of the area of present-day Jordan. The area lies along an important highway connecting Syria and the adjoining lands in the north; with Arabia and Egypt in the south. Located as such, the area was frequently conquered and held by various powers. The archaeological remains show evidence of cities being built, destroyed, and rebuilt as tribes moved from the north to conquer the south or vice versa. The recurrent and continuing battles and exploitations denuded the land and reduced the people to a state of poverty. Famines, epidemics, petty wars, and uprisings characterized conditions on both sides of the Jordan well into the nineteenth century.

It was in the nineteenth century that the East and West Bank territories of the River Jordan were undergoing distinctly different historical experiences—experiences that may explain much of the contrasting personality and mentality that characterize the fellahin (West Bank) on the one hand and the Bedouin (East Bank) on the other. Except for a small area between the Jordan and Yarmuk Rivers where some settlements were established, the peoples on the rest of the East Bank, or Transjordan, were largely unsettled, the land uncultivated, and the nomadic Bedouin patterns of life undisturbed by Turkish authorities. They remained basically independent of any external political or administrative authority and were loyal only to their sheiks and their tribes.

However, in the area that we call the West Bank Territory, life was considerably different. Most of the population was settled, living in villages, and working the lands. These people were at the mercy of Turkish authorities and tax collectors. The only alternative to submitting to the Turkish oppression and exploitation was to flee to the desert—hardly a viable alternative. During the nineteenth century, these peoples again came in contact with the Western world. In an earlier encounter, the Arabs were the highly cultured urbane people and the Franks were the barbarians, but in the nineteenth century, the descendents of the Crusaders appeared as representatives of a culture that in its material aspects seemed superior to that of the descendents of the Saracens. Before long, the banking institutions, civil and religious establishments, mercantile institutions, mining concessions, and the rudimentary public utilities were owned and controlled by foreigners. And so a territory loosely governed and without fixed boundaries passed into the hands of the British after the defeat of Turkey in 1918.

Since the Balfour Declaration issued on November 2, 1917, had contained a statement that "His Majesty's Government view with favor the establishment in Palestine of a national home for the Jewish People, and will use their best endeavors to facilitate the achievement of this object," it was felt that reference to this declaration should be incorporated into the British Mandate.[3] Therefore, prior to the League of Nations' approval, an article was included in the mandate that allowed Britain the right to withhold application of the Balfour Declaration to the territories east of the Jordan River. A thorough-going pacification program was undertaken, and Emir Abdullah eventually was able to subdue the desert peoples and begin to establish a unified government relying upon the leaders of the desert tribes to assume positions of responsibility. Territorial boundaries were negotiated over time and by installments, and beginning with the Organic Law of 1928, the formal basis of a constitutional representative government was prepared. Abdullah won the support and allegiance of the villagers and the Bedouin, and from these groups, he also recruited the Arab Legion. The urban nationalists were less enthusiastic in their support of the Emir, but the possibility of national independence and an elective government mollified them.

The outbreak of World War II did not directly affect Transjordan, but the country did greatly benefit by the fact that Britain, in need of reserve forces stationed in territories under its control, proceeded to build up and modernize the Arab Legion. Large numbers of Arabs fought in the British services as well.

In 1943–44, Britain made the implicit promise that she would grant Transjordan complete independence after the war, and in 1946, the United Nations was notified of this intent. The Treaty of Alliance, signed on March 22, 1946, recognized "Transjordan as a fully independent state and His Highness the Emir as the sovereign thereof."[4] There were provisions for military and technical assistance included in the treaty. In a second treaty negotiated in Amman in 1948, Britain's military prerogatives were reduced, but in exchange for certain options in event of war, Britain agreed to cover the entire cost of maintaining the Arab Legion.

On November 29, 1947, the United Nations General Assembly voted to recommend the partition of Palestine into an Arab and a Jewish state, with an economic union.

> The Arab state was to consist of Western Galilee, the east-central part of Palestine (Samaria and Judea, with the exception of a strip along the seashore, which was to form part of the Jewish state) from the Valley of Esdraelon down to Beersheba, a five-mile-wide strip along the Mediterranean from the latitude of Jerusalem down to the Egyptian frontier, and an irregular strip of land along the Egyptian border from the Mediterranean to about halfway to the Gulf of Aqaba–a total territory of about 5,000 square miles. Jerusalem and Bethlehem, with some adjoining territory, were to remain outside both states and form a trust territory under U.N. administration.[5]

The Jews accepted the resolution, but the Arabs rejected it and began to organize armed resistance. British troop withdrawals were completed by May 14, 1948, and the British mandatory government of Palestine was officially ended. On the same day the Jewish National Council declared the foundation of the independent State of Israel, which was officially recognized, in a matter of hours, by then U.S. President Harry S. Truman. The following day the Arab armies attacked. After a second truce was enforced, it was apparent that only King Abdullah's Legion had been able to hold its own against Israel. Abdullah was in control of the Old City of Jerusalem, and of two large areas extending from the Jordan River westward into the hill country of Samaria in the north and of Judea south of Jerusalem–that is, almost the whole of the territory that we refer to as the West Bank (see Figure 2-1). Though the Arab League opposed Abdullah's action, an armistice agreement between Israel and Transjordan confirmed Abdullah's hold over the territory. Abdullah renamed his country the Hashemite Kingdom of Jordan.

The annexation of the West Bank introduced changes in both the social structure and political life of Jordan. The Palestinian population, with the influx of the refugees, was twice as large as that of Jordan. But the main difference between the peoples was a result of the different cultural and social experiences they had during the Mandate period. The East Bankers lived under an Emirate where the old Muslim Middle Eastern traditions were undisturbed in the areas of

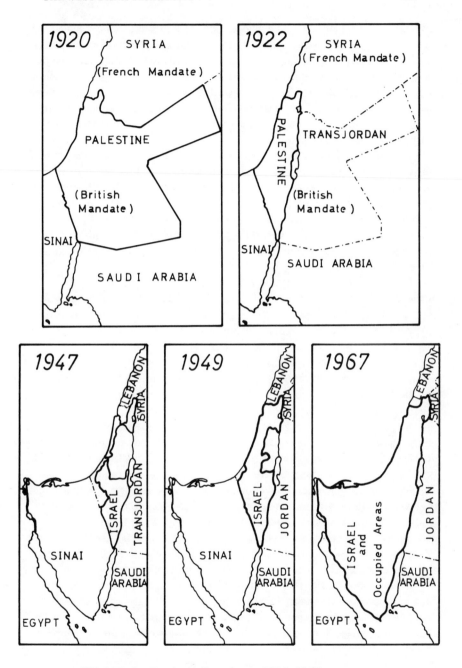

Figure 2–1. Border Adjustments, 1920–1967.

family, social, educational, and economic life. The nomadic, semi-nomadic, village, and agricultural infrastructures remained unchanged. On the other hand, the Palestinian Arabs were subject to direct and incisive influences exerted directly upon them by the Mandate government, the growing Jewish population, and the direct exposure to the Western world. As a whole, the West Bank population was more advanced in Westernization, more highly educated, more urbanized, and more experienced in political organization and activity. The resulting tensions were to be expected.

In many cases, the Palestinians with their special administrative skills were able to fulfill many needs in the new government but rivalries began to emerge. The Transjordanians resented the fact that the Palestinians, whose territory they had conquered and annexed, were able to take over, because of their superior qualifications, important positions in government, and professional life. The Palestinians resented the fact that though they represented two-thirds of the population, political and military power remained concentrated in the hands of the Transjordanians.

In spite of these internal problems, which frequently flared up in both major and minor disturbances, the Hashemite Kingdom of Jordan progressed well, almost wholly dependent on foreign aid for development, over the next nineteen years. Abdullah was assassinated in 1951, and, after a brief reign by his son Talah, his grandson Crown Prince Hussein was proclaimed king in 1952. Hussein has reigned since that time, on the whole moderately and effectively, and the fact that he is alive today in spite of periodic threats to his crown and life—from both internal and external sources—must attest in part to his ability as a diplomat.

But the tensions and rivalries of the early years of the Hashemite Kingdom of Jordan did not abate. The presence of large numbers of refugees on both sides of the Jordan, and the resentment felt in particular by the Palestinians towards Israel were a constant source of irritation in the political situation in Jordan. There were unceasing border incidents between Jordan and Israel, and although the Jordanian incursions into Israel were frequently small-scale attacks, the Israeli retaliation was slow in coming but always on a much larger scale. The impression left by such attacks as the ones on Kibya (October 1953) and Nahhalin (March 1954) was so intense that no moderate Jordanian politician ever dared advocate a compromise or a rapprochement with Israel.

In late 1966, relations with Israel underwent a marked deterioration as Arab raids into Israel, notably by the Syrian based al-Fatah and al-Asefa organizations, provoked sharp reprisals on Jordan. In December, there were armed clashes with Syria as Jordan attempted to prevent guerrilla infiltration through Jordan into Israel. Diplomatic relations with Syria were broken in May, but in the face of alleged Israeli military buildup, Arab unity was proclaimed prior to June 5, 1967.

In November 1966, after a massive Israeli attack on the village of Samua, disturbances erupted in the West Bank Territory and the Kingdom was on the verge of a civil war. The Palestinians charged that there was no Palestinian representation in the ranking positions of either the military or the police force and that the king was not interested in either defending or arming the border territories of the West Bank. A long curfew was imposed upon the West Bank, and after a series of discussions, Hussein promised to change his policies towards the West Bank and the Palestinians. It is important to note, however, that little positive action had been taken prior to June 1967 and that, as a matter of record, the Arab Legions did little to defend the territory, with the exception of Jerusalem, during the Six Day War. This failure to act has in no way aided the position of King Hussein nor increased his support among the West Bankers and the Palestinians.

It is beyond the scope of this study to examine the causes or course of the Six Day War. Suffice it to say that the Middle East has considered itself to be in a "state of war" since 1948 and that during this time, there were two periods when full-scale war was undertaken—during the Suez crisis in 1956 and again in 1967. When war did break out, Jordan was fully committed, and its forces were engaged almost immediately. By the third day of the Six Day War, Israeli forces had overrun the whole of Jordan west of the river to capture Bethlehem, Hebron, Jericho, Nablus, Ramallah, and Jenin, as well as the whole of Jerusalem. Of all the Arab states, Jordan suffered most heavily from the hostilities with 6,094 dead or missing, 200,000 new refugees for an already overburdened economy to support, and the loss of one-third of its most fertile land. Another legacy of the June War was a considerable increase in political instability in Jordan that was aggravated by the refugee problems and the activities of some of the guerrilla organizations bent on the overthrow of the Hashemite dynasty as a prelude to resuming the war with Israel. After a series of rebellions, revolts, and armed battles, the Jordanian Army took final measures in the summer of 1971 against the guerrilla strongholds and broke their power bases and influence in Jordan. King Hussein's authority was fully restored following a costly civil war-like struggle.

Though the fighting continued for six days, the course of the war was decided within the first few hours on June 5. From 7:30 a.m. on, the Israeli Air Force continually attacked Egyptian, Jordanian, and Syrian airfields and inflicted severe damage to both the fields and the aircraft on the ground. Even the Habbaniyah airfield in Iraq was attacked, and henceforth Israel had the immense advantage of complete mastery of the air. On June 6, the U.N. Security Council passed a resolution calling for a cease fire. On June 7, at 8 p.m., Israel and Jordan accepted the call; on June 8, Israel and Egypt accepted the cease fire; and finally on June 10, Israel and Syria agreed to the cease fire. At the conclusion of these agreements, Israel occupied all of the territory west of the Jordan River, the Gaza Strip on the coast, the Sinai peninsula, and the territory on the Syrian border known as the Golan Heights (see Figure 2-2). Within two

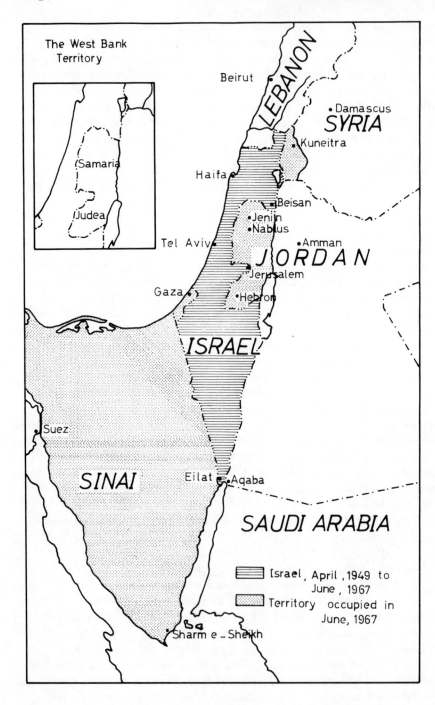

Figure 2-2.   Israel: 1949 Armistice Agreements and 1967 Cease Fire Lines.

weeks of the capture of Jerusalem, the Knesset (the Parliament of Israel) passed legislation making the Arab sector of the city an integral part of one municipal area.

A struggle developed within the United Nations. On July 11, Israel reported her acceptance of U.N. observers along the Suez Canal with the provision that observation posts were also established in the area held by the United Arab Republic. On the same day, Israel rejected a U.N. General Assembly resolution asking annulment of the unification of Jerusalem and said that the administration and municipal integration provided the legal basis for protection of the holy places. On July 14, the Assembly unanimously adopted a Pakistani resolution asking that Israel immediately rescind actions for unification of Jerusalem.

It soon became clear that the Assembly would not reach an effective agreement, and the Middle East question was referred back to the Security Council. The secretary general was instructed to work out with Israel and Egypt arrangements to station military observers in the Suez sector where Israel occupied the eastern bank and where shooting incidents were frequent. On November 22, 1967, the Security Council unanimously passed a British resolution that called for withdrawal of Israeli armed forces from territories occupied in the conflict; the acknowledgement of the sovereignty, territorial integrity, and political independence of every state in the area; and a just settlement of the refugee problem.[6]

In the meantime, a concentrated effort was being made to "normalize" living conditions in the occupied territories. In mid-July, excise duties were imposed upon local products of the West Bank region to equalize the prices between the occupied West Bank and "all other parts of the country" (Israel). In late July, the first groups of nearly 160 Jordanian refugees to return were officially repatriated to the occupied West Bank. On July 19, the West Bank courts began functioning in accordance with Jordanian law. And as early as August 2, the Israeli Director General of the Ministry of Agriculture, Ariel Amiad, outlined a new agricultural policy for the occupied West Bank. The Jordanian farmers were to be urged to shift to crops that would more easily exportable. The Ministry announced that a long-range plan was being prepared to facilitate the settlement of Arab refugees and to improve agricultural productivity in the occupied territories.[7]

Relations between Israel and its Arab neighbors remained extremely tense during the years following the Six Day War. Arab guerrillas, operating from bases in Jordan and Lebanon, committed numerous acts of sabotage in Israel and thereby provoked severe Israeli reprisals. Hostilities along the Suez Canal occurred with almost daily regularity, and there was intermittent fighting along the length of the Jordanian and Syrian borders. War-like activities increased in 1970 with Israeli bombers extending their raids to the vicinity of Cairo, as well as concentrating their efforts on the destruction of Soviet missile bases being established in the Canal area. In May, the Israeli Army made incursions into southern Lebanon to attack guerrilla bases, and in June, there was heavy fighting in the

Golan Heights against the Syrian Army. But during this same time, international activities directed at a cease fire were beginning to take shape.

On June 25, 1970, U.S. Secretary of State William Rogers launched a peace plan for the Middle East known as the Rogers Plan. A U.N. Mediator, Gunnar Jarring, conducted negotiations, and a cease-fire agreement was agreed upon by Israel, Egypt, and Jordan. The 90-day pact, which included a cease-fire agreement and a military standstill, came into effect on August 7. It was first extended until February 5, 1971, and a further extension remained in effect into 1973. Negotiations had hardly begun when charges of attacks and counterattacks were exchanged between Israel and Egypt, and Israel withdrew from the negotiations which were then suspended indefinitely. The talks were resumed in January 1971, but little further progress was made, other than it appeared that the talks were crystallizing around a proposal for the reopening of the Suez Canal and the retreat of Israeli troops for an unspecified distance into the Sinai Peninsula. As of the middle of 1973, no further discussions or agreements had been confirmed.

The fourth Arab–Israeli war started with a surprise attack launched by Egypt and Syria against Israel. The attack was made on Saturday, October 6, 1973–Yom Kippur (the Day of Atonement), the most sacred occasion in the Jewish religious calendar. There had been no political warning and the military warnings had not been fully evaluated by the intelligence specialists. The country was more unprepared psychologically than militarily. Israel took 72 hours to reach full mobilization strength, and, at first, the Israeli forces covering the Egyptian and Syrian frontiers were driven back. Israel launched a counterattack against Syria and by October 17 had driven to within 20 miles of Damascus. Then Israel directed her forces to the Sinai front. Egyptian forces had reacted too slowly to the counterattack, and on October 20, Israel executed a classic breakout from a bridgehead of armored warfare. By October 22, Israeli forces were within 50 miles of Cairo. Egypt secured a cease fire on October 22, but attempts of the Egyptian 3rd Army to break out led to renewed fighting. A final cease fire was negotiated on October 25, and on October 28, the direct negotiations (concerning prisoners of war) that began between Israel and Egypt constituted the first such contact since 1956.

This war was different from any previous Arab–Israeli encounters. Israel was forced to engage in relatively static battles of attrition rather than the mobile armored battles in which she excelled. The failure of the Israeli government to order mobilization until just before the war broke out created a major domestic political dispute. Israel appears to have underestimated the Arab's military capabilities, especially the morale of the troops, and she seems to have assumed that the Arabs would be as easily defeated in 1973 as in 1967. The Arabs, however, proved to be much more formidable opponents in 1973; they were able to take considerable losses and still keep on fighting. Military equipment and training provided by the U.S.S.R. had made a remarkable difference in the Syrian and Egyptian armies. Jordan and Iraq both came to the support of Syria after the war started, but neither committed their full forces.

The 1973 war, like all previous Arab–Israeli conflicts, ended politically inconclusively. All countries suffered heavy losses: Israel had over 4,000 killed and wounded; Egypt, 7,500; and Syria, 7,300.[8] On the initiative of the Soviet Union and the United States, peace talks were scheduled to be held in Geneva in December 1973. It was feared that the Arabs, having regained their self-respect, might be tempted to demand unacceptable concessions from Israel. Before the peace talks were effectively under way, Henry A. Kissinger, U.S. Secretary of State, had become an active intermediary between Israel and Egypt in bringing about a settlement—one in which neither side was forced to sacrifice or to lose face. Negotiations have continued on a variety of levels.

It had been feared that there might be an uprising within the West Bank Territory during or after the fighting in October, but none did occur. The population remained politically calm, and though there was a renewal of identity with the Arab cause and a corresponding increase in self-respect, few overt activities were recorded. Once peace negotiations were undertaken between Israel and Egypt, there appeared to be a renewed feeling of cautious optimism that some consideration might also be given to the future of the West Bank Territory. And then came the Rabat conference in October 1974. In spite of Jordanian objections, the Arab foreign ministers adopted a recommendation supporting establishment of a Palestinian state on the West Bank once Israel withdrew its troops from the area. The Palestine Liberation Organization (PLO) was recognized as having the right to create a Palestinian "national authority" on the West Bank. In November, King Hussein agreed to recognize a PLO government-in-exile and thus appeared to accept the general consensus in the Arab world, regardless of his previous position that he should be the one to negotiate with Israel on behalf of the Palestinians. Hussein declared that the Rabat decision would "compel Israel eventually to recognize the Palestinian reality."[9] The positions have been delineated, but the discussions have not gone forth.

Geography of the Territory

The West Bank Territory constitutes only 6 percent of the total area of Jordan; of approximately 2,350 square miles, the area is slightly smaller than the state of Delaware. It is divided by the Jerusalem corridor into a larger northern bulge which is roughly historical Samaria and a smaller southern area which is historical Judea. The central part of Samaria is a deeply dissected upland region with altitudes reaching 3,000 feet and with foothills falling down toward the east of the Jordan Valley and subsiding toward the west into the Sharon Plain (which is part of Israel). The only rock types exposed are limestone and chalky marl, with a few basalt dykes. Springs are not numerous and settlement is confined to the larger valleys, with the uplands being used only as pasture land. Many of the hillsides are planted with either crops or olive trees, and the ancient Roman terracing is still in use.

Judea is a barren, unbroken upland plateau with very few diversifying elements. Limestone and chalky marl are the predominant rock structures, often with no soil cover. Characteristic of the Judean wilderness are wide expanses of bare rock, numerous scattered boulders and scree, and small valleys carved in the hill slopes that are usually dry and barren and have numerous caves and underground drainage. Vegetation rarely consists of more than patches of scrub and thorns. On the Judean plateau, adequate soil coverage is rare, but where it does exist, it is of good quality. Cereals, fruits, and vegetables are grown, and conditions are particularly good for olives and grapes.

In the Samarian hills, olives and grapes are the leading crops, and cereals, figs, and some citrus fruit are also grown. On the dry, leeward side of the hills, sheep and goats (until banned by a Jordanian government decree) and cattle (used as a replacement for goat herds) graze.

The population in the West Bank is centered in and around a series of main towns which form an almost straight line from north to south in the middle of the uplands: Jenin, Nablus, Ramallah, Jerusalem, Bethlehem, and Hebron. The Judean Desert lies to the east of this line; barren, dusty, and practically uninhabited, it is an area in which only a few nomads can exist—with difficulty. Where there is adequate water, as in Jericho, irrigation allows for production on small intensely cultivated patches.

The climate of the hill country is similar to that of the eastern plateau: short, cool, rainy winters with occasional snowfall in the higher areas, as in Jerusalem, and long, hot, dry summers. In the hill country, there is an average of twenty inches of rainfall, and with relatively high humidity, evaporation is relatively low. The temperatures are mild, even, and rhythmic. The growing season lasts six to seven months with natural rainfall, but can be year-round with irrigation. In the Jordan Valley, there is less than two to five inches of rain annually, and the very low humidity results in a very high rate of evaporation. Temperatures are hot. There is virtually no rainfall farming season unless the area is immediately in the vicinity of an oasis, but the growing season can be year-round with irrigation. Generally, there is low productivity in the area, but potentially productive irrigation does exist.

In 1967, Jordan had an estimated population of 2.07 million, which included 977,000 West Bankers (40 percent) and over 720,000 refugees from Arab Palestine. Since the June 1967 war, some 350,000 persons from Israeli-occupied territories have become refugees on the East Bank. Though the West Bank constitutes less than 6 percent of the total area of Jordan (2,000 square miles within an area of 37,000 square miles), it contains about half of the best agricultural land in the entire country, most of the main urban centers (with the exception of Amman), and about 40 percent of the population. As of 1972, the West Bank had an estimated population of 634,000 inhabitants. This represents a 2.5 percent increase from 1971 (the rate of natural increase since immigration was not significant)[10] and is approximately 6.4 percent over the period from 1967 to 1972.

The geographical distribution and the mode of living of the population largely reflect the pattern of rainfall and cultivation. Nomads inhabit the desert and the steppe-country leading to the uplands, although a few are scattered through all other parts of the country. The settled population falls into two categories: rural and urban. The rural population dwells mainly in villages scattered throughout the areas where rainfall or irrigation make cultivation possible. The urban population is found in the larger towns and in the cities. Although these modes of living are fairly distinct in their pure forms, nomadism and village life merge among the semi-nomads, while the larger villages and smaller towns show characteristics of both rural and urban life.

Ethnically the population is homogeneous, nearly all being descendants of Semitic or mixed Arab-Semitic stock from northern Arabia. Over 93 percent of Jordanians are Muslim, predominantly of the Sunni branch of Islam. About 6 percent (100,000) of the population are Christians who have settled mainly around Jerusalem, Bethlehem, and Ramallah. The largest Christian Arab community is the Greek Orthodox, which numbers about 50,000. The rest are made up of Greek-Catholics, Roman Catholics (or Latin), and Protestants of various denominations. Non-Arab Christians include Armenians, Nestorians or Assyrians, and Syrian Orthodox. The Samaritans are an ancient Jewish sect who have lived in Nablus since the eighth century B.C. and who now number about 300.

There is a higher degree of urbanization among the Christian Arabs as compared with the Muslim Arab majority which is related to a number of differences. First, urban residence means that among the Christian Arabs there is a higher percentage of people engaged in non-agricultural occupations, such as commerce, crafts and industries, governmental service, professions, and so forth. Also greater concentration in these occupations means on the average, a better income and thus a higher socioeconomic position. The Christian Arabs are, on the average, better educated than the Muslims and have a higher literacy rate. These things have tended to magnify the difference between the East and West Bank populations.[11]

The Religion of Islam

No general description of the West Bank Territory as an introduction to our study would be complete without some discussion of the religion of Islam. On examining the data and history of the area, one frequently asks questions related to the practice of Islam: What is there in the teaching of Islam that makes consideration of manual labor unacceptable for an "educated" person? Why are

there no Christian refugee camps? Is there something in the practice or teaching
of Islam which has contributed to periods of stagnation and periods of slow development in the area? These are but a few of the questions that come to mind.

Any discussion of values as preconditions to development, must take religion into consideration. Religion must be studied for what it is among people:
"a ritualized and stratified complex of highly emotional beliefs and valuations
that give the sanction of sacredness, taboo and immutability to inherited institutional arrangements, modes of living, and attitudes."[12] Taken in this comprehensive sense, religion becomes a tremendous force for social inertia. Within
recent history in the Middle East, the predominant religion of Islam rarely has
induced social change, nor has it fostered realization of the ideals of modernization. Islam, a name used in the Koran in the sense of "surrender to God's will,"
is the name of the religion promulgated by Mohammad. One who accepts Islam
is a Muslim. There is a remarkable unity among Muslims both within themselves
and vis-à-vis the non-Muslim world, which thus justifies the concept of a "Muslim world." But there are also striking dissimilarities among Muslims, as both
cultural and religious differences exist among different regions: the Arabs and
the arabized Africans; the Turks and the Persians; the Pakistano-Indians, and the
Chinese. A prominent feature uniting the Muslim world in the twentieth century
has been religious unity which has rallied Muslims toward a strenuous and pro-
gressively successful endeavor to achieve or pursue independence from colonial
rule.

For the Muslims, the Koran is the Word of God; it confirms and consum-
mates earlier revealed books and thereby replaces them. The agent of revelation
is the Prophet Mohammad, the last of a series of messengers of God to man-
kind—from Adam through Abraham to Moses and Jesus (whose divinity as
recognized by Christians is strongly rejected). The sayings and deeds of Mohammad serve as a basis, besides the Koran, of the belief and practice of Islam. The
Koran is a forceful document basically expressing an *elan* of religious and social
justice. The early chapters contain grave warnings of imminent judgment, but
the later chapters are directed toward regulating the internal and external affairs
of the Muslim community-state.

In its original form, Islam was a religious movement which encompassed a
sociopolitical concept that found no separation between the church and the
state. Since Islam is a total way of life and admits of no division between religion
and state, all its institutions are, in this sense, religious. Thus the *zakat* tax is a
socioeconomic measure enforced by the state, but it is also one of the prime
religious duties. It is a tax on food grains, money, and so forth, payable each
year after one year's possession. When church and state were one, the collection
of the *zakat* tax was left to the state, but in many areas it is now the responsibility of the individual.

Education has occupied an important place in Muslim life as the Koran sets
high value on knowledge and learning. In actual practice, however, a sharp divi-

sion has existed between primary and higher education with the effect that there has been no standardized and systematic feeding of the higher level by the lower. Traditionally, only academic subjects have been taught, with no attention being paid to technical training and the pride of Islam has been its university system which produced the class of the *ulama* or learned men, the religious leaders of Islam. Originally, they were a powerful class and often played decisive roles in international affairs, but in modern times, they have gradually lost much ground vis-à-vis the Western-educated classes, although their hold on a vast body of conservative masses remains unshaken. One of the most crucial problems before modern Muslims is the creation of a new body of *ulama* capable of integrating tradition with modernity. In modern Islam, an almost complete cleavage has existed between the *ulama*, who know only the tradition, and the modern laity, who have been educated in and know only modern secular subjects.[13] Modern Islam has been divided by many movements, and the main points of agreement are with a positive activist orientation and a stress on the unity of the Muslim community. There has been little deep-reaching philosophical rethinking of Islam such as may affect the basic religious issues. Such problems as the status of women, slavery, political democracy, and the concrete issues of sociopolitical reform now confront the Muslims. Their relative inability to answer these questions must stem from the lack of integration between the traditional learning and the modern secular educational centers.

Social reform has, from the beginning of Islam, formed part of the core of Islamic teaching. It has been described as a socioeconomic reform movement backed by certain strong religio-ethical ideas about God, man, and the universe. Islam has laid a firm moral basis for a total, purposeful community with the intention of improving existing customary law of the Arabs. Usury and other forms of exorbitant economic exploitation are strictly forbidden. A rigorously moral state of affairs has been sought in family life and between the sexes.

Egalitarianism is, however, the most fundamental and dynamic element of the social ethic which Islam offers, although it is not always obvious in practice. All members of the faith, regardless of race, color, or social or economic status, are equal participants of the faith. There is no clerical instituion or laity division as in Christianity; although at times the *ulama* approach the influence of the cleric, they have never been instituted as clergy of God. The *ulama* obtain recognition on their own merits, but only to the extent that they exert intellectual and moral influence. As a result, a tremendous diversity of cultural patterns and social behavior has been absorbed and "islamized," and good custom has been recognized as a source of law. This diversity was incorporated by an alleged tradition of the Prophet: "Differences among my community are a mercy of God."

Many of the social developments of Islam were a result of the impact of different cultures on early Islamic society. During this early period, a period of acculturation as Islam spread over the world, much of the social ethic was developed and this led to a sense of fatalism, Messianism, indifference to public affairs, and a political docility and conformism, but at the same time, the idea of community was confirmed and reinvigorated.

During medieval times, as Islam spread throughout Arab and non-Arab countries, a form of new aristocratic class developed. In Iraq and Egypt, for example, the Muslims were there to serve as soldiers and did not engage in manual labor. At certain times, it was felt that Muslims should not be involved in agricultural work, though the Prophet surely could not have encouraged this as the Medinah population in his day must have been largely engaged in agricultural activities. In India, where a caste structure already existed, the conquering Muslim minority assumed administrative and military positions, and when the local menial classes were converted, the social stratification was intensified. The Muslims have never developed a strong commercial class. Some scholars maintain that Islam is basically an urban religion, and as late as the eighteenth century, orthodox Islam remained confined largely to the cities. This does not appear to be the case in the territories today, for it is in the villages that Islam seems to be a more vital part of the everyday life than in the urban areas. Another way of accounting for this may be that the cities have a higher percentage of secularly educated people for whom Islam has lost much of its significance.

The Islamic tradition appears to offer little to support the necessary preconditions for development. The emphasis upon academic training and the failure to support technical training and the medieval development of a class structure have helped to create a partially educated elite who will not work with their hands, but who have not the training to operate in managerial positions. The predeterminism of Islam—the willingness to subscribe almost anything to the "will of Allah"—has created a social immobility that only time and education can alleviate. Perhaps the great "awakening" of Islam will come once again when it enters a new period of acculturation. In the meantime, among the younger generations, the tenets of Islam are being put aside and the fear of a godless generation or society is developing. The burden of modernization lies heavily upon the leaders of Islam.

The Current Political "Climate"

Since the 1967 Six Day War, there has been considerable discussion as to what action or resolution there should be regarding the Israeli-occupied territories. Maintaining an occupation force and assuming the costs of running the municipal governments of the territories has put a considerable strain upon the already overburdened economy of Israel. But the situation is unique in that it is not only a political and/or economic problem, but it is also one deeply rooted in religious tradition.

At the beginning of this century, Zionism—the movement of Jewish national renaissance—declared two main targets: providing a refuge in the Land of Israel (Eretz Israel) for any Jew who wished or needed one and creating a new Jewish society in the Land of Israel based on justice, equality, and freedom.[14] The Zionist solution focused upon the idea of establishing a Jewish state in the Land of Israel. However, during the beginnings of the Zionist movement, the Land of Israel was not uninhabited even though its non-Jewish population, still living under Turkish rule, did not have self-government or sovereignty.

It is difficult to fathom a situation in which the world seemed to be unaware of this indigenous population. Even up until 1967, the Palestinians were a pawn in the strange chess match of Arab diplomacy. Although the guerilla movement probably did not represent the position of the Palestinian population within the occupied territories, that movement helped to establish for the world at large the existence of the Palestinian nation, and no future settlement of the conflict would be possible without the accord of the Palestinian population.

In 1968, when Yigal Allon, a member of the Israeli Cabinet, proposed that the West Bank be set up as an independent territory, the idea was not considered valid enough to even warrant much discussion.[15] In recent years, however, there has been, for the Middle East, a somewhat radical shift in thinking. King Hussein, in 1972, proposed a federation of states to be composed of the states of Palestine (the West Bank Territory) and Jordan's East Bank Territory.[16] The idea was immediately rejected by the Arab states, as it would have to be accomplished after some considerable negotiation and supposedly easing of position vis-à-vis Israel, but it was also rejected by Israel for more subtle and more far-reaching reasons. Nonetheless the most important point is that there had been a shift in public and governmental thinking which now made the consideration of a Palestinian state a possibility.[17]

Immediately after the Six Day War, the Israeli leadership generally refused to acknowledge the legitimate existence of the Palestinian claims. But by 1971, with a change in public opinion towards the Palestinian cause, it appeared that even among the older Israeli leadership, the attitude towards the Palestinians was visibly softening. They were at least willing to allow the Palestinians some possibility of self-determination, if peace were to be established. It was during this same period that there developed a growing spirit towards accommodation among the Palestinians within the West Bank and perhaps also the possibility of a proper climate to consider the establishment of a Palestinian state or nation.

But, as so often happens in the Middle East, before positive action could be taken, the decisions at Rabat catapulted the earlier considerations into obscurity. The PLO was given the "responsibility" of establishing a new state, and we are again in a waiting period. Questions such as whether the Palestinians are a people or a nation, though perhaps still relevant, are no longer being debated.

It has been suggested that a bi-national state could be established, but such a possibility cannot be considered. In any bi-national state, sooner or later, one group becomes the majority and the other, the minority. (The state of Lebanon

may be considered an exception, but in that state, although there are three religious parties within the government, all the people consider themselves Arabs
with a common language, culture and history.) It is unlikely that any Israeli or
any Arab would choose to be the minority in a bi-national state. Bi-nationalism
overlooks the dynamism of modern nationalism and would not take into account the heart of the problem, that both the Jews or Israelis and the Arabs have
a legitimate claim for nationhood and sovereignty. Cyprus, Nigeria, and Pakistan
all provide tragic examples of how poorly bi-nationalism can operate, and in
such established states as Canada and Belgium, bi-nationalism tends to institu-
tionalize rather than to resolve tensions, suspicions, and traumas.

It is difficult to try to describe the nature of the negotiations or their development, but it is probable that the solution would recall the general principle,
if not the detail, of the U.N. plan of 1947: since two national movements claim
the same territory, the only equitable solution would be partition. In 1975, as
opposed to 1947, the logical territorial claims are perhaps more obvious, if not
equitable.

Summary

The historical and cultural experiences of the Palestinian residents of the
West Bank Territory have made them a distinctly different people from the
East Bank residents of the Hashemite Kingdom of Jordan. It appears that there
is resistance on the part of the West Bankers to being absorbed once again into
the Kingdom, unless negotiations could produce a different political arrangement than existed in the pre-1967 period. Likewise, because of the different
historical, cultural, and religious experiences of the Palestinians vis-à-vis the
Israelis, there is great reluctance on the part of the West Bankers to becoming a
part of the State of Israel. The West Bankers are desirous of some form of self-
determination, although what form this should take appears to be open to discussion.

If, through negotiations among Israel, Jordan, and representatives of the
Palestinians, an independent state of Palestine were established, would such a
state, which would include the area of the West Bank Territory, be economically
viable? What has transpired since 1967 that would be an indication of growth
potential, trade relations, and viability? Has either the agricultural sector or the
industrial sector been developed to its full potential? What are the possibilities
for further development? Can the traditions of Islam and the inherited attitudes
towards education and manual labor be overcome so as to allow for the maximum potential development of the labor force? What are the various sociopolitical problems that will have to be solved before nationhood can be
established? And if nationhood is granted, can a new Palestine survive and be
economically viable? Let us examine each of these problems.

Notes

1. Material for this section has been drawn from a variety of sources including those footnoted, the *Encyclopedia Britannica*, miscellaneous archaeological reports, and the personal experience and observations of the author.
2. Raphael Patai, *The Kingdom of Jordan* (Princeton, N.J.: Princeton University Press, 1958).
3. Ibid., p. 34.
4. Ibid., p. 45.
5. Ibid., p. 47.
6. *The New York Times,* November 23, 1967.
7. Specific actions and projects for each of the sectors of the economy will be discussed below.
8. "The October War," *Encyclopedia Britannica, 1974 Book of the Year.*
9. *The International Herald Tribune,* November 5, 1974.
10. *The Economy of the Administered Areas 1972* (Jerusalem: Bank of Israel, 1974), p. 29.
11. Materials for the above section have been drawn from: Patai, *The Kingdom of Jordan;* George L. Harris, *Jordan* (New Haven, Conn.: Human Relations Area Press, 1958); *The First Census of Population and Housing* (Amman: The Government Press, 1961); and personal observations.
12. Gunnar Myrdal, *Asian Drama, An Inquiry into the Poverty of Nations* (New York: The Twentieth Century Fund, 1968), p. 69.
13. "Islam," *Encyclopedia Britannica,* Vol. 12, 14th edition (1972).
14. Shlomo Avineri, ed., *Israel and the Palestinians* (New York: St. Martins Press, Inc., 1971), p. 58.
15. *The New York Times,* October 14, 1969.
16. *The New York Times,* March 30, 1972.
17. See Shlomo Avineryi, *Israel and the Palestinians,* for an interesting documentation of this change in public opinion in a series of essays, interviews, and commentaries.

3

General Economic Development of the West Bank Territory

Main Economic Developments[1]

Real gross national product in the West Bank Territory has increased by an impressive amount since 1967: 24 percent from 1968 to 1969; 15 percent from 1969 to 1970; 18 percent from 1970 to 1971; and by approximately 28 percent from 1971 to 1972 (see Table 3-1). During this period the average annual rate of growth in Israel was about 9 percent. During the Six Day War and immediately afterwards, economic activity in the Territory was badly disrupted and this led for a relatively short period of time to a slump and considerable idleness of factors of production. Conditions were at their worst in the second half of 1967. During 1968 and 1969, the economic climate changed and forces developed that permitted an emergence from a short-term slump and a shift to a long-term high rate of economic growth as well as a rise in living standards to a level above that of the prewar era. Additional figures, through 1973, are given in Table 3-2.

Prior to the war, the economy of the West Bank Territory had been integrated into the economy of the Hashemite Kingdom of Jordan. The inhabitants were engaged primarily in agriculture and services; trade with adjoining regions took the form of exports of "surpluses" of these sectors and the importation of consumer goods and manufactured items. The war caused a sharp decline in the level of economic activity in the short run. First of all, economic ties were severed and commercial relations—beginning with agricultural produce— via the Jordan bridges were renewed only at a gradual pace. During the change in administration of the Territory, there was a temporary contraction of the sources of employment and income, for both civilian administration and the army had provided an important role in the economy prior to the war. The uncertainty and instability immediately following the war resulted in a sharp cutback in investments, which thus contributed to the slowdown in economic activity.

Another significant factor was the extensive emigration that took place during and immediately after the war. This resulted in a sharp reduction in the size of the local market as well as of the labor force. A countervailing factor in the immediate postwar period, however, was the large volume of purchases bought by Israeli tourists in the Territory, but this proved to be an effective market only in the short run. As inventories of imported goods were depleted, merchants were able to restock only with Israeli merchandise, and sales fell.

Large-scale unemployment was a short-run problem immediately after the

37

Table 3-1
Indicators of Economic Activity in Judea and Samaria, 1968–1971

	1968	1969	1970	1971	Percent increase or decrease (–) over preceding year		
					1968–69	1969–70	1970–71
Resources and Uses (1971 prices)							
Total Domestic Uses (IL million)	538	677	726	790	26	7	9
Gross National Product (IL million; market prices)	434	536	616	726	24	15	18
GNP per capita (IL)	749	901	1,017	1,123	20	13	15
Private Consumption per capita (IL)	781	915	974	1,008	17	6	3
Domestic Product per employed person (IL; market prices)	5,133	4,532	4,905	5,746	-12	8	17
Foreign Trade (IL million, current prices[a])							
Total Exports	148	173	211	350	17	22	66
Merchandise	97	109	110	150	12	1	36
Services	51	64	101	200	25	58	98
Total Imports	225	283	300	388	26	6	29
Merchandise from Jordan	17	25	12	14	47	-52	17
Merchandise from Israel	139	179	191	228	29	7	19
Population and Employment							
Mean Population (thousands)	579.1	594.6	605.5	619.0	2.7	1.8	2.2
Employed Persons (thousands)[b]	82.9	109.9	114.6	116.8	32.6	4.3	1.9
Unemployment (percent)	10.8	4.1	3.3	2.4	–	–	–
Employed Persons in Israel (thousands)	4.0	10.6	14.7	25.6	165.0	38.7	74.1
Prices and Wages							
Consumers Price Index	100.0	101.5	106.8	119.8	1.5	5.2	12.2
National Product Price Index	100.0	104.3	108.1	128.2	4.3	3.6	18.6
Average net Daily Wage (IL)[b]	–	6.7	7.9	10.3	–	17.9	30.4
Wages of Employed Persons in Israel (IL): Gross[c]	–	17.7	20.3	23.3	–	14.7	14.8
Net	–	10.1	11.8	13.5	–	16.8	14.4

[a]Excluding fruit and vegetables.
[b]Including persons employed in Israel.
[c]Total expenditure on labor per employed person.
Source: *The Economy of the Administered Areas 1971* (Jerusalem: Bank of Israel, 1972), p. 8.

Table 3-2

Indicators of Economic Activity in Judea and Samaria, 1968-1973[a]

	Average 1968-69	Average 1972-73[a]	Average annual increase (percent)
Resources and uses (1971 prices)			
Total domestic uses (IL million)	610	1,010	13
Gross national product (IL million, market prices)	500	920	17
National product per capita (IL market prices)	852	1,433	14
Gross domestic product (IL million)	434	634	10
Domestic product per employed person (IL, factor prices)	4,717	7,044	11
Private consumption per capita (IL)	835	1,223	10
Foreign Trade (IL million constant 1971 prices)			
Total exports	208	464	22
Of which: Goods	126	182	10
Services	82	282	36
Percent of goods exported to Israel in total goods exported	45	62	—
Total imports	308	545	15
Of which: Goods	244	403	13
Services	64	142	22
Percent of goods imported from Israel in total goods imported	79	86	—
Population and employment			
Mean population (thousands)	587	642	2
Employed persons from administered areas (thousands)	100	125	6
Employed in administered areas (thousands)	92	90	-1
Employed in Israel (thousands)	8	35	45
Unemployment (percent)	7	1	—
Prices and wages			
Consumers price index (excluding fruit, vegetables and housing)	100.0	156.8	11
Average net daily wage in areas (IL)[b]	6.0	15.1	26
Average net daily wage in Israel (IL)[b]	10.1	21.8	21

[a]Data for 1973 based on figures up to October with extrapolation for last quarter to discount the effect of the war

[b]Data on wages are for 1969 and 1973.

Source: *Economic Growth of the Administered Areas 1968-1973* (in Hebrew) (Jerusalem: Bank of Israel, 1974), p. 10.

war for several reasons. Emigration had reduced the labor force and also the "excess supply" particularly in the services branch. The economic significance of emigration lay not only in the fact that it diminished the problem of employment in the Territory and reduced the market, but as many of the refugees fled to the East Bank of the Jordan, the demand for exports to the East Bank expanded, particularly for agricultural produce. Soon after the war, Israel undertook to restore some of the traditional trading links (such as allowing trade via the Open Bridges—which trade also precluded a collapse of the Israeli agricultural sector) as well as to open new trading outlets within Israel and via Israel with Europe. Israel was able to provide an outlet for both goods and services from the territory.

The Israeli administration worked actively in two other fields to promote economic recovery. First, it initiated projects to promote employment and absorbed numerous public service workers and thereby provided a partial substitute for the economic activities of the previous administration. Some of these projects were actually of the "make-work" variety, which have been phased out, or labor-intensive projects, which have been replaced by capital-intensive projects as the available labor supply has decreased. Secondly, through an enlightened agricultural development program, Israel provided valuable technical assistance and resources. This involved not only educational programs but direct investment in agricultural development.

Economic activity in the West Bank Territory slowed down from 1969 to 1970, although production still grew more than in Israel. There were several reasons for the slower rate of growth. Since rapid growth of 1968–69 came after a year of especially low economic activity and high unemployment as a result of the war, the growth began from a higher level. Secondly, 1969 had been an excellent crop year, whereas in 1970 there was an extended drought and due to the cyclical nature of production, it was a low year for the olive crop in particular, and this affected both agricultural and industrial output (olive presses). During 1970, it would appear that most of the unemployed had found work, for the rise in the participation rate for men ceased, and unemployment among the men levelled off at 3.5 percent. And finally, there were indications of the fact (which is most important for future planning as full employment is achieved and the capital stock is more fully utilized) that the economy of the Territory will continue to grow at a slower rate. Since there was little increase in the stock of fixed capital, the increase in domestic product depended largely on additional investment in machinery, equipment, and structures. Between 8 and 10 percent of total resources was provided for investment, compared with about 16 percent in Israel.[2]

The growth rate was also slowing down in 1969–70. Remittances, particularly those from Israel, began to be a main element of the change in the national income. But part of the slackening of the growth rate in 1970 must be attributed to the limited supply of manpower available. Because of the near full employment condition and the relatively slow rate of growth expected in the number of employed persons, future growth will depend largely upon changes in the sector structure, in the composition of employment, and in production methods. Each of these is a function of the availability of increased fixed investment.

Evidences of economic integration between Israel and the West Bank Territory (and with Gaza) were obvious in 1970.

> Some three-quarters of the merchandise trade of the administered areas was with or through Israel, compared with less than two-thirds in 1968. Income from work in Israel accounted for about 15 percent of total national product, as against only 3 percent in 1968. In 1968–70 such income accounted for 37 percent of the product increment in the areas. Residents working in Israel provided more than one-third of the total rise in Israeli employment in 1970.[3]

Economic cooperation between the West Bank and Israel was most noticeably reflected in the structural changes in agriculture and employment. As a result of Israeli demand, average wages of workers in the administered areas increased faster than they did in Israel. Closing the wage gap, however, will be a slow process for it involves changes in the skill and sector composition of the labor force and it seems apparent that the comparative advantage of the Territory in labor-intensive goods will persist for several years. In 1969, the net daily wages in Israel were 3.7 times those paid in the West Bank; in 1970, 3.2; and in 1971, 3.0.[4] The gap continued to decrease in 1972.

During 1970, economic ties with Israel became stronger while the ties of Judea and Samaria with Jordan were weakened, as evidenced by the steep decline in trade over the Jordan bridges. There were several causes for this decline: animal disease in the Arab world precluded import of animals into the Territory; severe drought conditions caused lower production; and the unstable security and political situation in Jordan (both internally and with the neighboring Arab countries), and the cholera outbreak in the Middle East tended to dampen economic exchanges. The trade balance with Jordan showed an export surplus as in 1969. Personal and institutional unilateral transfers from Jordan and other Arab countries continued to rise, these transfers being mainly in cash but also in kind. They effectively increased the money supply and the stock of Jordanian dinars and other foreign currency.

Real gross national product grew by 18 percent during 1970–71. This high rate resulted mainly from demand in Israel for the Territory's labor and from a good crop year. The level of employment in the Territory declined (1969: 99,300; 1970: 99,900; 1971: 91,200) while the number employed in Israel continued to rise (1969: 10,600; 1970: 14,700; 1971: 25,600). In 1972, the relevant figures were 90,300 employed within the Territory, and 34,900 employed in Israel. The increase in the labor supply resulted from a growth in the working-age labor force and from a higher participation rate. A virtual full employment level was achieved, and this created problems for expansion of the economy in the Territory. The number of persons employed decreased mainly in agriculture (partly as a result of labor-saving devices and methods of production), industry, and construction. Thus the growth of output in these branches must be attributed to a remarkable increase in productivity per employed person as a result of a good agricultural year and of technological improvements.

Fixed investment in the Territory is still low, although it grew by about 33 percent, from 1970 to 1971, after a previous year's drop of 9 percent. Gross investment was about 11 percent of total domestic resources (product plus import surplus). In 1972, total investment in fixed assets grew nearly 50 percent, but it still accounts for only about 14 percent of total domestic resources. This is a little more than half the rate in Israel and lower than in most developing countries in the Middle East.

However, as real incomes grew, so did prices increase, especially in 1971 and 1972 (see Figure 3-1). National product prices in the Territory rose by about 19 percent between 1970 and 1971, compared with 13 percent in Israel. The expanding trade relations between the Territory and Israel led to an adjustment of changing prices and wages. The gap in wages between the two economies is being narrowed. The average daily wage for work in the Territory has continued to rise, and at a rate exceeding the growth of wages in Israel.

In 1972, the consumer price index rose by 15 percent in the Territory, against a 13 percent rise in Israel. The daily wage for workers within the Territory rose by 40 percent, while those for workers crossing into Israel, rose by 28 percent. This latter rate still exceeded the Israeli average pay rise.[5]

The August 1971 devaluation accounted for some of the rapid increase in prices, for the Israeli lire (IL) value of the Jordanian dinar was raised. Conversion of dinars into Israeli lire rose from 2.5 million dinars in 1970 to about 9 million dinars in 1971.[6] This increase in conversions was made possible by a growing export surplus to Jordan and from the unilateral transfers from Jordan. The latter, however, decreased by IL 14 million, because the Jordanian government halted salary payments to some of its exofficials in June 1971. There was also an increase in exported services that resulted primarily from summer visits of Arabs to the Territory, the number of which doubled in 1971.

The export surplus to Jordan is more than offset by the import surplus from Israel and other countries. The Territory is a net importer of dinars, but they also import goods for which Israel must pay in foreign currency, goods not produced in Israel (such as rice, vehicles, spare parts for vehicles and machinery, and so forth), and goods produced in Israel that have an import component. The estimated proportion of these two types of goods in 1971, by using coefficients from input–output tables, gives an overall coefficient of about 35 percent.[7] That is to say, the areas' (Judea, Samaria, and the Gaza Strip) imports from Israel in the two years (1970, 1971) caused Israel to pay over $30 million in foreign currency each year; part of the areas' exports to Israel may substitute for Israel's imports from abroad.

Unilateral transfers from the government of Israel to the West Bank Terri-

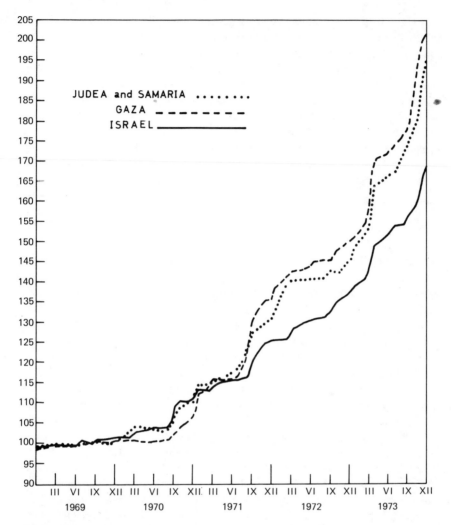

Figure 3-1. Consumer Price Index: Judea and Samaria, The Gaza Strip, and Israel. (1969 = 100)

Note: Fruits, vegetables, and housing are excluded.

Source: *The Economy of the Administered Areas 1968-1973* (in Hebrew) (Jerusalem: Bank of Israel, 1974), p. 19.

tory cover the excess of expenditures over income in the military government's budget and export incentives to residents (see Foreign Trade below) other than through the military government's budget. There are other budgetary incomes and expenditures that are not reflected in the military government's budget, such as customs paid on goods imported through Israel's ports.

    The economic merger of the three regions—Israel, Judea and Samaria, and the Gaza Strip—into a single economy has continued. This integration takes the form of continuous adjustments in the structure of production, trade in goods, services, and production factors, transfers of means of payments, and prices. There is still a fairly wide gap between the standard of living in the administered areas, however, and that existing in Israel, even among the Israeli Arabs, although the gap is closing. The gradually fading borders among the regions "is also evident in the increasing statistical problems involved in gathering the necessary data for economic analysis. Consequently, the reliability of the estimates included in the separate national accounts of each region is affected."[8] This integration, as it affects data, would also account for some of the discrepancies that appear in reports of various branches of the government and the Bank of Israel.

Resources, Uses, and Incomes[9]

Product and the Import Surplus

As stated above, the real national products of Judea and Samaria increased by 18 percent from 1970 to 1971 following previous increases of 15 percent (1969–70) and 24 percent (1968–69) (see Table 3-3). In 1971, national product per capita in Judea and Samaria was still only about one-seventh of Israel's national product per capita. A comparison of national product per employed person shows that it was four times higher in Israel than in the administered areas as a whole for 1971. An adjustment of previous data and preliminary data for 1972 show an increase in gross national product to be 22 percent between 1970 and 1971, and 28 percent from 1971 to 1972.

While the import surplus of the areas dropped in 1971, the share of national product in total domestic resources (consumption plus investment) rose. In Judea and Samaria, the rise was from 81 percent in 1968 to 85 percent in 1970, to 92 percent in 1971. Total national product in the Territory financed almost all private and public consumption and investment, while exports (including the export of labor) financed most of the areas' imports. This was accomplished at the expense of investment, which remains low in comparison with other economies growing at such a rapid pace.

Private Income and Consumption

Private disposable income in the West Bank Territory, in current prices and in real terms, rose steadily through 1972. Private consumption did not grow as rapidly. In current prices, incomes rose by about 190 percent from 1968 to 1972, whereas private consumption grew by only 160 percent (see Table 3-4). This would indicate a substantial increase in savings, from a low of 7 percent of disposable income from all sources in 1968 to 21 percent in 1972.

Table 3-3
Resources and Uses in Judea and Samaria, 1968–1971 (IL millions, 1971 prices)

	1968	1969	1970	1971	Percent change between		
					1968 & 1969	1969 & 1970	1970 & 1971
Private Consumption	452	544	590	624	20	8	6
Public Consumption	57	63	72	81	11	14	12
Gross Investment	29	70	64	85	141	-9	33
Total Domestic Uses	538	677	726	790	26	7	9
Imports[a]	284	352	350	416	24	-1	19
Exports[b]	180	211	240	352	17	14	47
Import Surplus	104	141	110	64	36	-22	-42
Gross National Product	434	536	616	726	24	15	18
Total Resources	538	677	726	790	26	7	9

[a]Imports include import duties as well as foreign factor payments (Israelis employed in the administered area).
[b]Exports include export incentives and subsidies as well as incomes from abroad of domestic production factors.
Source: *The Economy of the Administered Areas 1971* (Jerusalem: Bank of Israel, 1972), p. 14.

Table 3-4
Private Income in Judea and Samaria, 1968-1972 (IL millions,
current prices)

	1968	1969	1970	1971	1972
Gross National Product (at market prices)	348	440	511	737	1,164
plus Transfers and Subsidies from the Public Sector	2	3	2	2	3
less Receipts of the Public Sector from Taxes and Transfers	23	35	42	65	94
Private Disposable Income from Internal Sources	327	408	471	674	1,073
Transfers to Individuals from Abroad	72	79	101	92	92
Private Disposable Income from All Sources	399	487	572	766	1,165
Private Consumption	359	452	496	632	923
Private Consumption as Percent of Disposable Income from All Sources	90	93	87	82	79
Gross Private Savings Out of All Resources (percent)	10	7	13	18	21

Source: *The Economy of the Administered Areas 1972* (Jerusalem: Bank of Israel, 1974),
p. 13.

There are several difficulties in collecting accurate data on income and
consumption (see the discussion in Chapter 6), but the results recorded by the
Bank of Israel appear to be consistent with expectations. During the 1968-69
period the economy was still recovering from the 1967 war and was in a process
of adjusting to a new level of economic activity with new markets and demands
for labor. During this period, private consumption was 90 percent and above of
all disposable income, but this was not to be a long-run relationship. In 1970 and
1971, there appears to be a growing lag in adjusting private consumption to
disposable income due to the slow adjustment to a higher level of consumption,
to new commodities, and to unfamiliar consumption patterns. This action may
be typical, particularly when the process of rising incomes coincides with a
marked increase in prices which makes it difficult for individuals to realize that
their real income has risen. Persons in contact with residents of the Territory
reported that residents seemed to believe that all wages and prices would automatically rise by 20 percent after the devaluation of August 1971.[10] Both of
these instances may be attributed to the basic naiveté of the residents' under-
standing of income-price relationships.

There may be other ways to account for the rise in savings such as a general
shift to higher income levels. There seems to have been a particularly sharp
increase in the incomes of high-income earners, such as citrus growers and large
exporters, whose savings rate is far higher than average.[11] Some savings were also
directed toward improving housing conditions, particularly in 1971 when there
was a relatively large increase in private investment in dwellings (see Chapter 5).

Balance-of-payments indicators show a rising trend of savings through the accumulation of cash and possible accumulation of gold in considerable amounts. The accumulation of means of payment appears to be the main expression of private savings in spite of the rise in investment in dwellings and business premises (see the Monetary System below).

Real private consumption per capita consequently rose by only 2 to 3 percent; total per capita consumption of services even declined slightly. In quantitative terms, the decrease was mainly in consumption of services rendered by non-profit institutions, primarily United Nations Relief Works Agency (UNRWA), which had to restrict its activities in 1970–72 because of budget difficulties.

Gross Investment

The rate of growth of real gross fixed investment has varied significantly between 1968 and 1971; it grew by 138 percent between 1968/69, fell by 7 percent in 1970, and then rose by 33 percent in 1971 (see Table 3-5). In 1969, investment expanded as private building and purchases of equipment recovered from the low 1968 level that reflected the prevailing uncertainty at the time. The investment recovery was also related to increased technological innovations in the agricultural sector. The private sector increased its dwelling investment slightly in 1971, while public sector investments (the Israeli Administration and local authorities) remained stable at the 1969 level.

There may be a downward bias in the investment estimates because of an underestimate of machinery and equipment imported from Israel. Since 1969, when investment in machinery began to rise (both imports of second-hand equipment from Israel and new equipment from abroad), the increase appears not to be wholly reflected in the data. Such equipment is required for the con-

Table 3-5
Gross Investment in Judea and Samaria, 1968–1971 (IL millions, 1971 prices)

	1968	1969	1970	1971
a. Public Sector Investment	17	24	24	26
b. Private Sector Investment	12	35	49	59
Structures	8	18	29	33
Machinery, Equipment, and Vehicles	4	17	20	26
Fixed Investment	29	59	73	85
c. Changes in Inventories	0	10	–9	0
Total Gross Investment (a + b + c)	29	69	64	85

Source: *The Economy of the Administered Areas 1971* (Jerusalem: Bank of Israel, 1972), p. 16.

tinued development of existing industrial plants, for the mechanization of agriculture, for the development of new enterprises, and for replacement of obsolete equipment. This kind of development does not require substantial amounts of capital for structures because of the existence of a stock of structures vacant since 1967 and because it is usually possible to add equipment to existing plants without expanding the plants themselves. This is probably why total private sector investments in non-dwelling structures and works did not rise at a faster rate. At the end of 1967, there were also a considerable number of vacant dwellings that were filled in subsequent years, before there was an increased demand for more housing units.

Public sector investments include construction of roads, construction and equipping of schools and other public institutions, development of water resources, afforestation and land betterment, development of electricity and telephone networks, and construction of packaging and freezing centers. Public sector investment remained relatively stable since 1969, so its share in total fixed investment declined from about 35 percent of total gross investment in 1969 to about 30 percent in 1971. This is partly accounted for by an increase in private investment and partly attributed to the elimination of the need for public "make-work" projects as full employment levels were reached.

Part of the public investment in 1971 was in construction of dwellings and other renovation work within refugee camps, both in the West Bank and in the Gaza Strip, that was financed by the "Trust Fund for Economic Development and Rehabilitation of Refugees" (see Chapter 7, The Refugees). The fund is maintained by foreign contributions and the Government of Israel, and income from the fund financed works during 1971 of approximately IL 4 million.[12] Works financed on this scale can only improve living conditions to a very small degree.

The change in inventories again reflects the highly variable olive crop; in 1969, there was a bumper crop but in 1970, a meager crop. The 1969 crop meant a high level of olive oil production (about IL 35 million at producer prices). Part of this was kept in stock and consumed in 1970.

The total addition to fixed investment has not grown sufficiently to guarantee rapid economic growth in the future. It was derived largely from investment in machinery, equipment, and vehicles that were needed to replace obsolete or worn-out equipment. In 1971, investment was about 11 percent of domestic uses, compared with 10 percent in the two preceding years. In Israel, investment during the same period was between 22 and 24 percent of domestic uses. The West Bank is lagging far behind other developing countries, even in the Middle East where the following averages are recorded: Egypt (1969), 13 percent; Jordan (1969), 22 percent; Syria (1971), 15 percent; and Iraq (1969), 20 percent.[13] A higher percentage of domestic uses must be given over to investment, for this is a basic condition for establishing rapid and lasting economic development. If we accept the standard of a rate of investment equal to 12 to 15 percent of net national income as being necessary for an economy to diversify and advance, we see that there must be greater emphasis placed on investment within the Territory (see Chapter 5).

Development by Economic Sector

The most outstanding feature of sector composition in national product, both in its development since 1968 and in 1971, was the decline in the weight of domestic product in the administered areas. Net income of residents employed in Israel rose by 14 percent in 1970 and by about 21 percent in 1971 (see Tables 3-6 and 3-7). The entire period is marked by wide fluctuations in the share of income originating in agriculture, which reflects natural growing conditions. Between 1969 and 1971, there was no change in the share of income originating from industry, and since 1969, only a minor change in construction. The significant change in the share of income from construction between 1968 and 1969 reflected a resurgence of economic activity and a using up of structures vacated during the Six Day War. There appears to be little transition from agriculture to industry, which is usually considered a prerequisite for economic development and involves considerable capital investment, technological ability, and experience. It is difficult to see how this transition can be effected as long as cheap labor is drawn off for construction and industry in Israel.

Real domestic product per employed person rose in 1970 by only 6 percent and the number of locally employed persons declined. In 1971, real domestic product rose steeply—by 17 percent. This increase was achieved without any significant increase in capital stocks, and it was accompanied by a drop in the number of employed persons working in the Territory. This increase probably

Table 3-6
Branch Composition of Product in the Administered Areas,
1968-1971 (percent)

	1968	1969	1970	1971
Agriculture	34	38	32	37
Industry	7	8	8	8
Construction	3	5	6	6
Government and Local Authorities	18	17	18	17
Trade, Transport and Other Services	38	32	36	32
Total Domestic Product	100	100	100	100
Domestic Product	99	92	86	79
Net Factor Payments from Abroad	1	8	14	21
Total National Product (all branches)	100	100	100	100

Source: *The Economy of the Administered Areas 1971* (Jerusalem: Bank of Israel, 1972), p. 19.

Table 3-7
Branch Composition of National Product at Factor Cost, Judea and
Samaria, 1970-1972 (IL millions, 1971 prices[a])

	1970	1971	1972	Percent change over preceding year	
				1970/71	1971/72
Agriculture[b]	163	205	291	26	42
Industry	46	51	60	11	18
Construction	28	30	48	7	60
Government and Local Authorities[c]	81	84	88	4	5
Trade, Transport, and Other Services	172	167	190	−3	14
Total Domestic Product	490	537	677	10	26
Net Incomes of Production Factors	88	162	222	84	37
Gross National Product (factor cost)	578	699	899	21	29

[a]With the exception of agriculture, product computed for 1970 in 1971 prices using the derived price index of total gross domestic product.
[b]Data on agriculture in this table refer to calendar years.
[c]Including non-profit institutions as well as electricity and water services provided by local authorities.
Sources: *The Economy of the Administered Areas 1971* (Jerusalem: Bank of Israel, 1972), p. 20; *The Economy of the Administered Areas 1972* (Jerusalem: Bank of Israel, 1974), p. 16.

reflects several things: a decline in disguised unemployment as many workers found jobs in Israel; an excellent crop year in which climatic conditions favored high production; and overall improvement in efficiency, a part of which must be attributed to greater use of more efficient equipment on the farms.[14]

Foreign Trade

Main Developments

Immediately after the Six Day War, all the conditions that we have discussed were also paramount in regard to the foreign trade sector of the economy: a break in traditional trading links, a decline in potential market due to emigration, reduction in employment opportunities in the public sector, and general political and economic instability. However, soon new trading relations were made possible between the West Bank and the Gaza Strip and Israel, as well as the possibility of re-establishing trade with the East Bank of Jordan via the Open Bridges.

The major factor which enabled the economy to find an outlet for its surplus productive capacity was made available with the policy to reopen the Jordan bridges. When trade was permitted between the Territory and Israel, subject to limitations, a second outlet was provided as well as the possibility of a greatly expanded outlet for labor. The establishment of trade relations with Israel expanded the area's markets and improved its terms of trade. With the opening of new trade outlets, the costs of certain imports could be reduced and the return on some exports increased. An outstanding example of the improved terms of trade is the export of labor services to Israel, which earned the Territory a high income relative to alternative uses of this resource.

Another important factor which affects the structure of trade is the system of customs duties, subsidies, and quotas in force. Customs duties are levied on imports from Jordan and all countries except Israel at the standard Israeli rate. Exports to countries other than Israel are subsidized on condition that the foreign currency proceeds are converted into Israeli pounds. In the early years, there were limitations on exports to Israel so as to provide administrative protection for Israeli agriculture; as stated earlier, as the agricultural sector has become more integrated, these restrictions have been cancelled.

The development of the international trade of the West Bank Territory to its present level and scope has been a gradual process, entailing an adjustment to the changing trade opportunities. As exports have expanded and as other factors have stimulated economic activity in the area, there has been a rise in incomes and consumption, and hence also of imports (see Table 3-8).

During the second half of 1967, trade with Israel was very limited, with the major item being Israeli tourism in the area. The bulk of trade with Jordan consisted of olive oil and agricultural produce, whereas imports from the East Bank were negligible. During 1968 and 1969 trade relations between Israel and the administered areas grew rapidly. By 1968 exports to Israel were up to IL 45 million, almost 50 percent of the area's total exports; approximately half of the sum represented income from work in Israel (i.e., the export of labor services). Imports consisted largely of staple foodstuffs, fuel, and various manufactured goods, which it did not pay to buy abroad via the Jordan bridges after customs duties were equalized.

The rapid development of trade between Israel and the West Bank Territory must be attributed to the degree of economic integration that had taken place since the war. Although defined as international trade, these relations are more in the nature of trade between adjoining regions of a single economy since customs barriers and restrictions imposed by transportation costs in international commerce do not exist. The geographical proximity, the use of the same currency in trade transactions, and the absence of customs barriers (particularly in later years) have all helped to create close commercial ties covering a wide range of goods and services that are typical of the interregional trade of a single economy.

Commercial relations between the West Bank Territory and Jordan developed

Table 3-8
Balance of Payments of Judea and Samaria, 1969–1972 (IL millions, current prices)

	1969		1970		1971		1972	
	Credit	Debit	Credit	Debit	Credit	Debit	Credit	Debit
Total	288	288	352	352	484	484	680	680
Total Merchandise and Services	166	265	211	300	343	389	542	569
Merchandise	103	211	110	227	143	284	212	415
Services	63	54	101	73	200	105	330	154
Transport	–	7	–	8	–	11	–	17
Insurance	1	2	3	5	6	7	8	11
Foreign travel	12	28	9	23	19	19	26	34
Investment income	3	–	3	–	3	1	3	11
Government	–	5	–	6	–	7	–	7
Miscellaneous	47	12	86	31	172	60	293	84
labor	47	7	86	8	172	13	293	15
other	–	5	–	23	–	47	–	69
Unilateral Transfers	122	4	141	14	141	24	138	42
By Private Institutions[a]	84	4	101	14	92	24	72	42
Government of Israel	38	–	40	–	49	–	66	–
Net Capital Movements, Errors, and Omissions	–	19	–	38	–	71	–	69

[a]Includes transfers from the Jordanian government.

Sources: *The Economy of the Administered Areas 1970* (Jerusalem: Bank of Israel, 1971), p. 28; *The Economy of the Administered Areas 1971* (Jerusalem: Bank of Israel, 1972), p. 30; and *The Economy of the Administered Areas 1972* (Jerusalem: Bank of Israel, 1974), p. 25.

more slowly, at least partly due to the restrictive customs duties levied by the Israeli government which favored trade between the Territory and Israel. Exports to Jordan consist mostly of fruit, vegetables, and processed agricultural produce. These exports are no smaller than in the prewar period, but purchases from Israel have been substituted for imports from Jordan.

In 1969, there continued to be a deficit on the current account, which condition existed in the prewar years as well. Most of the gap has been covered by unilateral transfers to individuals and government transfers to make up the deficit in the domestic budget. Transfers in 1968 and 1969 exceeded the current account deficit, so there was an accumulation of reserves in the West Bank Territory.

In 1970, there was continuation of the substitution of Israeli imports for the imports from Jordan and overseas and a growth in the exports of labor services to Israel. Both of these elements established closer economic ties between the Israeli economy and the West Bank Territory. Trade between the Territory and the Gaza Strip also expanded. There are no complete data on this trade but it includes agricultural produce and olive oil from the West Bank, fish and citrus from Gaza, labor services from Gaza to the West Bank, and tourism in both directions. The Bank of Israel refers to this process of integration as "a common market of three regions . . . with a uniform customs barrier between them and the rest of the world, while the restraints on interregional trade are gradually disappearing."[15]

The year 1970 was one of slower growth of both production and employment in the West Bank. Thus, there was a slight decline in merchandise exports; merchandise imports rose slightly; and income from the export of labor services grew more moderately than in 1969. In 1970, as mentioned above, there was a decline in agricultural output, and this led to a decline in exports to Jordan of olive oil, olives, vegetables, and other field crops. Exports overseas included some vegetables but mainly consisted of objets d'art, including ornaments and mother-of-pearl and olivewood handicrafts (sold mainly in the United States).

The main effect on imports results from the rise in private consumption. The reasons for the drop in trade with Jordan have been discussed above: livestock diseases led to the prohibition of livestock imports, mainly sheep, and thus to a decline in imports; the drought in Jordan brought about a decline in the import of cereals; the unstable political-security situation in Jordan (particularly during the month of and the period immediately following the war against the terrorists); and the cholera outbreak all affected trade adversely.

In 1970, the West Bank had a trade surplus with Jordan of IL 28 million, which was similar to the surplus amount of the two preceding years (see Table 3-9). The import surplus with Israel in 1970 was about IL 123 million (down from IL 134 million in 1969), and was financed mainly by incomes from the export of labor services and by unilateral transfers of the Government of Israel and various institutions. West Bank merchants were paid in dinars for the surplus

Table 3-9
Trade Balance of Judea and Samaria, 1968–1972 (IL millions, current prices)

	1968		1969		1970		1971		1972	
	Exports	*Imports*	*Exports*	*Imports*	*Exports*	*Imports*	*Exports*	*Imports*	*Exports*	*Imports*
Overseas	1	20	1	22	2	24	2	43	2	54
Jordan	51	17	63	25	40	12	68	14	107	19
Israel	45	139	45	179	68	191	73	227	104	342
Total	97	176	109	226	110	227	143	284	213	415

Sources: *The Economy of the Administered Areas 1971* (Jerusalem: Bank of Israel, 1972), p. 31, and *The Economy of the Administered Areas 1972* (Jerusalem: Bank of Israel, 1974), p. 27.

exports, part of which were hoarded by the residents. The Jordanian government transferred dinars to the region mainly in the form of salaries to civil servants. Additional sums were transferred by private persons mainly in the form of family support. Private transfers grew at an estimated IL 15 million in 1970, while Jordanian government transfers remained at their previous level of IL 30 million. Since only a small portion of these dinars were actually converted into Israeli lire (although export subsidies are only granted to exporters who convert their dinars to Israeli currency), the stock of dinars held by the region's residents evidently continued to grow in 1970. The service import surplus with Jordan (including net travel expenses from the administered areas to Jordan) was estimated at IL 3 million by the Bank of Israel and therefore could be a source of demand for only a small portion of the dinars. Hoarding of dinars may also have been one of the causes of the decline in the exchange rate of the dinar on the free market to only 4 percent above the official rate.[16]

A significant part of the West Bank Territory's foreign trade is foreign travel which includes visits of persons from Arab countries to their families in the West Bank and visits of the region's residents to Israel, Jordan, and other Arab countries. This tourism entails transactions in foreign currencies. There was a considerable increase in 1970 in receipts from foreign visitors but residents of the Territory made fewer visits to the Arab countries so that the import surplus declined from about IL 16 million in 1969 to IL 14 million in 1970. Based on sample surveys, it is estimated that each Arab tourist brings along an average of about $250, part of which is privately transferred to relatives and part of which is used to finance his visit in the Territory and Israel.[17]

In 1971, the West Bank's balance-of-payment deficit rose by over 20 percent, whereas the surplus in the services account rose from IL 28 million in 1970 to IL 95 million in 1971, which is an increase of some 240 percent. Both income of residents employed in Israel and receipt from foreign travel doubled. Fewer residents traveled abroad and thus expenditures for foreign travel decreased by approximately IL 4 million. In 1972, the trade deficit increased by some 45 percent; in the same period, the surplus in the services sector rose to IL 81 million, which is an increase of about 85 percent.

The current deficit was financed by unilateral private, institutional, and Government of Israel transfers. In mid-1971, the Jordanian government stopped paying salaries to some ex-Jordanian officials, so total unilateral transfers stood at the same level as in 1970. The transfer from the Government of Israel rose by some 23 percent—from IL 40 million in 1970 to IL 49 million in 1971. This resulted largely from an increase in salaries paid to employees of the military government to compensate for the elimination of the transfers from Jordan and for the considerable price increases that took place during 1971.

Net transfers to Judea and Samaria dropped from IL 127 million to IL 117 million. This was caused primarily by an increase in income tax rates and national insurance payments of area residents working in Israel, deductions for which are made at the source.

Trade via the Jordan bridges increased to about 54 percent of total exports of goods from the West Bank. The region's export surplus of goods to Jordan rose by 86 percent in 1971, to reach about 5 million dinars. The export surplus continued to grow in 1972. This further increased the residents' incomes in dinars. In 1971, the rate of conversion into Israeli lire increased due to special export incentives dependent upon conversion and the August 1971 devaluation of the lire (see Monetary System below).

As stated above, the export of goods is directly affected by the cyclical element in olive yields; yields were high in 1971, so olive oil exports (constituting about 10 percent of total exports) more than doubled, totaling IL 15 million. There was also an increase of more than 40 percent in the export of dairy produce, totaling IL 15.5 million. Exports of goods overseas was less than IL 2 million in both 1971 and 1972 and consisted mainly of handicrafts as in 1970.

As a result of the growth of domestic products, which required greater inputs and investments, imports from overseas rose substantially—from about IL 24 million in 1970 to about IL 54 million in 1972. The nominal value of imports from Israel also rose, but most of this increase reflected the steep price increases in the period. The import of goods from Jordan continued to decline from about 11 percent of total imports in 1969 to about 4 percent in 1972. These imports included cereals, pulses, and seed.

In summary, the volume of trade continued to grow in 1972. Trade with Israel was increased due to stronger economic ties being established between the two economies. Exports to Jordan increased substantially as a result of high yields of olives, citrus, and other fruit, as well as vegetables. Industrial exports also increased as a result of the agricultural productivity: these exports were of processed goods such as olive oil and milk products. The trade deficit was somewhat offset by the export surplus in services which resulted from the rapid and continuous increase in exports of labor services to Israel. There was an increase in services imported as well, which reflected a greater demand for insurance, health, and transportation services by the residents of the West Bank. Imports from Jordan and from overseas grew only slightly; these consist of foodstuffs and investment assets. In 1972, there was a decrease in unilateral transfers from private institutions while at the same time, transfers from the Government of Israel, through the military government, were increased.

Trade with Israel[18]

The economic ties between Israel and the administered areas are reflected in the balance-of-payments figures (see Table 3–10). The process of economic integration among the economies continued into 1971, although Israel did not have to bear an increase in economic burden. Total imports of the administered areas from Israel in 1971 were about IL 356 million. Over 80 percent of these imports were industrial goods, especially foodstuffs (flour and sugar), fuel,

Table 3-10
Trade Balance of the Administered Areas, by Type of Goods, 1969-1971 (IL millions, current prices)

	Overseas			Jordan			Israel		
	1969	1970	1971	1969	1970	1971	1969	1970[a]	1971[b]
Exports									
Agricultural Produce	21	24	55	30	32	30	11	18	17
Industrial Goods	1	1	2	39	28	51	41	58	84
Total	22	25	57	69	60	81	52	76	101
Imports									
Agricultural Produce[b]	27	31	39	17	5	5	42	61	64
Industrial Goods	11	13	30	8	8	9	219	230	292
Total	38	44	69	25	13	14	261	291	356

[a]Estimates.
[b]Foodstuffs, including cereals, flour, oils, sugar, pulses, and milk powder.

Source: *The Economy of the Administered Areas 1971* (Jerusalem: Bank of Israel, 1972), p. 32.

vehicles, and clothing. Agricultural goods imported from Israel were wheat, barley, rice, fruits, and vegetables that were valued at about IL 64 million. Some of
these goods were imported indirectly from Israel from overseas and others consisted of goods produced in Israel with imported inputs. Some products, such as
cigarettes, are both imported from and exported to Israel; the West Bank exports
Turkish type cigarettes that are cheaper than those produced in Israel itself. The
areas export building materials, such as stone, floor tiles, and blocks, as well as
clothing and textiles, some of which are products finished by subcontractors in
the areas.

In 1971, goods exported from the areas to Israel rose by 30 percent; the
import surplus amounted to IL 250 million as compared with IL 215 million in
the preceding year. Total goods and services exported from the areas to Israel
rose by some 70 percent, a major part of which was accounted for by the export
of labor.

Both the increase in income and an increase in the number of residents
working in Israel increased the volume of expenditures made by residents in
Israel. The Bank of Israel reports on a survey which "revealed that a resident of
the administered areas working in Israel spends about one-third of his net wages
on purchases of goods and services in Israel."[19]

In 1972, the volume of trade between the areas and Israel increased by
about 50 percent. This was accounted for by the continued export of labor to
Israel and the import of industrial products from Israel. More work is also being
subcontracted by Israeli firms to plants within the areas. These products include
building materials, such as tiles and building blocks, and clothing made from
Israeli materials. Although the trade deficit increased, this was offset by the
growth in income from labor, which also helped to reduce the current deficit
between 1971 and 1972.

Exports to Israel are predominantly of industrial goods; less than 15 percent
of the exports were agricultural products. Imports from Israel included basic
food stuffs, goods for secondary processing, vehicles, fuel, and electrical appli-
ances. Industrial goods accounted for less than 14 percent of total imports.

Trade over the Jordan Bridges

Trade of the administered areas over the Jordan bridges has undergone some
considerable changes since 1968 (see Table 3-11). Exports from the areas
declined in 1970 primarily as a result of several factors mentioned above, but
also because after the war with the terrorists, neighboring Arab countries severed
diplomatic relationships with Jordan and Jordan cut back imports that would
normally have been sent on to these Arab countries. This embargo was lifted in
1971, and export trade increased by 30 percent. Variations in the components
of the exports can be accounted for by many factors: the cyclical nature of
olive yields; increased productivity of citrus, particularly in the Gaza Strip;

Table 3-11

Trade of the Administered Areas, via The Jordan Bridges, by Commodity Group, 1967-1971

	1967	1968	1969	1970	1971
			EXPORTS		
Total Exports	34.6	54.3	69.0	60.2	80.6
Agricultural Produce	8.2	25.0	28.9	31.1	28.0
Citrus	3.1	9.8	11.6	18.5	18.6
Other Fruit	2.2	6.7	8.5	6.3	6.3
Olives	1.3	0.8	0.3	–	0.1
Vegetables	1.6	7.7	8.5	6.3	3.0
Industrial Exports	26.4	29.8	40.1	29.1	52.6
Olive oil	20.1	8.7	17.2	5.8	15.0
Dairy Produce	–	6.8	9.0	10.8	15.5
Soap	–	4.0	4.2	44.6	6.7
Stones	–	1.5	1.1	0.8	0.5
Plastic Products	–	0.7	0.8	0.8	1.4
Others	6.3	7.6	7.8	6.3	13.5
			IMPORTS		
Total Imports	0.8	18.2	24.9	12.8	14.1
Livestock	–	5.8	8.1	2.6	–
Cereals and Pulses	–	6.2	7.3	1.7	3.0
Seed and Feed	–	1.2	1.4	0.7	1.2
Foodstuffs	–	1.4	1.4	1.0	2.7
Textiles and Cotton	–	0.3	0.5	0.5	0.5
Paper and Printed Material	–	0.1	0.3	0.2	0.3
Machines and Spare Parts	–	0.2	0.7	0.4	0.2
Others	–	3.0	5.2	5.7	6.2

Source: *The Economy of the Administered Areas 1971* (Jerusalem: Bank of Israel, 1972), p. 32.

improved productivity in the dairy industry as a result of improved herds and methods of transport; and variation in productivity as a result of climatic conditions.

Imports have not increased as one would have anticipated because improved trading relations have been established with Israel. Many goods are also cheaper in Israel, as a result of customs duties that are levied on imports from Jordan.

In 1972, goods exported over the Jordan bridges continued to expand by about 50 percent in current prices. Most of the increase was in exports of agricultural produce to Jordan and other Arab countries.

The Monetary Sector

There are certain distinct characteristics that have been identified within the monetary system throughout the period of 1968 to 1972. First, there was no active banking system in operation. The Arab banks were closed at the beginning of the Six Day War, and although they were given permission to reopen several months later, none did. Branches of Israeli banks were established within the West Bank Territory in late 1967. But even into 1972 the rapidly growing activity of these banks was from such a low base as to leave them with a small share in total monetary activity. Currency remains the chief component of the money supply, and there are two currencies in circulation: the Israeli lire and the Jordanian dinar. The third variable in the monetary sector is the market exchange rate between the two currencies. Under these circumstances, the money supply can be increased only by creating a surplus on current and capital accounts in the balance of payments with the rest of the world. This is done in relation to Israel and the East Bank.

The second characteristic is a high propensity to invest in financial assets, or, as a matter of fact, to hoard dinars and other foreign currencies. It is probable that political and economic uncertainties of the Territory underlie the desire to hold currency, but this very accumulation continues to be a barrier to an increase in investment that is so desperately needed.

The third characteristic is a general reluctance to hold Israeli lire. During the archaeological expeditions in 1968 and 1970, for instance, we had to offer a "bonus" to the workers to accept pay in lire, and this "bonus" usually went to the money changers who converted the pay into dinars on the spot. Currency was held only in amounts necessary to carry out transactions with Israeli residents, while saving and hoarding were done in dinars. This explains the relatively small amount of lire in circulation within the Territory, as well as the fluctuations in the rate of exchange between the two currencies.

In 1970, there was some increase in the amount of public deposits and some increase in the amount of credit extended by the banks. The expansion in credit continued into 1971 with most of the credit stemming from government deposits designated specifically for "directed credit" loans for operating capital in agriculture, industry, and services. Loans were granted to residents only on approval from the military government and were subject to approval guaranteed by the Government of Israel. Up until January 1973, banks could only extend directed credit loans because, first of all, there was a maximum 9 percent interest rate on loans established by the Jordanian government and there was no security that the loans would be repaid. In January 1973, Israeli banks were allowed to lend money freely to local residents on their own initiative at a competitive interest rate (the Jordanian law was no longer being enforced). The government guarantees 90 percent of all loans and only those loans exceeding IL 10,000 need approval of the authorities.[20]

There are no complete data on the flows of the means of payment, but the Bank of Israel Research Department suggests some trends:

> Up to 1971 there seems to have been a constant growth in the accumulation of dinars and other foreign currency by residents of the administered areas. On the other hand, no particular rise was observed in the

accumulation of Israel pounds. The turning point was in 1971, especially after the August devaluation, which led to a sizable rise in the amount of currency held by the public, mainly in Israel pounds. This change reflects, *inter alia,* a further tightening of trade relationships in goods, services and production factors between Israel and the administered areas, and a reduction in residents' expectations of a political change in the near future.[21]

In 1971, there was an increase in demand for Israeli pounds brought about by a rise in the conversion of dinars. Over 9 million dinars were converted, as opposed to 2.5 million dinars in 1970. Several reasons for this increase can be cited: rapid price increases in Israel, a change in the rate of exchange, and additional premiums offered for exports.[22] In order for an exporter in the administered areas to be eligible for these incentives, he must convert his dinars into lire. The average effective rate for official conversion (which includes the export premium) was IL 11.76 per dinar, which was higher than the rate on the free market at least until August 1971 (the prevailing free market rate was IL 10 per dinar). The free rate rose to IL 12.17 towards the end of 1971, which was just 3 percent above the official rate. In 1972, conversion privileges entitled exporters to export incentives, which raised the exchange rate of the dinar to approximately the free market rate of IL 12.7 per dinar. About 9.5 million dinars were converted in 1972, compared with 8.7 million dinars in 1971.[23]

There were no major changes in banking activity during 1972; Israeli branch banks did more business, but their relative share in overall monetary activity remained low. It would appear that currency in circulation is still the main component of the total means of payment (probably more than 90 percent).[24] Total deposits of residents doubled during 1972, but as credit to the public grew only slightly, deposit balances were increased.

It is difficult to draw substantive conclusions concerning the monetary sector. The preferred medium of exchange within the Territory is the Jordanian dinar, but it must be remembered that the dinar is a hard currency for it is a member of the sterling block currencies. The Israeli lire is non-convertible, and the residents tend to hold it in quantities sufficient only to meet the needs of daily transactions with Israeli residents and suppliers. The accumulation of currency appears to be the main expression of private saving in spite of an increase in the investment sector. There may be certain sociopolitical ramifications to this decision, but it also appears to reflect an attitude of the Arab toward the monetary sector. Traditionally, the measure of one's wealth was in terms of the volume of real estate held and any accumulation of currency was sent out of the country for safe investment. Those West Bankers who had their assets frozen in Arab banks during the Six Day War also exhibit certain precautionary tendencies toward the banking system. It is interesting to speculate whether or not the reopening of an Arab bank in the Territory would significantly affect current monetary trends.

Notes

1. Data for this chapter are derived from a variety of sources: published and unpublished reports from the Central Bureau of Statistics; publications and reports from the Research Department of the Bank of Israel; *The Israel Economist; The Jerusalem Post* and *The New York Times.* Data for 1972 are preliminary.
2. *The Economy of the Administered Areas 1970* (Jerusalem: Bank of Israel, 1971), p. 5.
3. Ibid., p. 8.
4. Ibid.
5. *The Economy of the Administered Areas 1972* (Jerusalem: Bank of Israel, 1974), p. 14.
6. *The Economy of the Administered Areas 1971* (Jerusalem: Bank of Israel, 1972), p. 10.
7. Ibid., p. 11.
8. Ibid. /
9. The following discussion is based on data prepared and published by the Bank of Israel.
10. *The Economy of the Administered Areas 1971,* p. 15.
11. Ibid.
12. "Refugee Turning Point," *The Israel Economist,* Vol. XXVI, No. 6 (June 1970), p. 129.
13. *The Economy of the Administered Areas 1971,* p. 17.
14. All of these factors are discussed in greater detail in Chapters 4, 5, and 6.
15. *The Economy of the Administered Areas 1970,* p. 26.
16. Ibid., p. 31.
17. Ibid.
18. The following discussion concerns trade between Israel and the administered areas, which include the Gaza Strip, Judea, and Samaria.
19. *The Economy of the Administered Areas 1971,* p. 33.
20. "Israel Guarantees Loans in Administered Areas," *The Israel Economist,* Vol. XXIX, No. 1 (January 1973), p. 20.
21. *The Economy of the Administered Areas 1971,* p. 45.
22. Ibid., p. 47.
23. *The Economy of the Administered Areas 1972,* p. 12.
24. Ibid.

4 The Agricultural Sector

Introduction

Agriculture is a major sector of the economic and social structure of all Middle Eastern countries and especially of the West Bank Territory. The potential of agricultural resources, combined with modern technology, offers many countries an opportunity to escape the vicious cycle of poverty, excessive dependence on agriculture, high birth and death rates, low capital accumulation, and poverty. The obstacles to sustained and rapid increases in agricultural output are great and many are lodged deeply in social and political structures. Stable governments must be established so that long-term resource development and agriculture improvement programs can be undertaken. There must be an improvement in the general infrastructure—transportation, communication, education, financial institutions—as an essential element in both achieving the potential levels of production and exploiting them profitably. Continued improvements within agriculture itself are necessary. And finally, the new attitudes toward knowledge, working relationships with one's friends and with others, and a willingness to modify custom and inherited practices that are no longer functionally efficient are not only necessary, but are most difficult of all to either measure or to achieve.[1]

Agriculture in the West Bank Territory is still a curious and complex mixture of ancient and fully modern technology. Tractors and an occasional combine reap much of the land planted to grain, but there can still be seen women and children pulling meager barley crops from the soil as they harvest the grain for human use and the roots, as well as the stalks, for livestock feed. In some sectors of the West Bank, chemicals for the control of insects, plant disease, and weeds are used extensively, but over large areas, chemicals are not in use and weeds choke out gains. Although there are some modern dairies and chicken producing units, nomads continue to drive herds of sheep and occasionally goats across sparse grassland.

For many reasons, including the above, agriculture prior to 1967 was not as productive as it might have been, nor was livestock production. Most livestock was not fed or pastured on crop farms, but grazed natural pastures and grain stubble the year around. Often too much livestock was kept in relation to the grazing capacity. The animals tended to obtain food sufficient only for their maintenance, leaving little margin for growth or fattening. Many of the

63

animals were diseased and the particular breeds of animals, though well-adapted to the harsh conditions, lacked the capacity to grow rapidly and to multiply even when conditions were more favorable.

The human input into agriculture is largely a function of the general standard of living, the level of nutrition or health, as well as of the disposition of the populace towards work. Much of the agricultural sector is still highly labor intensive, and modernization of the sector must deal with the problem of the displacement of human labor by the introduction and use of machinery and other technological measures necessary to increase agricultural output.

Agricultural Resources and Inputs

Before dealing with many of these problems, it is necessary to review something of the natural resources of the territory as they affect agriculture. Of the 5,500 square kilometers in Judea and Samaria, nearly 40 percent are cultivated, although less than 2 percent are irrigated. Statistics on total agricultural area vary greatly and may reflect yearly changes in climatic conditions. Rainfall is highly variable from one year to the next, and cultivated acreage expands and contracts with the amount of rain received.

The area is mostly arid. A relatively high temperature, a high percentage of sunshine, variability in general frequency of precipitation, and sparseness of vegetation all make this a region of high evaporation. In the summer, the hot drying winds frequently cause severe damage to growing crops, and high natural evaporation leads to severe salt accumulation in the soil wherever water is applied and allowed to evaporate.

The soils are relatively well supplied with nutrient elements other than nitrogen, the low content of which reflects a very low level of organic matter in the soils. The soil has a fairly high content of clay particles, which makes the soil difficult to work with hand tools or with animal power, as it is sticky when wet and cracks deeply when dry.

In the higher rainfall area, from the center of the Territory north, the soils from limestone and marl are favorable for growth of winter grain and can do well in carrying crops into early and mid-summer without irrigation or with only limited supplemental water. Where the area is hilly, much of the surface is exposed to rock. But if there is sufficient soil depth, and if rock terraces can be built, crops can be and are now being grown. For instance, many of the steeper areas have been rock terraced for production of olives. Other areas of thin soils could be managed for grazing. Thus the area of cultivation could be expanded and present farm management practices could be greatly improved.

Toward the Jordan Valley, the soil complex changes to steep rocky lithosols that have some grazing value but are of limited value for crop production. In some of the valleys, soils are deep and there is some water for irrigation.

These areas are cultivated and the available water is used. Much of the soil in the Jordan Valley is salty and requires considerable leaching prior to agricultural production. The valley is very dry and hot, but where there is a water source, such as at Jericho, the land can be highly productive.

In 1967, the Central Bureau of Statistics of the State of Israel conducted a population census in the administered territories. The census revealed that 51,000 (42 percent) of the 119,200 households in Judea and Samaria were found to have farms. The farm population amounted to 283,700 persons or 47 percent of the total population.[2] Fruit plantations were found in 68 percent of all farms, and in 26 percent, they were found the sole branch of agriculture. Field crops were grown by about 58 percent of the farms, and exclusively so by about 13 percent. Vegetables were grown by 29 percent of the farms with 3 percent specializing exclusively in truck farming while livestock—cattle and sheep—were maintained by 23 percent of the farms, of which about 4 percent specialized exclusively in animal husbandry.

Only one crop per year is grown on most of the irrigated area, with the net result that about 1.25 crops per year are grown on the land as a whole. It has been estimated that this figure could be raised to 1.5 crops per acre per year, which would mean that, on the average, a second crop be raised on every other acre.[3] Over one-third of the land in agricultural holdings lies fallow in the winter and more than one-half during the summer. Where soil and water conditions are favorable, two crops are usually grown: a winter crop of mainly barley or wheat and a summer crop, such as maize, tomatoes, or melons. Basically, agriculture is characterized by the application of little capital to the land.

The dry-farm area of the West Bank Territory is in the highlands under conditions of rainfall that range up to 24 inches of rainfall per annum. The crops of this area are mostly wheat and barley though such other crops as olives, lentils, vetch, tomatoes, grapes, and melons are also grown. Some tobacco, planted after the last spring rain, is also produced. Olives are grown on the rougher land in the dry-farm areas. Olive production from year to year is very erratic, but despite this, olives form an important part of the country's agricultural produce. Better management, including a "fertility program" could lead to some stabilization of the annual production.[4] There are good potential grazing areas in the higher rainfall regions of the West Bank, where the land is too rough or too steep for cultivation, but there is a need for better management. Overgrazing has not been controlled nor have the pasture lands been managed for optimum production.

In September of 1967, the Registry Office recorded 147 tractors in use in the West Bank. There was not only an inadequate number of tractors but they were put to poor use. A Food and Agriculture Organization report on Jordan in 1967 stated that the tractors were mainly wheeled tractors of 40 horsepower and over. Their use was largely confined to the grain fields of the north, where their usefulness was limited in that they tended to bring marginal land into use rather than contribute to better cultivation of areas already being exploited.[5]

One of the problems in the Middle East is that the tractors are imported from various countries, and there is great diversity of tractor models, sizes, and types. Maintenance throughout the area is poor; there is a shortage of trained men to service the equipment and a shortage of spare parts for the great variety of tractors. Much of the other machinery that is in use is relatively simple—that is, drawn either by animal power or by hand. Such simple machines and tools, which are generally locally made, utilize age-old designs and traditional materials.

Another form of agricultural input that must be considered is the use of fertilizers, pesticides, and other chemicals. Although there are little data available, it can be assumed that in general there is insufficient use of any fertilizers and chemicals. In the middle East, soil organic-matter levels are very low and only small amounts of nitrogen and phosphorus (so necessary for high yields of wheat and other grains) are made available each year for plant growth by natural microbial decomposition. If nitrogen cannot be furnished by the soil, it must be supplied as animal manure or added as purchased mineral fertilizer. Potassium is available in reasonable amounts, but if high yields are to be expected for long periods of time, it is likely that some additional application may be necessary. Increased fertilizer use must be accompanied by better soil preparation and chemical control of weeds and plant diseases.

Jordan, as a whole, has low total fertilizer use in contrast to Israel, which uses all three kinds of fertilizer—nitrogen, phosphate, and potash—at relatively high rates. Israel produces potash fertilizer derived from evaporation of saline brines of the Dead Sea. There is an export surplus that moves in international trade and is available to the West Bank. Phosphate fertilizer is also produced in both Israel and Jordan, with export surpluses. Israel produces the nitrogenous fertilizer it uses, with no significant import or export, though some is available for the West Bank.[6] While supplies are available, there is need for an increased understanding of the need and use of fertilizers, as well as some assistance in the purchase thereof.

Because of its system of small, owner-operated farms and the relatively small number of large landowners and sharecroppers, land tenure in Jordan is less of a problem for agricultural development than it is in neighboring Arab states. Approximately 70 percent of the farmers till their own soil. Most farmers live in villages rather than on the land worked although land is their most prized possession. Fragmentation of holdings is characteristic, and land is usually owned in several parcels which may be inconveniently distant from one another. The average size of the West Bank farm is 30 to 50 dunams (one dunam equals approximately 0.24 acres) with a few as large as 200 dunams. There are only a few large land holders who tend to sublet their land in small plots to tenant farmers. The landowner and the tenant each get a specified percentage of the return from the land. Leases are usually short, a fact which removes the incentive to invest and improve.

Water is probably the main concern of the farmer. Water sources are of two types: water that falls on the region in the form of rain or snow, a minor part of which later shows up in the flow of streams and springs; and water that is carried into the region by major rivers, which either arise outside of the region or originate along the extreme northern border as does the Jordan River. The Jordan and its tributaries are divided among Israel, Syria, and Jordan. It is a small stream with a total supply of 1.25 million acre-feet for the whole system. There are some miscellaneous areas of underground water supplies of great importance, such as those at Jericho. The greatest handicap to the area is the lack of rainfall. A high rate of evaporation, the irregularity of precipitation, and a negligible dewfall reinforce the effects of scarcity of rain. Practically all precipitation comes during the winter and early spring. The Palestinian hills and the northern sector receive the most abundant rainfall and are, therefore, the most productive areas in the territory.

Agriculture, pre-June 1967[7]

The agricultural capital stock as of June 1967 consisted mainly of fruit tree plantations, most of which were not irrigated. They covered an area of about 340,000 dunams, but this included between 60,000 and 65,000 dunams of trees that were too young to bear fruit. About half the total area were vineyards, and fig and almond groves constituted a large portion of the remaining half. Olive groves covered over 600,000 dunams. The stock of livestock consisted of about 1.8 million head of sheep, some 72,000 head of cattle—mostly of local stock—and about a million fowl. There is no estimate of the number of goats, which was still considerable even though the Jordanian government had undertaken a long-term project of replacing goat herds with cattle. As noted above, there was relatively little farm machinery (the Economic Planning Authority had originally estimated some 1,000 tractors for approximately 60,000 farms, but the census corrected this number to about 147). Most of the work was done with the aid of approximately 50,000 work animals, mostly donkeys. Cattle were also used for pulling plows, tilling, and so forth.

The agricultural output in 1966 was estimated at 17 million Jordanian dinars (at the rate of exchange JD 1 equals $2.80, the value was $47.6 million). Approximately one-quarter of the output was derived from the production of fruit, one-fifth from vegetables, one-third from livestock, and the rest from field crops. Because of fluctuations in the amount of annual rainfall, in recent years prior to 1966, the annual output varied from 14 million dinars in a drought year to 18 million dinars in a year with a good rainfall.

Field crops consisted mostly of wheat, barley, and other grain crops. All the wheat is winter wheat, for the cool winter climate is more congenial to wheat than the hot summer climate of the area. Wheat has long occupied most of the rainfed lands capable of growing economical yields. But year-to-year variations are significant and almost wholly a function of the total precipitation. The relationship between wheat yield and annual rainfall in Jordan provides a typical example. Not only does more rain mean higher wheat yield, but the increase in yield is more than proportionate to the increase in rain—an increase of 10 points in the rain index leads to an increase of about 17 points in the wheat yield index.[8] This may well understate the relationship, as in years of low rainfall, marginal areas are not harvested, for the return would not compensate for the cost of harvesting, so these areas do not even enter the yield statistics. This relationship is derived from data for natural rain, but the same results could possibly be obtained by better conservation of the moisture that does fall— that is, for example, more efficient fallowing as a means of increasing available moisture or perhaps increasing the amount of irrigation.

Barley is another ancient crop of the Middle East, for it is generally similar to wheat in its requirements for moisture and climate. It is also a winter crop, grown on rainfed lands. As with wheat, the production of barley was highly variable in the West Bank. In a good year, the output of barley could reach about 80,000 tons, while in a dry year, it would drop to about 35,000 tons. This variability in the production of barley, a feed grain, was not conducive to stable livestock feeding operations.

Vegetables and melons are grown in all parts of the West Bank, but particularly in the Nablus-Jenin area where rainfall is plentiful and irrigation is practiced in some of the fields. The various vegetables all have some seasonal characteristics, due in part to their climatic requirements. It is not clear whether the official statistics report all vegetables grown, including those which the farmers consume in their own families or villages, or whether they report primarily marketed vegetables. About 20 percent of the truck farm output consists of watermelons, another 20 percent of tomatoes, with other vegetables making up the rest. About half the vegetables produced in the entire Kingdom of Jordan were grown in the West Bank. The quantitative output of most varieties measured about half that of Israel's truck farms. The lack of a vegetable-processing industry reduced the possibilities for balancing seasonal production with seasonal demand.

The main fruit varieties grown are grapes, olives, and citrus fruits. Vineyards are concentrated in the Hebron area, citrus orchards in the area of Kalkilya-Tulkarem and the Jordan valley, and olives are scattered over the entire mountain district, but especially in the Nablus-Ramallah area. Olives and grapes are ancient crops in this ancient land. The West Bank used to produce most of Jordan's olives—about two or three times as much as are grown in Israel, and the grape harvest amounted to over 40,000 tons per year—about the same as Israel's harvest. Each is a deep-rooted crop, capable of drawing soil moisture from deep levels to sustain itself, and therefore able to produce fruit during the long rainless summers. The trees and vines are usually on terraced land, except near Hebron where large fields of vines are cultivated. Many of the olive trees are quite old and yield poorly. Since these are each long-lived plants, the acreage —though not the yield—is stable from year to year.

The citrus industry has not been exploited although it was in the process of being expanded during the period prior to June 1967. Israel, however, has expanded its acreage greatly and today citrus is an important earner of foreign exchange for Israel. The oranges are of very high quality, yields are high, and the fruit has been marketed in Western Europe.

A wide variety of fruits, including the famed Lebanese apples, are found in the hill country. Grapefruit, lemons, bananas, mandarins and tangerines, as well as guavas are also grown.

As with the vegetables, there is relatively little processing for use outside of the fresh season. Some wine is made, olive oil and its by-products are of importance, but nothing is accomplished on the scale that characterizes the processing industry in Israel. Yields of citrus compare favorably with the United States in both Israel and Jordan.

Thus the West Bank raises some high-value crops, such as fruits and vegetables, but its total crop acreage is dominated by large areas of cereals—which are usually relatively low-valued per acre, especially where such low yields are obtained.

The output of the livestock industry was estimated at 6 million dinars for 1966, but a member of the Economic Planning Authority cautioned that this figure may have been too high. About one-third of this figure was meat—mainly mutton—another third was milk, about one-sixth eggs, and the remainder various by-products. The West Bank supplied about 40 percent of Jordan's entire livestock and dairy produce although the quantity was still very small when compared with Israel's output.

Most of the cattle are native breeds, and they are allowed open grazing, though they are less well suited to this than sheep or goats. They are used for a number of functions: as work animals, for milk production, and they, as well as their offspring, for meat. Sheep are an important source of milk as well as of wool and meat. Goats are another important source of milk, and they also produce mohair and meat. Goats have a long, very bad reputation for destructiveness in grazing on natural ranges. They will eat many types of forage that neither cattle nor sheep will, and, as they are physically more active than sheep, they may actually climb small trees to eat leaves. Much of the fault for overgrazing, however, lies not with the particular animal, but rather with the lack of management of the land. There has been an increasing production of poultry in the Middle East in general and particularly in Israel and in Jordan. Some of the increase is commercial broiler production, but much is from small flocks on farms.

In many of the grazing regions, the owner of the livestock uses the land without firm land tenure. The first man on the land with his livestock gets the grass. Under these circumstances, no livestock operator has any interest in

either managing or conserving forage. Overgrazing of range is an inevitable conse-
quence of insecure land tenure, and overgrazing means that the animals are
poorly fed. Often weeds are allowed to grow on fallow land and the animals
are turned loose to graze on the weeds. The primary function of fallow in the
grain-fallow rotation program is the accumulation of moisture. But this function
is completely lost if weeds are allowed to grow for they use the moisture. More-
over, the weeds are a poor livestock feed both in volume and quality. More feed
for livestock and more grain could be produced, at lower cost, if some of the
lower-yielding land were retired from grain production and planted to permanent grasses, and on the better lands, a strict grain-fallow rotation were practiced.

With the exceptions of a few districts and products, subsistence farming
was the rule, with only part of the output reaching the market. Grain crops
were produced primarily for domestic consumption, mostly by the rural population, and except in a particularly good year, the West Bank did not produce
enough to meet its own requirements. In 1965, for instance, it imported almost
two million dinars worth of grain. Vegetables were raised both for private consumption on the farm and for sale. Olives were sold to the edible oil and soap
industries.

Livestock was raised for on-the-farm consumption, and only small quantities ever reached the urban market. This necessitated supplementary import
of meat, milk, fish, and eggs, which totaled about one million dinars in 1965.
Imports of other foodstuffs, such as sugar, tea, and coffee, amounted to nearly
two million dinars in the same year.

The West Bank exported vegetables and fruit both to the East Bank and to
neighboring Arab states. In 1965, sales from the West to the East Bank were
estimated at 1.5 million dinars with sales being divided evenly between vegetables (tomatoes, potatoes, watermelons) and fruit (citrus and grapes). In that
same year, the West Bank exported to foreign countries about 1.5 million dinars
in vegetables and some fruit.

Trading in produce was concentrated in the hands of a few large wholesalers in the larger urban centers of Hebron, Jerusalem, Ramallah, Nablus, and
Jenin. The transaction between the farmer and wholesaler was made either in
the field or in town, and the produce was hauled in the wholesaler's trucks. The
wholesalers distributed the produce through municipal auction markets. Between one-third and one-half of the retail price went to the producer. In recent
years, there has been no clear upward or downward price trend, although there
were significant annual and seasonal fluctuations that depended on the size of
the output.

Agricultural development programs in the West Bank were designed to expand production by increasing the water supply, creating better land utilization
schemes, expanding plantations, and introducing more advanced methods of
farming. These programs required large capital investments, but as capital re-

sources of Jordan were limited and there was very little private capital available for agriculture, aid had to be obtained from abroad. The development program planned for 1967–1970 estimated a total investment of 5.5 million dinars for the country of Jordan, part of which was expected to come from the World Bank. An additional 30 million dinars were to be invested in the development of water resources.

Farm credit to be used for development and investment was extended by the Agricultural Credit Corporation, which was established in 1961. Medium- and long-term loans were granted to finance projects conforming to the overall development program. The interest rate was originally set at 5 percent, but was scheduled to rise to 6 percent in 1967 or 1968. Short-term operating capital loans at 7 to 8 percent interest were available from farm cooperatives that were affiliated with a central corporation operating on credit received from the Agricultural Credit Corporation. Short-term loans could also be obtained from commercial banks at an interest rate of 8 to 9 percent. Some of the non-institutional sources—such as wholesalers, landowners, and distributors—also offered funds, but they usually charged a very high rate of interest.

Agriculture, post-June 1967

The foundation of Moshe Dayan's administrative policy in all the occupied territories was first to get the public services going and then to reactivate municipalities and other institutions in their previous Jordanian form. On Thursday, June 8, the formation administrative unit started functioning in Nablus, and on Sunday, June 11, a young Operations Officer, Eytan Israeli, was appointed Formation Agricultural Officer. Eytan had been educated at the Kadoori Agricultural School and had recently returned from a four-year U.N. agricultural advisory position in West Africa. It was great good fortune for all concerned that this man was chosen to run what became a most successful agricultural rehabilitation program.

The agricultural year of 1966–67 had been one of record production. After a long, hard, very wet winter, spring came quickly and the hot weather turned the countryside into a green fertile area. It was a year of bumper crops for both Israel and Jordan. But the fields in the West Bank had not been tended for upwards of 11 days when Eytan was appointed Agricultural Officer and they were in desperate need of harvesting or whole crops would be lost. At the same time, the supplies of food in the towns and villages were running very low. Eytan met first with the mayor of Nablus, and within two days he had reassembled the staff of the Jordanian Department of Agriculture, Nablus District. He seemed to operate more out of a concern for the problems of agriculture than for the duties of an occupying administrator. In spite of strict curfew regulations, men were allowed to begin working the wells and water machinery to keep the cattle from dying of thirst. By June 14, the non-curfewed hours for farm workers had been increased from the usual three hours to twelve hours, so the fields could be worked and the harvest reaped.

On June 18, an evaluation of the agricultural sector was presented to the Israeli Director General of the Department of Agriculture. On the West Bank there were approximately two million acres under cultivation. It was the high season of agriculture and most of the vegetable and fruit crops, as well as the wheat, were ripening. The war and the razing of the bridges over the Jordan had cut off the West Bank commercially from the Arab countries. Between a half and two-thirds of the agricultural produce sold in the past to markets east of the Jordan would become surplus, while there would be a shortage of everything that the West Bank had previously imported from the East Bank or via Akaba. Shortages of wheat and barley, as well as minor shortages of other grains and legumes, could be met by Israel from its own warehouses or by imports. But the anticipated surplus of about 120,000 tons of agricultural produce could not be absorbed by Israel without destabilizing its own economy. Sale of West Bank produce was strictly forbidden in Israel; since the produce was not only abundant, but also much cheaper, it was feared that sales might result in the collapse of the Israeli agricultural sector.

Long- and medium-range objectives were quite clear: planning was to prevent surpluses and to integrate the West Bank agricultural production into the Israeli economy. But the short-range problem seemed insoluble. Various economic ministries of the government sought a solution by improvisation: part of the surplus would be abosrbed by the Israeli canning industry for preserves, juices, and canned fruits; part would be bought up with subsidies and destroyed; part would be sold in European markets; part sold to Zahal (the Army) and social welfare institutions in the occupied territories and Israel. In spite of this it was clear to the Ministry of Agriculture that no satisfactory solution had been found and that from an economic point of view the West Bank was in for difficult times. Many, including Dayan, understood that the imminent economic difficulties would serve as a convenient background for renewed activities of the Arab terrorist organizations, for economic crises are fuel for any underground movement. It appeared that Israel might forfeit its military victory in the agricultural market.[9]

The short-run solution to the problem was suggested to Eytan Israeli by a wealthy Arab farmer who saw his large holding of ripe produce being lost for lack of a market. In the summer, the Jordan river is very low and in the middle valley there are several places where trucks could easily ford the river. Without receiving official permission from Jerusalem, the Nablus command allowed two trucks from Jenin to deliver tomatoes to the river. At the river the produce was off-loaded and reloaded onto trucks from Amman and a Jenin merchant accompanied the trucks toward market. Tomatoes were selling for 10 fils a kilo in the West Bank and the first shipment to Amman sold for 80 fils a kilo. More trucks were "allowed" to cross and, when it became obvious how desirable the arrangement was, official permission was requested from the Command in Jerusalem. The official report for the week of July 16–22 read as follows:

> Four hundred trucks and tractors have crossed to the East by the end
> of the week, at the rate of about one hundred a day. Apart from tak-
> ing bribes, the Jordanian guards are not interfering in any way. To
> speed up the procedure, trucks and tractors should be allowed to drive
> to the market and should not be required to off-load and transfer the
> goods to vehicles from the East Bank.[10]

Thus began the "open bridges" policy that opened up the import–export market for the West Bank. West Bankers benefited in numerous ways by this trade. It was found, for instance, that the propane gas systems of Israel and Jordan were not compatible and as the tanks were being emptied, no refills were available. When trucks were returning from Amman, they were able to carry back much needed supplies of propane gas, and soon more than produce was being exchanged via the open bridges.

By August, the beginnings of an agricultural revolution had taken place in the West Bank. The farmers had discovered a new world of modern agriculture, and the Israeli agricultural experts were enthusiastically embarking on a challenge of which they had never dreamed: to advance the backward agriculture in "one fell swoop." Instructors of the Israeli Ministry of Agriculture spread out in teams throughout the West Bank. They discovered that the strains of wheat and other crops were virtually unchanged in 20 years; in the same period Israel had begun to develop her own agricultural potential. The West Bank wheat, for instance, was an unselected, traditional hybrid while Israel had meticulously cultivated strains suitable to her own conditions.

An agricultural plan was undertaken to conduct a vigorous policy of improvement of plant varieties and cultivation methods on the West Bank. Improved varieties would be more readily marketable both in Israel and for the export market and would provide greater yields at better prices. New varieties developed in Israel were introduced: the Ayalon and Rehovot 13 tomatoes, Beit Alpha cucumbers, and barley of the Omar strain, as well as the Florence-Aurore wheat strain that yielded over three times the yield per dunam of the average Jordanian strain. Cultivation of these improved strains necessitated increased care in handling as well as in using chemical fertilizers, such as nitrogen sulphate and phosphorus, which were supplied by the chemical industries in Israel.

The Higher Agricultural Council was established, as well as six public boards similar to those in Israel, to examine the execution of policy of improved farming and the dissemination of technology. About seven of the more prominent personalities in the West Bank agricultural community were involved in these boards, which included boards for citrus, fruit and grapes, tobacco, corn, poultry and dairy farming, and olive oil. All this was accomplished by August 1967.

During winter, the Jordan River would become too swollen for the trucks to ford the river, so the Israeli government cooperated with the Jordanian government. Jordan built a Bailey bridge across the river and Israel paved the road to the bridge. But plans were formulated by Israel in the event that the bridges might be closed and an alternative marketing schedule was drawn up for such an event. When Jordan and her neighboring Arab states severed diplomatic relationships in July 1971, the alternate scheme was put into effect and was operated successfully. The scheme was similar to the improvised scheme of 1967.

A more serious problem was facing the dairy farmers, as many of the West Bank cows were infected with bovine brucellosis and tuberculosis. Israelis were apprehensive that their own herds might become infected, so in 1968, a combined commission of West Bank and Israeli veterinary surgeons was established. The chief veterinarian of the West Bank, Dr. Hatem Kamel, was given the task and the finances to put into effect the Jordanian supervisory laws. All cows were branded and blood samples were taken from each. After analysis, the combined commission of Israeli and Palestinian vets would decide which cows were to be destroyed and how much compensation would be paid the owners. Within a few years the West Bank should have healthy dairy herds.

As early as 1968, a new problem was threatening the agricultural sector: profits were declining at a rapid rate. Farmers had been encouraged to adopt a new crop program that involved changing from watermelon production and other high-water-content produce to leguminous crops in order to reduce the dependence of the West Bank agricultural economy upon Jordan and the markets to the east. Preservable crops, such as beans, sesame, and cotton, had been introduced. Should the bridges be closed and the eastern markets sealed off, the West Bank farmer would not be threatened with disaster, as the crops could be stored for marketing at a later date or in another market. Unemployment had been a problem in the West Bank in 1967 and 1968, so labor-intensive crops had been chosen. Initially, the crop program showed good results.

As the Israeli economy began to demand more labor from the West Bank, unemployment declined and wages rose to a level double those prevailing in Jordan. Farmers had to increase farm hands' pay until it too had doubled. As wages constituted half the production costs of unirrigated crops, costs increased by 25 percent, while income from produce sold in Jordan remained constant. During this same period imports from Israel replaced previous cheaper sources, which also caused a rise in prices. Shirts, pencils, fuel, construction materials, and consumer goods imported from Israel were double the price of former Jordanian goods.

A deep-rooted social and economic transformation was beginning. The owners of marginal farms were the first victims, as they, unable to pay the higher wages and meet the high costs, either gave up farming completely, or left the farm to the women and children and went out to find other work in Israel. This was the beginning of the process of urbanization via migration. Large farm owners were faced with the increasing cost problem and sought a short-run solution of returning to their traditional crops, including watermelon, which required the least amount of labor. But the growers would again be dependent upon the bridges across the Jordan or upon marketing in Israel, which already had sufficient quantities under cultivation. It became necessary to integrate the West Bank and the Israeli economies so as to arrive at a two-way traffic of agricultural produce and to develop West Bank agriculture so that yields would increase, thereby increasing sales, which would help to solve the problem of rising input costs. This decision of the Ministry of Agriculture was an outcome of circumstances and not a result of a preconceived policy.

A five-year plan for the West Bank was formulated, and it depended heavily upon increasing educational and training programs and extension services to the West Bank. Two instructors were appointed from Israel, one for irrigation crops and another for vegetables; these men would provide training for the Palestinians selected to serve as chief instructors. The West Bank Department of Agriculture hired 22 Arab agronomists, some of whom had returned from universities abroad (mostly from Cairo) and some of whom had been employed as teachers and clerks in other departments. Courses for practical work and theoretical study were instituted, and a new section for agricultural development was established in the West Bank Agricultural Department.

Thus, all of the structural changes that were introduced by the Israeli Department of Agriculture followed the necessary routes for agricultural development. In reviewing the first five years of progress, Mr. Assael Ben-David, the Ministry of Agriculture official who replaced Eytan Israeli as agricultural officer on the West Bank, summed up as follows:

> Passing through the fields of Judea and Samaria one sees crops which were never grown there before, such as tomatoes for industry, early onions for export, sugar beet, peanuts, cotton, among others . . . . In Judea and Samaria today tractors can be seen ploughing and spreading chemical fertilizers; the tractors are also used in spraying operations and in other parts one sees the farmers spraying their orchards, using special back packs. This sight shows that there has been a very important change in the farmers' thinking and in his systems of work.
>
> Visiting the Jordan Valley or the Jenin region one sees the extensive use of irrigation systems, both drip and sprinkler, and sees large areas covered in plastic (as plant protection material). The visitor begins to realize that what has happened here is not a slow, evolutionary development, but a revolutionary leap forward in the development of the region's agriculture.[11]

Experimental stations were either reactivated or new ones set up and demonstration plots were planted in or near many of the villages. The farmers were able to see how new systems of work, new varieties of crops, use of pesticides and fertilizers, and the use of plant protection materials were able to increase yields. As many as 16 agriculture experts were eventually attached to the Military Government and by 1972, 150 Arab instructors, 70 of whom were university graduates, were working in the Territory. An extension center was established in Ramallah for training instructors in technological improvements as developed by Israel's farmers and agricultural research institutes. In 1972, a land enrichment program was undertaken, and the positive response of the Arab farmers was beyond the expectations of the Israeli instructors.

In attempting to control the spread of disease among the livestock, imports from Jordan were forbidden by the Military Government. The Territory was not self-sufficient in the production of livestock for their own use, so Israel allowed the import of sheep from Rumania. Farmers were encouraged to allow their own sheep to reach a weight of 50 to 70 kilos instead of slaughtering them at a weight of 15 to 18 kilos. It is estimated that within three to four years increased production will meet the needs of the West Bank population.[12] The potential increase in livestock production represents the farmers' acceptance of Israeli technological developments in special foodstuffs and proper veterinary services.

In 1971, a program for the rehabilitation of the orchards was undertaken. Olive production is the second largest branch of agriculture, as there are 600,000 dunams planted with some 6 million olive trees. Efforts were also extended to improving the production of almond and pistachio nuts. Special machinery was introduced for use in the hilly areas, where many of the orchards are located, as the increasing wages of hired labor had made it uneconomical to continue farming the hilly areas. The results of this program are only beginning to be realized.

As stated above, there were three stages to Israel's agricultural policy on the West Bank. The first was to return conditions to as near normal as possible; this was achieved quite rapidly. The second stage was to improve existing practices and production. This was achieved through the introduction and training in use of fertilizers and pesticides and improved plant protection materials; the introduction of new varieties and strains of crops, as well as crop rotation and crop substitution programs; a continuing emphasis upon the necessity of education through both Israeli and Arab agronomists, extensive demonstration plots, special training sessions on location, and the use of trade fairs to introduce new methods and equipment to the local farmers.

The third stage of the agricultural policy was to find new markets for the produce. Originally, transport across the Jordan opened up an export trade for the Territory, but there was always the possibility that the bridges might be closed. Alternative marketing schemes were developed. First, the farmer had the possibility of the local market and the Gaza Strip. Over the five year period, both markets have grown in their need for quality, quantity, and variety of food. Also as more of the marginal farms were closed out as the men found work in Israel, this increased the need for higher production on the existing farm land. Secondly, the Israeli market was opened to the West Bank produce in 1971. Prior to this time, Israelis bought in the territory or else produce was sent in via a black market organization, in which case the farmer did not benefit from the higher prices prevailing in Israel. In Israel, all produce is marketed through a central board, and quantity and prices are well controlled. In July 1971, restrictions were eased on the sale of fruit grown in Judea and Samaria in an effort to assist the Arab farmers who had lost most of their markets when Syria and Iraq closed their borders with Jordan. Jordan suspended most importing as she was able to absorb only a small quantity of the usual imports of fruit. Restrictions on sales of produce in Israel were abolished completely at the beginning of September. This coincided with the decision of the Arab League to implement a boycott of farm products from the administered areas. The league claimed the Israeli goods, disguised as goods from the areas, were being shipped into the Arab states. This claim was denied by all in the West Bank and Israel. It is interesting to note the quantities of produce involved: Judea and Samaria were permitted to send 15 tons of plums a day to Israel in addition to the then current daily quota of 10 tons to Jerusalem. It was estimated that the total production of plums would be 3,500 tons, as compared to the previous year's production of 2,100 tons, all of which was exported to Jordan. As of August 1, the West Bank farmers were permitted to sell 25 tons of grapes a day to Israel, and in subsequent months, restrictions were slowly relaxed as the agricultural sectors became more integrated.[13]

The third market available to the farmers was Jordan and via Jordan, other Arab countries that had been the natural customers of the West Bank in the pre-war period. This was an unreliable market, as explained above, and trade with Jordan by 1972 was down approximately 20 percent as the farmers found and developed more reliable markets in Israel or in Europe. Also, Jordan had imposed an import tax which reduced further the farmer's profits from this market.

The fourth market was a totally new market for the West Bank farmer. As the variety and quality of the crops improved, Agrexco, the Israel agricultural export marketing company, began to operate in the West Bank. They first took over and modernized a packing plant in Jericho and subsequently established packing plants and cold storage houses in other parts of the Territory. In 1972, 1,200 tons of early onions were exported to Europe as well as avocados, tomatoes, melons and watermelons and peppers.[14] The farmers received the same prices as the Israeli farmers, and these prices were well above those received in either the local market or the Arab market via Jordan.

Improvements in other aspects of the general infrastructure were also being made. Israel is cited as an outstanding practitioner of the proper implementation of a theory of spatial organization.[15] The main objectives of Israel spatial design are settlement, defense, resource development, and conservation. With the exception of defense, at least in the evaluation of the Israelis, each of these goals may be applied to the development of the West Bank Territory. In the tradition of August Lösch,[16] the overall goal of spatial and locational design would be for every rural producer to be within convenient travel time of some adequately competitive selling place for his produce, some equally competitive source of consumers' and producers' goods, and some adequately diversified service center. These market centers are only the basic building blocks of a much more complex hierarchy of central places capable of bringing the entire spatial economic structure together in a truly functional sense. The market centers are already well established in the Territory and are the prewar markets of Jenin, Nablus, and Hebron. Jerusalem was the most important distributive center, but her position vis-à-vis the West Bank is now considerably changed (see Chapter 7). Israel has made extensive improvements in the road systems connecting these centers as well as in the feeder road systems from the villages to the centers. Whether further spatial development will be undertaken remains open to question. Some light industrial development has taken place within the market centers, and cottage industries have been encouraged in more rural centers, but, if Israel is to continue to employ the number of laborers from the West Bank, which she has to date (some 40,000), it is unlikely that much effort will be made to encourage the development of either the settlement service centers or the regional service centers as the Israeli plan originally envisaged. One finds that the contrasts between rural and urban areas is becoming more evident in Israel itself, and there is considerable back flow from the rural areas to the urbanized centers, particularly to the coastal zones. As agriculture tends to become more capital intensive and the fraction of the work force engaged in farming declines, the same trend is taking place in the Territory. One main difference exists, however; the labor force that works in Israel is bussed across the green line on a daily basis, but it is still necessary for the laborer to be in one of the centers from which the buses leave. No settlement of West Bank Arabs within Israel is allowed.

In the Israeli government budgets for the 1968–69 and for 1969–70, specific sums were allocated for Judea and Samaria. *The Israel Economist* reported that in 1968–69, 2.96 million Israeli lire were spent on the administered areas, large sums of which were devoted to agricultural research and to direct assistance to the area's agricultural development. It is not specified what percentage of this money went to the Gaza Strip and what percentage to the Territory. In the 1969–70 budget, IL 4.36 million was designated for Judea and Samaria as follows:

2.00 million for development of water sources;
.54 million for agricultural development (as for pasture land development);

.74 million on water surveys;

.53 million on water surveys in specified agricultural branches;

.50 million for loans to agriculturalists and for establishment of
packing houses and cold storage houses.[17]

In 1970, extensive efforts were directed toward various water development
schemes. Most of the population of Judea and Samaria had previously been dependent upon well water and water accumulated in cisterns. Pipe lines were laid
connecting various villages and drilling efforts by the Israelis yielded good results
in the regions of Salfit, Tubas, Axoun, Sebastia, Samoa, and Nablus. A Master
Plan for the Supply of Drinking Water was drawn up and the projected needs for
the Territory were based on the assumption that over the next decade or two,
the living standards of the Arabs inhabiting the region would reach the standards
prevailing among the Arabs of Galilee. Water conservation programs were also
undertaken aimed at improving the use of water among the Arabs (e.g., requirements for citrus groves in the Arab part of the Jordan valley are nearly 4,000
cubic meters per dunam as compared with 1,200 cubic meters per dunam in
the Beisan valley Jewish settlements). Water development in Judea and Samaria
is financed by funds supplied by the Military Government, and the work is carried out under the auspices of the Israel Ministry of Agriculture. Upon completion, the water networks are transferred to the local authorities.[18]

It is difficult to derive exact figures from subsequent budget presentations,
as the sums designated for the Territroy are included in a variety of lines.

The Israeli banks opened up offices in the Territroy when it became apparent that the Jordanian branches would not be reopened. These banks are
empowered to extend credit to the public, most of which is "directed credit"
designated for operating capital in agriculture, industry, and services. This credit
rose from IL 300,000 in 1967 to IL 11,598,000 in 1971, but this credit is the
total for all the administered areas and no breakdown according to territory or
sector is available.[19] In January 1973, the Israeli government passed legislation
enabling the banks to lend money to the Arabs on loans other than on "directed
credit" loans. Directed credit loans needed the approval of the authorities, but
they were fully guaranteed. The more liberal loan regulations waived the interest
rate ceiling (as Jordanian law applied in the Territory, there was a 9 percent ceiling on interest rates) and provided a guarantee of 90 percent of all loans.[20] This
should encourage increased use of the credit system.

Development theory predicts that there are two basic problems that must
be dealt with in agriculture in most of the economically less advanced countries:
the growth of agricultural productivity, which we have been discussing; and land
tenure reform, or the redistribution of land ownership. As stated above, the
average size of the West Bank farm is 30 to 50 dunams, with a few larger farms
of up to 200 dunams; these larger areas are usually sublet to tenant farmers.
Little effort has been expended in the area of land tenure reform for several
reasons. Many of the small holdings are farmed in a cooperative manner by mem-

bers of villages or adjacent rural areas. Machinery is used on a cooperative basis, and returns for production are recorded on a traditional informal basis. Also, it is very difficult to determine clear title to much of the land under cultivation in the Territory. In discussions with members of the United States Consul General's office in Jerusalem, this very problem was raised. The U.S. government has been investigating land ownership questions, and any clear decisions in this problem are not evident. Much of the land appears to belong to the Jordanian government but has been extended on a loan-use basis. As deaths have occurred or tenant farmers have moved, the use of the land would pass to other members of the family, tribe, or village. It appears that now many people no longer know whether they in fact own the land or are using the land on a "loan basis" from the government. As long as areas are farmed in a somewhat cooperative arrangement, the necessity of extensive land tenure reform has been outside the interest of the Israeli government.

In an interesting study on "Agrarian Reform and Urbanization in the Middle East," Elias H. Tuma found that agrarian reform policies have frequently run counter to the logical relationship between agricultural development and urbanization without providing adequate compensatory aids to development. Agrarian reform has frequently favored urban areas at the expense of rural areas, contrary to its basic objectives, and "has thus created an artificial demographic stability which has handicapped rural change and economic development."[21] Tuma uses the term agrarian reform to mean any rapid and conscious improvement in the agrarian structure, which includes land tenure, the pattern of farming, the terms of holding and scale of farm operation, and rural credit.[22] It is a matter of controversy whether development in general—and development of agriculture in particular—should precede, accompany, or follow urbanization. It is commonly argued that development should precede urbanization—assuming that in sparsely populated areas, rural labor is needed to produce more food and raw material for the country, while in densely populated areas, rural labor should remain in the countryside until the urban economy has developed and become capable of absorbing them. Agrarian reform should be one mechanism of implementing this policy, but it appears not to have been wholly successful in its implementation in the Middle East. In conclusion, Tuma offers various "Implications and Alternatives."[23] Certain agrarian reforms, such as land tenure security, membership in cooperatives, low technology in agriculture, and traditional family ties have inhibited migration. Other measures used to consciously discourage migration have failed to improve rural conditions sufficiently to remove the "pull and push" factors tending to migration. Tuma suggests alternative measures for consideration in order to promote development: (1) increase labor productivity, which will generate higher incomes and hence more savings; (2) allow investment policy to be guided by the expected marginal productivity of capital and by its impact on the utilization of other factors of production; (3) create non-agricultural job opportunities in rural areas to stem migration to the urban centers;

(4) increase capital formation by utilizing the underemployed and the unemployed rural labor force with little or no investment of scarce capital resources in such projects as land improvement, irrigation, afforestation, building of roads and schools, and slum clearing, and (5) place more emphasis on the pattern of cultivation and aids to labor productivity and less emphasis on institutional arrangements, such as land tenure security and membership in cooperatives. The income from the land is what has significance, not the land itself.

Israel is one of the five Middle Eastern countries that Tuma studies, the others being Iran, Iraq, Syria, and the UAR. Israel does stand out in contrast to the time-tradition bound ways of the Arab countries. It must be noted that in the administration of the Territory, Israel has laid emphasis on the alternative measures that Tuma suggests: emphasizing productivity increases, creating non-agricultural job opportunities, using the underemployed or unemployed rural labor force in local projects, encouraging capital investment where marginal productivity of capital is greatest, and emphasizing the returns which can be generated from the crops rather than being concerned with institutional arrangements, in spite of Israel's exemplary work in this aspect of agrarian reform. On the other hand, the type of migration which the industrial and agricultural sectors of the Israeli economy have encouraged is the daily bussing of tens of thousands of West Bankers across the green line; these workers are the core of the unskilled labor market in Israel.

Productivity and Potential[24]

The value of agricultural output in Judea and Samaria in 1967-68 was IL 135 million; in 1971-72, the value of the output had risen to IL 280 million in current prices. During this same period, the farmer's daily wage increased from IL 14.20 to IL 31 per day.[25] But a new feature was being evidenced in the agricultural sectors of Israel and the administered areas: an attempt was being made to include all three economies (Israel, the West Bank, and the Gaza Strip) in a common agricultural planning scheme. Crop specialization has been introduced according to the relative advantages of each region. Watermelons grown in the areas have been reduced and melons are imported from Israel; vegetables for winter exports are grown in the Jordan Valley; Hebron grapes are used to supplement needs of the wine and juice producers in Israel. The incomes of the farmers who have participated in the crop specialization schemes have increased and have also served as incentives for others to participate.

In 1970, the first suggestions were made towards establishing free trade between Israel and Judea and Samaria in agricultural commodities. Until December 1971, supervision teams were at the check points from the West Bank to Israel to ensure that only the necessary amounts of produce entered and that surpluses endangering the Israeli farmer were not created. However, in December the teams were removed for a trial period of four months, and when that period expired, it was decided not to reinstate the inspection. In 1972, the Israeli Ministry of Agriculture requested that a single marketing system be established. The proposal suggested recognizing West Bank wholesalers as licensed and called for the collection of a levy for agricultural production councils on all produce sent to Israel, the determination of a single price system for Israeli and West Bank produce, and the setting of minimum prices. To date, the military administration has opposed this out of concern that the levies may increase the price of goods, but it appears that this opposition may be temporary and integration among the sectors is continuing.

The volume of real agricultural output in Judea and Samaria during the agricultural year October 1970 to September 1971 rose by 14.2 percent, a total in value of IL 227 million (see Table 4-1). The average annual growth rate between 1967–68 and 1970–71 was 10 percent—a figure that reflects, among other things, a 10 percent decline in output during 1969–70 when there was a severe drought that, combined with average annual yield fluctuations, produced a decrease in olive yield by 72 percent and in field crops by 23 percent. The climatic conditions in 1970–71 were far improved for agriculture, which, again combined with the cyclical element in olive yields, produced an increase in the olive crop at a real rate of 100 percent; this contributed more than 9 percent to the real growth of total agricultural output.[26]

Agricultural output registered a 28 percent real increase between 1970–71 and 1971–72. This reflected primarily the large increase in olive production, which accounts for about one-fifth of the Territory's product. There were also plentiful rains during the latter season.[27]

In 1970–71, field crop output increased by over 40 percent, this being accounted for by a large increase in the output of sesame (one of the new crops introduced in the Territory) and the improved strains of wheat. Wheat output increased from 80–150 kilograms per dunam to 300–400 kilograms per dunam. The output of ground nuts increased; this is another crop to which special attention was directed as a potential export crop. There was an increase in yields per dunam, as well as an expansion of acreage planted, from 500 dunams in 1970 to 1,200 dunams in 1971. In 1969, there had been an overproduction of tobacco (used in cigarette factories in the West Bank and Israel) by 500 tons, so in 1970 the acreage of tobacco was reduced—an example of planning that prior to 1967 had not been operative. The area devoted to sugar beets has been increased, and with additional input, there has been a fourhold increase in income per dunam. However, there was a general decline in field crop prices of 7 percent in 1970–71.

The decrease in the production of melons and watermelons reflects another of the structural changes introduced by the Ministry of Agriculture: the shift away from low-income crops and crops that must be marketed immediately. The supply did not meet the demand for melons in the Territory, so water-

Table 4-1
Agricultural Output, 1967–1971 (IL millions, current prices)

	1967–68	1968–69	1969–70	1970–71	Percent change over preceding year in volume of output 1970–71
1. Value of Output	135.0	180.4	171.9	227.4	14.2
Field Crops	11.0	21.5	18.4	25.5	48.4
Watermelons	6.0	4.6	2.1	3.2	9.5
Vegetables and Potatoes	19.5	23.5	27.0	32.4	-2.2
Fruit	51.4	71.7	54.2	86.1	36.2
Livestock and Their Produce	45.0	56.4	67.2	76.7	-5.8
Afforestation and Orchards	2.1	2.7	3.0	3.5	6.8
2. Purchased Inputs	21.4	27.0	30.9	35.3	—
3. Income Originating in Agriculture (1 less 2)	133.6	135.4	141.0	192.1	14.2
Percent Change over preceding year in volume of agricultural output	—	26.5	-10.2	14.2	—

Source: *The Economy of the Administered Areas 1971* (Jerusalem: Bank of Israel, 1972), p. 21.

melons were imported from Israel. Certain sectors of Israel have been specifically designated for watermelon production as part of the crop specialization
program.

In the vegetable sector, the most significant change was an increase of 43
percent in onion yields, a crop of traditionally high quality, which is now designated for European export. In 1971–72, production of tomatoes, cucumbers,
eggplants, marrows, onions, hot peppers, celery, okra, beans, and strawberries
continued to expand. These products were sent to industry and made available
for export.

The fruit sector, which includes olive, deciduous, citrus, and banana trees,
continues to account for over a third of the West Bank's total agricultural output. There was a 36 percent real increase in this sector in 1970–71. As mentioned above, this was accounted for by an increase in both olive and grape
yields. Part of the increasing yield in grapes, figs, and plums is being marketed
to industrial plants in Israel. Citrus output rose at a real rate of 8 percent, but
there was a sharp drop in prices and thus the income of citrus growers fell. This
was caused primarily by an increase in competition from the Gaza Strip, which
increased its citrus production by 23 percent during this same period.[28] Fruit
production continued to expand in 1972 by about 15 percent. Part of the
output was exported to Jordan, and part was sent to industry in Israel.[29]

Due to the increased competition of Israeli producers and agricultural
specialization, the output of beef and poultry decreased by about 12 percent
after a real increase of 6 percent in the previous period (accounted for primarily
by an increase in poultry). The sheep-fattening plan sponsored by the Ministry
of Agriculture and the Military Government has not yet prevented the decline
in the output of mutton. This decline, as well as the limiting of the import of
sheep from Jordan, due to an increase in diseases in Jordan, caused meat prices
in the West Bank to soar. It is also possible that the number of herds and herders
are decreasing as more laborers go to work in Israel. There was a 6 percent reduction in milk output, accompanied by a 35 percent rise in prices. It was
necessary to continue to import sheep from Rumania during this period, and it
is not known when the domestic supply will be able to meet demand. There was
overall a 6 percent decline in livestock output over the previous year.

It is important to note the increase in purchased inputs from a value of
IL 21.4 million in 1967–68 to a value of IL 42.0 million in 1971–72. Purchased
inputs include chicks purchased in Israel, poultry equipment, fertilizers, pesticides, feeding stuffs for livestock and seed. This reflects directly the results of
the education and training programs of the Israeli and Arab agronomists as the
use of chemical fertilizers, pesticides, special strains of seeds, and improved feeding stuffs has become part of the agricultural plan. Only 5 percent of the cultivated area in the Territory is irrigated.

The product per employed person in agriculture in the West Bank rose by
about 37 percent in 1970–71, which followed a decrease of 2 percent in 1969–

70. This occurred in a period when there was a decrease in the total number of persons employed in agriculture from 42,000 to 37,000 and so reflects both a year of good climatic conditions as well as increased productivity per employed person as a result of greater mechanization and various technological improvements.[30]

Total income of farm owners originating in agriculture rose by over 40 percent in 1969–70 after having declined considerably in the previous year. Average income per farm rose from IL 2,070 in 1969–70 to IL 3,000 in 1970–71. Income per cultivated dunam rose to IL 105, from IL 47 in the preceding year. However, wages of persons employed in agriculture rose by only 3 percent, which reflected the structural problem discussed above.[31] These severe fluctuations in incomes are typical of farming and agricultural sectors that must rely almost exclusively upon natural conditions.

In an extremely comprehensive study of *The Agricultural Potential of the Middle East,*[32] the authors examined the various Middle Eastern countries as to current and potential agricultural development. Many of the most important prerequisites for improvement of output that they indicated are necessary are the very improvements we have been discussing: increased use of input factors, specialization in high value export crops with reduction in production of cereal crops, improvement in marketing conditions especially for the export sector, general overall improvement in the agricultural infrastructure, and the need for developing intraregional trade. Their discussion of the country of the Hashemite Kingdom of Jordan includes all the territory within the borders as of pre-June 1967. No attempt is made to segregate the West Bank Territory from the country as a whole. However, in discussing the overall potential for the country, some specific projections can be applied to the Territory. In estimating potential development, several assumptions are made. It is assumed that some 225,000 acres of the driest land previously used for crops on the East Bank be reseeded or allowed to revert to grass for pasturage. It was suggested that because of the problems of moisture and weed control on fallow land (during fallow periods the land was allowed to grow up with weeds that used the water and thus defeated the purpose of fallow periods), the alternate crop-fallow system on unirrigated crop land be abandoned in favor of annual cropping with increased use of fertilizers. The Clawson-Landsberg-Alexander study suggests a new strain of wheat be adapted for general use, one similar to the wheat introduced by Israel. Variations in crop yields will still arise because of climatic conditions, but they estimate that the variations will be around a higher level. Additional irrigation, increased use of fertilizers, controlled grazing, and good management practices are also assumed.

> With these changes, wheat production would increase more than threefold; barley, somewhat less than double; lentils and other legumes, more than five-fold; and forage crops substantially. Only modest in-

creases in acreage of fruits and vegetables were assumed but larger
increases are technically possible if demand warrants.[33]

They predict a 50 percent increase in yields for vegetables and fruits, most of
which are grown in the West Bank Territory. No time dimension is established
for meeting this potential increase, but the authors generally talk in terms of
decades.

In view of these estimates, the development of the West Bank Territory
has been quite adequate. The wheat yield has increased by 2 to 2.5 times. Real
product in agriculture rose by 26.5 percent in 1968–69, declined in 1969–70 by
10 percent, and rose again in 1970–71 by 14.2 percent, for a net increase 1968–
69 to 1970–71 of 30.5 percent. This increase was achieved in three agricultural
years, not over a period of decades. As stated above, the 1969–70 decline was
accounted for by a drought, which mainly affected field crops where the real
decline was almost 23 percent and by the cyclical nature of the olive crop. The
latter phenomenon was exacerbated by the shortage of water, which resulted in a
decline in olive production of 72 percent.[34] In 1969–70, as a result of the decline in output value and the rise in purchased inputs and wages, farmers' nominal incomes fell by 12 percent.[35] In 1970–71, however, there was a sharp re-
bound when total income of farm owners originating in agriculture rose by over
40 percent, and the average income per farm rose by 31 percent.[36] As stressed in
the Clawson-Landsberg-Alexander study, this severe fluctuation in incomes is
typical of farms that rely almost exclusively on natural conditions.

Rapid progress has been made, but we should not expect such increases in
productivity to continue indefinitely. The past few years have been ones of
quantum leaps in introduction and use of modern agricultural technology, better
use of fertilizers and pesticides, plant protection materials, improved strains of
crops, and improved marketing conditions. Many of the marginal farms have
already been closed or have been incorporated into larger farm units, and although the cultivated area has declined, total yield has increased. The agricultural sector has become more mechanized as the number of tractors has
increased from 147 to 640,[37] and cooperative societies are making use of
reapers and combines rented from Israeli agricultural societies. In conversations
with representatives of the Department of Agriculture at Nablus in 1973, I
found them reluctant to estimate future productivity increases. They continually
stressed that total output was so dependent upon the climatic conditions and
when pressed to assume a year's natural conditions similar to 1970–71, they
talked generally in terms of an 8 to 10 percent annual increase in productivity
in the short run. I was unable to gain more information from them as to how
this estimate was made, what factors were considered, and so forth.

Now that many of the short-term programs are operating successfully, the
number of demonstration plots is being reduced. Training and plant improvement techniques are being taught in the most rural of areas, and almost the total

agricultural community has been in contact with the training agronomists. The longer-term projects will have to concentrate on better irrigation systems and on new water supplies, as well as on soil enrichment programs. These projects will require a large capital investment, and at this time Israel is not willing or able to make such an investment, as she faces similar problems in her own agricultural sector. As the economies become more integrated, this major problem will have to be solved. Only if the sector can begin to "control" the natural climatic conditions can any degree of stability be introduced into this, the most important productive sector of the economy.

Prospects for the Future

There are still a variety of problems that must be faced when evaluating the prospects for the agricultural sector of the West Bank Territory. Although even the most rural of the farmers have been eager to accept new methods of production, new strains of seed, crop rotation programs, increased use of fertilizers, pesticides, and other chemicals, many farms are still far from producing efficiently. In the larger, more heavily farmed areas, crop specialization programs have been successfully introduced but in the areas of small farm concentrations little specialization has been undertaken. These latter farms are frequently marginally farmed and before the maximum productivity can be achieved within the sector all farms will have to come under the regulation or advisement of the agricultural boards. This will involve a continuing emphasis upon special training programs and the use of demonstration plots and trade fairs, for instance, as means of educating the local farmers.

Although there has been considerable improvement in agricultural productivity in field crops and vegetables, less emphasis has been put upon the improvement of the fruit sector. One reason is that any improvement in this sector must be measured in terms of years not in terms of an agricultural season. Many of the fruit plantations are in need of improvement, which will require additional capital investment to develop the stock of fruit trees. This involves improving the current stock as well as introducing new stock and expanding the orchards and vineyards. Continuing educational programs will have to be instituted even though in the past, more care was extended to the orchards than to cultivated fields. As an integrated agricultural plan is implemented, it may be necessary to introduce some specialization into this sector also.

Programs directed at the improvement of the livestock must go forward. Progress has already been made towards improving cattle and sheep herds and eliminating the various diseases that have precluded maximum growth of the animals. Attempts are being made to provide pasturage areas so that grazing can be controlled and so that both the livestock and the land will benefit. As long as sheep can be imported to meet the local demands of the population, herders will

benefit from allowing their sheep to grow to heavier weights. It may be necessary to more closely control grazing, to eliminate goats from the Territory as
was planned by the Jordanian government, and to experiment with different
breeds of animals that might be more productive in the Territory. Local farmers
are benefiting greatly from the experience of the chicken farmers in Israel, and
production in this sector is increasing.

There are, however, many constraints upon the full development of the
agricultural sector. Most of the constraints are a result of insufficient supplies of
capital investment. There is a desperate need for additional sources of water and
irrigation systems, but finding water and then supplying it to the fields involves
large expenditures of money. There is a need for additional agricultural equipment and for improvements in the use of the equipment. Much of the current
equipment is old, poorly maintained, and not always well suited to the uses to
which it is put. There should be some standardization of the equipment so spare
parts and adequately trained maintenance personnel will be available, as needed.
An attempt is being made to standardize the equipment, but this can be achieved
only over a long period of time. In the meantime, the possibility of renting
equipment from Israeli agricultural settlements will be a short-run solution to
the problem.

Much of the land in cultivation, as well as the orchards and vineyards, has
been extensively farmed over generations, and the quality of the soil is not good.
In some areas, old Roman terracing is still in use, and it may be assumed that
these areas have been subjected to intensive cultivation over many years. Capital
investment in land nutrients and chemicals will be a continuing need for the Territory. Many of these can be supplied by Israel, which has export surpluses of
most needed chemicals and fertilizers. Continued emphasis must be placed on
the advantages of and necessity of the use of fertilizer.

The evidence of the slow development of the agricultural sector in the
period 1948 to 1967 bears out the absolute need for continued research and
development expenditures. However, with limited capital resources, it is pref-
erable, at least in the short run, to concentrate expenditures on direct improvements in the sector. As long as there is cooperation and participation between
the agricultural departments of the Territory and Israel, the local farmers will
benefit from the extensive research and development that is being undertaken
in Israel.

Much of the West Bank Territory cannot be developed for agriculture because of the natural terrain, but there is one area that could be beneficially developed with adequate capital investment. The Jordan Valley has a climate that
would allow for year-round farming, but the Valley lacks water resources. If new
sources of water could be found or if irrigation systems could be developed for
the Valley, the potential productivity of the agricultural sector of the West Bank
Territory could be greatly increased. But the lack of capital is the economic constraint. However, there is a more serious constraint—a political constraint—that

might preclude the control of the Valley by the residents of the Territory (see Chapter 7).

Israel has developed a plan to integrate the agricultural sectors of Israel, the Gaza Strip, and the West Bank Territory. The various trade barriers that were established in 1967–68 have been eliminated, and the area is operating as a single market. Crop specialization programs have been instituted, and there is virtual free trade among the three areas. The Territory is no longer even as self-sufficient in produce as it was in pre-1967, for some commodities that are food staples are no longer grown but are imported from Israel. Land previously planted in watermelons, for instance, is now used for growing cotton, which is exported to Europe. Any political settlement within the Territory would have to take into consideration the implications of the integration of the agricultural sectors.

It is in the agricultural sector where the greatest development has taken place, but can an area become economically viable if it is dependent upon the agricultural sector for growth and development? As we have shown, because of the lack of adequate water resources and irrigation, productivity is mostly a function of current climatic conditions. Few countries, with perhaps the exception of Denmark, have been able to grow into a modern, market-organized, viable economic unit relying primarily upon development of the agricultural sector.

Before and immediately after the Six Day War, the Territory depended upon trading relations with Jordan, and via Amman, with other Arab countries. There has been a shift in recent years caused partly by the customs regulations imposed by Israel. The Territory is now exporting considerably more to Israel, the Gaza Strip, and via Agrexco, to the world. Any type of political settlement will have to take this demand condition into consideration.

There has been impressive development within the agricultural sector since 1967. There are many important problems yet to be solved. The most important economic constraint upon development is lack of adequate capital for investment. The most important political constraint will be defined in terms of maintenance of current trading partners and the development of new trading relationships.

Notes

1. Marion Clawson, Hans H. Landsberg, and Lyle T. Alexander, *The Agricultural Potential of the Middle East* (New York: American Elsevier Publishing Co., Inc., 1971), p. 1.
2. *Census of Population, 1967,* conducted by the Central Bureau of Statistics; Publication No. 12 (Jerusalem: Central Bureau of Statistics, 1970), p. 18.
3. Clawson et al., *The Agricultural Potential,* p. 32.

4. Ibid., p. 33.
5. *FAO Mediterranean Development Project, Jordan Country Report* (Rome: FAO, 1967).
6. Clawson et al., *The Agricultural Potential,* p. 44.
7. Data on the West Bank for the period prior to June 1967 are not readily available, for the Jordan Bureau of Statistics has not published information by region. The Economic Planning Authority of the Prime Minister's Office in Israel has prepared a series of papers and studies on the West Bank and much of the following information is drawn from these studies (unpublished), from the *Economic Survey of the West Bank* (Jerusalem, December 1967), and from interviews with members of the Authority.
8. *FAO Mediterranean Development Project, Jordan Country Report,* p. 52.
9. Shabtai Teveth, *The Cursed Blessing* (New York: Random House, Inc., 1971), Chapter 10, pp. 90–95.
10. Ibid., p. 148.
11. "The West Bank's Agricultural Revolution," *The Jerusalem Post Magazine,* June 2, 1972, p. 10.
12. Ibid.
13. "More Fruit to Come from Judaea & Samaria," *The Jerusalem Post,* July 28, 1971.
14. *The Jerusalem Post Magazine,* June 2, 1972, p. 10.
15. E.A.J. Johnson, *The Organization of Space in Developing Countries* (Cambridge, Mass.: Harvard University Press, 1970), Chapter 9.
16. August Lösch, *The Economics of Location,* 2nd rev. ed., translated by Wolfgang F. Stolper (New Haven, Conn.: Yale University Press, 1954).
17. *The Israel Economist,* Vol, XXV, No. 3 (March 1969), p. 61.
18. *The Israel Economist,* Vol, XXVI, No. 5 (May 1970), pp. 122–23.
19. *The Economy of the Administered Areas 1970* (Jerusalem: Bank of Israel, 1971), p. 46.
20. *The Israel Economist,* Vol. XXIX, No. 1 (January 1973), p. 20.
21. Elias H. Tuma, "Agrarian Reform and Urbanization in the Middle East," *Middle East Journal,* Vol. 24, No. 2 (Spring, 1970), p. 163.
22. Ibid., p. 164.
23. Ibid., pp. 175–77.
24. The data on which the following discussion is based are derived from many sources: the Central Bureau of Statistics preliminary and published reports, the Bank of Israel (including its reviews of the economy of the administered areas, 1969, 1970, 1971, and 1972), and various articles in *The Jerusalem Post* and *The Israel Economist.* Complete data are available through 1971, and preliminary data are available for 1972.
25. "West Bank Farm Output Doubles in Four Years," *The Israel Economist,* Vol. XXIX, No. 2 (February, 1973), p. 54. These are preliminary data for 1971–72.
26. *The Economy of the Administered Areas 1971* (Jerusalem: Bank of Israel, 1972), p. 22.
27. *The Economy of the Administered Areas 1972* (Jerusalem: Bank of Israel, 1974), p. 17.

28. *The Economy of the Administered Areas 1971,* p. 23.
29. *The Economy of the Administered Areas 1972,* p. 19.
30. *The Economy of the Administered Areas 1971,* p. 23.
31. Ibid.
32. Clawson et al., *The Agricultural Potential,* 1971.
33. Ibid., p. 134.
34. *The Economy of the Administered Areas 1970,* p. 18.
35. Ibid., p. 19.
36. Ibid., p. 23.
37. "Five Years Israel Administration in Judea and Samaria," *The Israel Economist,* Vol. XXVIII, No. 9–10 (September–October 1972), p. 244.

5 The Industrial Sector

Introduction

As is true for other developing nations, the West Bank Territory faces a variety of limitations and constraints upon development of the industrial sector. These limitations include the lack of skilled labor, the lack of capital, the lack of markets, and the scarcity of foreign exchange.

In an effort to meet a rising need for labor in both construction and industry, Israel has established a variety of training programs within the West Bank Territory. Most of these programs were geared towards basic job skills, but in recent months, efforts have been made to also increase job skills through training programs for skilled labor. The improvement of the labor force has not been for use within the Territory, but rather to meet the labor demands within Israel's economy. Developing nations usually have an abundant supply of low-cost labor, but this condition does not exist within the Territory. Wages have risen to equal those paid in Israel, and still there is a shortage of labor for local projects. As the Israeli economy has been expanding, more labor has been required, and there is virtual full employment within the Territory.

The West Bank Territory has had considerable difficulty in attracting capital investment, both in the pre- and postwar periods. This is one of the great problems that one faces when trying to analyze the capital sources available for industrialization. There has been an historical tendency for the wealthy to invest their savings outside of the Arab world. Residents of the Territory express exasperation with a Westerner who cannot understand how risky it would be to invest within the Arab world when its history has been one of instability, both politically and economically. Capital would only be attracted to the Territory if investors could be given some assurance that the possibility of stability, at least in the period long enough for a reasonable return to be earned on the investment, lay in the future. This attitude seems to contradict another that is common within the Middle East: time is relative, and if one looks over the long span of of the existence of the Arab within the area, it is an existence for the Palestinian, at least, that has never known freedom or lack of foreign domination; yet the existence has been perdurable. Something of economic determinism has perhaps assuaged the long-term fatalism of the population. This is another conflict of the cultural and developmental attitudes.

The West Bank Territory should not suffer from lack of markets, for as long as the bridges are open, she is free to trade with the Arab world, her natural prewar trading partners, via Jordan. Since 1967, she has the additional market outlets of the Israeli economy and, via Israel, foreign non-Arab markets. Potentially, the markets are available if the industrial sector can be developed to produce the commodities required for trade.

It appears that there is a scarcity of foreign exchange, although as discussed in Chapter 3, little is known about the monetary sector. Most funds tend to be held in Jordanian dinars or other currencies and Israeli lire appear to be held in quantities sufficient only to meet short-term trading needs.

Prior to 1967, the Jordanian government concentrated its industrial development efforts on the East Bank. Few programs included investments in the industries of the West Bank. The small enterprises were of a workshop nature rather than of a factory character. Since 1967, there has been little concern about developing the industrial sector, and programs have not been established to encourage development. In both periods, political reasons were dominant over economic considerations.

Industry, pre-1967

In 1957, the International Bank for Reconstruction and Development published an extensive study on the Hashemite Kingdom of Jordan. The summary report on industry began: "The limited local supply of industrial raw materials of suitable quality, the high cost of power and the small size of the Jordan market all severly restrict the scope for industrialization."[1] Jordan was burdened with high transport costs, so industrial expansion, which required imported raw materials or was dependent upon a market abroad, was almost totally precluded. This protection created by high transport costs should have created relatively favorable conditions for industries processing local raw materials to be sold within Jordan. The report indicated that industrial expansion had been taking place within recent years and that it was being supported by private initiative, technical and financial assistance of foreign agencies, as well as by protective measures and promotional activities of the government. The progress made in agricultural and mineral development tended to provide new opportunities for manufacturing enterprises, not only directly but indirectly by generating additional purchasing power and broadening the market for consumer goods.

The report considered several possible fields in which expansion was feasible. In view of anticipated participation in an export program, there should be an increase in the quality of the olive crop and an increase in the refinery capacity. The tanning capacity should be increased and modernized in order to improve the quality and value of sheep and goat skins. An improved program for by-product usage would accompany this phase. Small-scale spinning and weaving of wool, as well as experimental weaving mills were suggested as possible areas of expansion. Other projects, applicable to the West Bank, included the expansion of the dairy products industry, of fruit and vegetable canning, of the manufacturing of glazed clay pipes, roof tiles, and other commercial pottery, and expansion of the industries manufacturing articles bought by tourists (embroideries, jewelry, and so forth).

Jordan's industrial development between 1948 and 1967 was accomplished almost entirely as a result of private initiative. Certain local industries were favored by the expansion of the local market, the cheap and abundant labor supply, and the shelter of high transport costs. But conditions continued to be difficult particularly with respect to procurement of raw materials, transportation, water and power supplies, and credit facilities. In summing up the industrial sector, the World Bank mission points out

> . . . many difficulties inherent in Jordan's geographical location, present frontiers and poor endowment of natural resources are bound to remain, in the absence of marked changes in the political picture or discoveries of new wealth. The mission regrets that it cannot, for these reasons, envisage wide perspectives for industrial development. Agriculture (including mineral development) form the main base for Jordan's industrial potential.[2]

Foreign technical assistance as well as capital was needed. The most useful technical assistance for Jordan's manufacturing industry was suggested to involve the improvement of its local raw material supply. This would require an educational program for cultivators of industrial crops, mine operators, and other raw material suppliers, and for those responsible for handling of raw materials. Industrialists would have to be instructed in appropriate purchasing practices, proper storage, and efficient processing, including economic utilization of by-products. Technical assistance would be needed in the use, maintenance, and repair of machinery. The development of industrial power supplies and the study of water source development and use would be of extreme importance. And finally, the mission states the necessity of an extension of industrial vocational training and a re-emphasis in secondary education.

In the 1950s, two firms were established through combined private initiative, foreign technical assistance, and government action: Jordan Cement Factories Company and Jordan Vegetable Oil Industries Company. Promotion was principally undertaken by the government, which participated substantially in providing capital. It appears that it was extremely difficult to raise private funds for large projects unless there was government participation, and this situation still exists today. Private capital held a majority share in each of the companies, as well as a majority of the seats on the Boards of Directors.

In all the years of Jordanian rule, not a single investment was authorized for the West Bank that amounted to more than 10,000 Jordanian dinars (1 JD equals $2.80).[3] Of the $884,000,000 invested in 1966, two-thirds was invested on the

East Bank, which was rapidly becoming the center for all the country's sizeable industries, such as oil refining, cement, and phosphate.[4] The West Bank was relegated to agriculture. With Amman as the commercial center, the Jordanian government was able to control the flow of funds, and as a matter of policy, gave East Bank merchants priorities in such matters as import quotas and buying privileges. The government was thought to be blocking loans to West Bank projects and all this resulted in a continual flow of economic concerns and labor eastwards. The West Bank had only 22 percent of Jordan's industry and 16 percent of her transport, though half of Jordan's population lived in the Territory.

The Jordanian Development Plan, 1964–1970, was basically concerned with the East Bank. The role of the West Bank was to produce simple basic goods to supply the elementary needs of its population, and the industrial establishments, with few exceptions, were of the workshop form with small work forces.

Industrial Development, post-1967

Because of the lack of published data, it will be necessary to rely upon various summaries of the administered areas published periodically by *The Israel Economist* and the Bank of Israel.[5] The first data published about the economic activity of the administered areas appeared in August–September 1970, and they indicated that there was a sharp increase in economic activity in the areas in 1969 that brought about a 25 percent rise in gross national product in real terms and a 22.5 percent increase in the GNP per capita. The increase in agricultural production and the increased employment of inhabitants of the areas in Israel together contributed to a 60 percent rise in GNP, so 40 percent of the increase could be attributed to the industrial sector and to government. In this same period, gross investment increased from IL 23 million to IL 33 million (at 1969 prices) in Judea and Samaria alone. About half of the investments came from the public sector, such as the Military Government and the local authorities, with the remainder coming from private sources.[6]

As in many developing countries, industry centers around processing primary raw materials and agricultural products grown in the region, so there is a direct relationship between crop yields and change in industrial output. Olive oil is the prime example: in 1969, an excellent crop year, sales of olive oil constituted about 31 percent of total industrial sales (excluding mines and quarries) in the West Bank. In 1971, olive presses accounted for only 26 percent of total industrial sales (see Table 5-1). In 1969, other agricultural products provided raw material for the food, beverages, and tobacco branch, which amounted to 45 percent of West Bank manufacturing sales. The production of cigarettes and samneh (from sesame) for export is especially important. The remaining one-quarter consists of all other industrial branches together, including the production of soap and plastic goods (6 percent of the total) and textiles, clothing, and footwear (also 6 percent).

Table 5-1
Distribution of Sales in Manufacturing, Judea and Samaria, 1969 and
1971 (percent)

	1969	*1971*
Food, Beverages, and Tobacco	47	47
Olive Presses[a]	31	26
Textiles	3	3
Clothing	2	3
Leather and Leather Products	1	1
Wood and Wood Products	2	2
Paper, Paper Products, Printing and Publishing	3	3
Chemicals, Fuel, Rubber and Plastics	6	8
Non-metallic Minerals	1	2
Basic Metals and Metal Products	4	4
Machinery, Electrical Appliances, and Vehicles	—	1
Total Industry	100	100

[a]Production value of olive oil after deduction of IL 8 million in 1969 and IL 4 million in 1971 due to stock accumulation.

Source: *The Economy of the Administered Areas 1971* (Jerusalem: Bank of Israel, 1972), p. 25.

Industrial development continued in 1970 with both the existing plants and the establishment of new plants. The activity was related to closer economic ties with Israel and to the growth of real income and local demand for industrial products within the Territory. Israeli firms continued subcontracting relationships with West Bank firms in the areas of clothing, food (candy), building materials (floor tiles and blocks), plastic (mattresses), and metal fabricating. By 1970, a shortage of manpower had begun to develop as workers preferred to work in Israel for higher wages. This shortage seems to have moderated the increase in industrial production.[7]

Industrial production in 1971 rose by only 11 percent, and this increase was attained in spite of a decline in the number of persons employed in the industrial sector. The Research Department of the Bank of Israel believed that the main factor restraining the further development of industry in 1971 was probably the shift of workers to industrial and construction jobs in Israel, where wages were double those paid in the areas.[8] However, equally important must be the attitude of the Israeli government towards development of the territory and the lack of capital available for industrial development (see below). The transition to capital-intensive production methods is a lengthy process, requires investors and entrepreneurs, as well as training and comprehensive expertise in all stages of production and management. Few technological improvements have been introduced, and no efforts towards improved development, such as those expended in the agricultural sector, have been exerted in the industrial sector.

Structural changes in industry reflect, among other things, a decrease in olive yields and a subsequent decrease in the production of olive oil. This was due to natural conditions. The expansion of clothing in total output is explained by a widespread increase in subcontracted work carried out in Judea and Samaria for Israeli firms. Also, the increasing demand of Israel's construction industry (as well as the local construction industry) explains the relative growth in building materials and increased sales of plastics and non-metallic minerals, which include building blocks and tiles. These increases were accomplished by direct purchases and subcontracting agreements with Israeli construction companies.

Thus, over the five-year period from 1967, the real industrial product continued to rise, but at a decreasing rate. In June 1972, *The Israel Economist* reported that 45 new plants had been established in Judea and Samaria in the previous five years and 55 more had expanded. Over 8,000 workers were employed in industry, as compared with 2,500 in 1968.[9] However, there were still only five factories employing more than 100 people.

In 1972, industrial production grew by 18 percent, though there was no significant change in the number of people employed. This represented an increase in productivity estimated at 20 percent. Expansion of production resulted from a very good crop year and especially from the very large olive crop. Production of olive oil accounts for about one-third of the Territory's industrial production. However, industry still accounts for only 9 percent of total domestic product.[10]

Construction

One indication of the relative security and stability in the West Bank Territory in the period from 1967 to 1972 may be in the increase in private construction for dwelling purposes. This expansion was facilitated by the increase in residents' disposable income. However, construction has not yet returned to its prewar level, and though there is incomplete data for comparison, building starts in Nablus in 1964, for example, were equal to total urban construction in the West Bank in 1970. This can be partially accounted for by the fact that the large emigration that took place during and immediately after the Six Day War, left a number of structures that became fully utilized over the following years.

In 1971, building starts rose by 80 percent to reach 185 thousand square meters in Judea and Samaria. This still represents a modest branch of development. Building starts are less than 4 percent of the figure for Israel in the same period, however, and building costs per square meter are lower in the Territory than in Israel since a large portion of dwellings are actually built by the owner and his family in their leisure time. Taking into account the lower wages paid in the areas, the lower costs of materials and the different composition of inputs, the Bank of Israel estimates building costs at IL 200–250 per square meter, compared with IL 500 per square meter in Israel, excluding the cost of land.[11] This figure may be somewhat inaccurate—actually understated—as many builders forego the services of a contractor and recruit the necessary skilled labor themselves. This is true for not only the rural areas where half the construction is carried out, but also in the urban areas.

In 1971, total investment in construction in fixed prices rose by 12 percent. There were mutually offsetting trends in the sector for as the construction of dwellings rose sharply, earthworks and road building carried out by the Military Government and the local authorities decreased somewhat. Building in other branches remained more or less constant and at a low level.

In 1972, the expansion of construction continued mainly in the construction of private dwellings, for public construction declined in Judea and Samaria. Building starts in 1972 rose by about 45 percent.[12]

The expansion in building activity during 1971 and 1972 was achieved although the number of residents employed in construction declined by about one-third, according to the Survey of Families (see Table 5-2). The growth implied in output per employed person in this sector can be partially explained by the familial methods of construction described above. Also, construction workers employed in Israel work an average of 21 days a month and thus are free to work on a private basis during the remaining days within the Territory. Another factor has been the increase in the substitutability between labor and machines, especially in construction and maintenance of roads and other public works. Immediately after the war, thousands of unemployed laborers were hired on "make work" projects involving road improvements, rebuilding and rehabilitating government structures, and various public work projects. As unemployment declined, improved methods were employed and more and more public works were carried out with modern machinery, which thus displaced labor. While the number of persons engaged in construction declined in 1971, the number employed in construction and public works in Israel increased significantly

Table 5-2

Construction in Judea and Samaria, 1967–1971

	1967	1968	1969	1970	1971
	(thousands of square meters)				
Building Starts (Total)	43	67	123	140	224
Dwellings	41	51	88	101	185
Other	2	16	35	39	39
	(thousands of square meters)				
Building Completions (Total)	3	79	93	109	166
Dwellings	3	63	71	76	134
Other	–	16	22	33	32
	(IL millions: 1971 prices)				
Total Investment in Construction	–	25	42	52	58

Source: *The Economy of the Administered Areas 1971* (Jerusalem: Bank of Israel, 1972), p. 26.

(approximately 8,400 to 14,600) (see Table 6-3). A resident working in Israel netted about IL 15 per day compared to IL 9 earned by an employee working in the Territory. It is quite easy to understand the exodus of construction workers from the West Bank to Israel.

The Role of the Israeli Government in Industrial Development

In the postwar period up to 1974, there has been a dramatic development in the economic sectors handled by the military administration. The agricultural economy of Judea and Samaria developed beyond expectations and at a greater pace than the rate of employment of West Bank laborers in Israel. During the same period the industrial sector failed to develop to any great extent. This imbalance was created because the government failed to develop any firm plan regarding the territories; the two ministers involved–the Defense Minister, Moshe Dayan, and the Finance Minister, Pinhas Sapir–carried out their own concepts in their respective spheres of responsibility. As a generalization, it may be said that in all areas handled by the Finance Ministry–investments, encouraging new enterprises, development of technological infrastructure, and so forth– very little has been accomplished since 1968.[13] Dayan had called for the establishment of partnerships of capital and investments, the establishment of firms and the development of an infrastructure; but the government instructed the Ministerial Committee for Economic Affairs to examine the question, and, in general, investors were provided with second-class incentives with the result that the West Bank has not become an attractive place for investment. Consequently, there are few joint projects of Israelis and Arabs, and the development of industry and services has lagged behind that of agriculture. The Finance Ministry maintained that the income and expenditure of the West Bank budget should be balanced.

In 1968, the Military Government submitted a development budget of IL 100 million, but the proposal was not accepted and only piecemeal development budgets have been approved. In 1971, the government provided loans for industrial development in the administered areas (Judea, Samaria, and Gaza) worth IL 8 million, and in 1972, worth IL 16 million, which were considerably different from the amount originally requested.[14]

The Labour Party of the government, on more than one occasion, had been involved in discussions about future policy concerning Arabs in the administered areas. One faction was led by Pinhas Sapir who was concerned about the Israeli economy becoming dependent on the thousands of Arab laborers from the areas, as well as the dangers of Israel being responsible for upwards of 950,000 Arabs in the areas. Moshe Dayan, on the other hand, maintained that a way to existence with the Arabs of the territories could be found without undermining the character of the State of Israel. He continued to demand decisions that would outline the path he should follow in the areas—that is, decisions on economic, social, and cultural questions. Even if the crucial question of Jordanian, Palestinian, or Israeli sovereignty in Judea and Samaria were tabled, decisions on daily relations could not be delayed, since material issues such as the establishment of industrial factories, extension of the electrical grid, and investment in ports (in Gaza) were dependent upon them.

> The possibility of differentiation between the final political decision
> (mapdrawing) and the determination of the network of relations with
> the inhabitants of the areas stems from Israel's recognition that whatever
> the final political settlement will be, it will be a settlement that will not
> be bound up with sealing off the frontiers hermetically between the
> inhabitants of Israel, Jordan and the other Arab countries.[15]

This is to say that decisions made today regarding economic ties would be valid in any settlement.

Dayan's policy with regard to the areas was one that had been carried out de facto and it appeared to have the following aims:

> 1. Bringing economic prosperity to the Administered Areas, either by
> local development (mainly by fostering agriculture), or by minimum
> Israeli investment, or by strengthening the ties with Arab states, or by
> finding employment for the areas in Israel.
> 2. A gradual blurring over of the status of 1948 refugees by finding
> employment for the inhabitants of the areas and turning them into
> productive workers and by convincing municipalities to include refugee
> camps in their tax system and provide services in return.
> 3. Provision of as much [sic] autonomy to the inhabitants of the
> areas in conducting their internal affairs.
> 4. The assurance of as close a mutual contact as possible between
> inhabitants of the areas and Israel on the one hand and with the Arab
> states on the other.[16]

This policy had succeeded beyond all expectations, a fact which even Dayan's opponents conceded, and there had been a definite relaxation of tension and the creation of a basis of Jewish–Arab coexistence. But Dayan could not continue carrying out de facto policies without a formal party and government decision; the most urgent questions concerned investment in the areas and the removal of the economic barriers still existing between Israel and the areas.

The question of investment and the problem concerning the number of workers from the areas working in Israel were, and are, directly related. The creation of jobs in Judea and Samaria (and in the Gaza Strip) on a wage level that is not inferior to that prevalent in Israel would encourage the workers to return to the Territory. Obviously, they cannot find employment within the agricultural sector, which has continually reduced the amount of labor with technological improvements, and it would therefore be necessary to establish industrial enterprises in the Territory that could employ tens of thousands of workers.

But, from where will the necessary capital investment come? There are probably three possible sources. One source is Arab capital both from within the areas and the Arab states. The Israeli government has continued to encourage investment from without the area in the form of loans. However, it appears that apart from political difficulty (there may be opposition to indirectly aiding Israel by developing the areas), there seem to be no interested investors. The problem of encouraging Arab investments within the Arab world is again evidenced. The same reluctance towards investment appears to be evident among the residents. I know personally of several wealthy Arabs who are living in the Territory but investing within Jordan and other Arab countries, as they feel that their investment will be less subject to political instability. And now that travel between the countries has become more convenient, there may be a greater movement of capital out of the areas into Jordan. The lack of entrepreneurial ability is another important factor in this dearth of Arab investment.

The second source is international capital. Various efforts have been made in this area, and there are signs that certain foundations and giant industrial companies may be prepared to establish plants in an area where there is relatively cheap labor, accessible marketing outlets and a neighboring industrial base (Israel) that is capable of aiding such developing firms.[17] But as in all developing countries, it is nearly impossible to encourage foreign capital unless there is some degree of political stability (perhaps hinging upon some decision of the Israeli government regarding the future policy towards the areas) and some hope of internally generated investment as well.

The third source is Israel. It would be nearly impossible to place this burden upon the State of Israel, which is already hardpressed to meet the rising investment needs of her own population. And this was at the heart of the debate between Dayan and Sapir. Dayan's supporters argued that if Israel did not want the political, social, and economic problems of the demographic nature suggested by Sapir, then the only alternative was to move the sources of employment to the areas. And they argued that there was no reason to believe that the return on the investment would be any less than the return already reaped by increased vocational training.

Thus, Dayan argued for increasing the budgetary allotments for development of the West Bank Territory and the Gaza Strip. Secondly, there must be a reduction of protection of Israeli producers in trade between Israel and the areas. At present, there is no limit on the transit of industrial and agricultural produce from Israel to Judea and Samaria, but customs are levied on the "import" of stone from Hebron to Jerusalem, for instance, and there are restrictions on the import of fruit and vegetables from the areas to Israel, though these are gradually being relaxed as an integrated agricultural sector is developed. Besides the question of discrimination, there is the advantage of economic efficiency that would result from economic integration.

Thus, separation between socioeconomic and political planning is impossible. It may be hoped that the removal of economic barriers will increase the flow of trade with Jordan and the rest of the Arab world and that the Territory might serve as a transit area; economic relations might then lead to some political movement, if not settlement. Any change in the economic relations is in effect the creation of political realities.

The Public Sector

There has been a constant rise in the share of expenditures being covered by domestic revenues as evidenced by a comparison between the incomes of the public sector in the West Bank Territory and its expenditures on consumption and investment (see Table 5-3). Revenues from taxes were only 35 percent of total expenditures in 1968 but rose to 45 percent in 1971, and to 59 percent in 1972.[18]

The public sector's demand surplus, which has accelerated economic activity

Table 5-3
The Demand Surplus of the Public Sector, 1969–70, 1970–71, and 1971–72 (IL millions, current prices)

	1969–70	1970–71	1971–72
a. Revenue			
Direct taxes	2	2	2
Indirect taxes	36	43	57
Other revenue	3	3	4
Total *Revenue*	40	48	66
b. *Expenditure*			
Consumption[a]	56	65	81
Investment	19	21	26
Transfers and Subsidies	3	2	2
Total Expenditure	78	88	109
c. *Demand Surplus*			
(b minus a)	38	40	43
d. *Net Credit*			
Errors and Omissions	–2	–2	–3
e. *Financing*			
From the Administration	36	38	40

[a]Current purchases less sales. Excluding expenditures on defence and penitentiary services that are defined as part of Israel's public consumption.

Source: *The Economy of the Administered Areas 1971* (Jerusalem: Bank of Israel, 1972), p. 27.

in the past, has not varied greatly since 1968. The surplus is financed by transfers from the Israel government. The item "net credit" by the public sector is obtained as a residual from the computation of the demand surplus and its financing; it includes the errors and omissions of other items. No significance should therefore be attached to annual fluctuations in this item.

Income from direct taxes increased substantially; these include income tax and national insurance collected at the source from residents of the areas employed in Israel. Indirect taxes more or less follow the trend of local product growth, but there have been efforts made to improve the collection methods, and there has been some increase in tax rates to adjust to the Israeli rates. Collection of taxes is carried out almost exclusively by the Israeli Administration, which passes on part of the property and fuel taxes to the local authorities.

Though the composition of expenditures did not change significantly in 1971, there has been a change over the past four years. A considerable proportion of investment in the Territory is undertaken by the public sector. The Administration's ordinary budget expenditures are mainly for education, health, internal affairs and welfare. Ordinary municipal expenditures are primarily on town engineering and sanitation (about 60 percent). The residual is largely for current administrative expenses.

There are some aspects of revenues and expenditures that are not accounted for by these data, such as the indirect revenues of the Israel public sector from residents of the Territory. These receipts are not included in the government budget; they are derived primarily from customs on goods imported by residents through Israel's ports, and indirect taxes on goods and services purchased in Israel. There are, of course, also indirect subsidies to residents of the Territory when they purchase subsidized goods such as milk, flour, poultry and eggs, or imported goods on which the exchange rate is particularly low. No reasonable estimate of the size of these taxes and subsidies is available because of lack of data.

Prospects for the Future

The potential for industrial development within the West Bank Territory will be a function of the amount of investment capital that can be attracted. The Arabs themselves appear to be reluctant to invest, and even the oil-rich countries are now concentrating on developing their own economies, rather than strengthening the Arab world as a whole. It will be extremely difficult to attract foreign capital until there is some political settlement within the Territory. And Israel is unlikely to be able to afford the massive capital flows that would be necessary to spur meaningful industrial development because of the increasing demands being made upon her own economy.

A second major roadblock in the way of industrial development is the lack of a professionally trained managerial class and of the entrepreneurial spirit. Here again, the cultural heritage of the population is a hindrance to development. It appears to be more possible to train and develop a skilled laboring class than either managerial or entrepreneurial classes. For with intensive retraining, Israel is improving the quality of a traditional laboring class. The Territory suffered a severe loss during and just after the Six Day War when thousands of the well-educated and professionally and semi-professionally trained population left the Territory to seek job opportunities in other parts of the world. It is difficult to know how to attract these personnel back, for without them there can be only a long-term hope of creating a managerial class—a long-term prospect that involves intensive education.

Efforts are being made by the Israel government to improve the infrastructure so necessary for development. The transportation and communication systems are being improved, although the latter needs massive improvement to serve the needs of the community adequately. New generating equipment has been obtained by some communities, such as Nablus, with special import rights being granted to the community by the Military Government. In other areas, arrangements have been made for linking up communities in the Territory to the Israeli electric grid, such as in Kalkilya and Hebron.[19] As both the communications and electrical tie-ups are made with Israel, the economic links become more secure, and perhaps more permanent.

In the labor sector, the Histadrut is discussing the possibility of integrating Arabs from Judea and Samaria working in Israel into trade unions and the Histadrut insurance funds. The Histadrut claims that such a development would ensure the Arabs of social benefits and of an appropriate wage level.[20]

In many respects the conditions necessary for development have not changed substantially from those existing when the World Bank Mission prepared its study. At that time the Mission was unable to envisage wide perspectives for industrial development and suggested that "agriculture would form the main base for Jordan's industrial potential." Current development within the Territory seems to confirm the Mission's expectations. Much of the industrial development is related to the canning, packing, and preserving of fruits and vegetables, as well as to supplying needs of larger establishments, on a subcontracting arrangement, within Israel. No new industrial factories have been established. Existing industries such as the Hebron glass industry, those industries catering to the tourist trade, and those supplying products of the cottage-type industries have expanded, but the expansion has been in the nature of workshop-type factories or of small establishments that subcontract their work to laborers who work in homes and return the finished product to the factory for distribution.

There are few current data available concerning the potential for mineral development and exploitation within the West Bank Territory. It has recently been reported that oil has been discovered near Ramallah, but no firm information is available on the estimated size of the deposit. Those mineral deposits that are known include ochre, which is found in small spotty deposits and is not of general commercial importance although it might have some use in paint pigments and cement coloring. High quality white barite deposits have been found near Bethlehem, but not enough work has been done to enable an estimate of the size of the reserve or the economics of recovery. Barite is suitable for use in chemicals and probably as a weighting material in oil well drilling mud. It is also used in many oil fields to seal off wells to water and to prevent the loss of oil gas. Salt is produced by solar evaporation from Dead Sea brines in salt pans south of Jericho. In the prewar days, a potash works had been proposed and salt would have been a principal by-product of the potash works. It is unlikely that there will be any encouragement from Israel for the undertaking of the potash works since Israel is establishing a giant industrial development on the southern shores of the Dead Sea to use the organic compounds of chlorine and bromine derived from the Dead Sea to produce fertilizers and fumigating materials, as well as metals and minerals for the production of magnesium, aluminium, and petrochemicals. Ironically, the founder of the chemical industry at the Dead Sea, Moshe Novomieski, not only envisaged the mass manufacture of potash, bromides, and magnesium, but also planned to go into partnership with Emir Abdullah to establish an industry on the widest possible economic basis. According to the original plan, it was to have been possible to establish greater political under-standing and a degree of economic coexistence between the Arabs and the Jews, something which is still needed in the area today. The rest of Jordan's mineral deposits lie east of the Jordan River.[21]

Economic theory stresses the need for industrialization in order to achieve high levels of growth. In the early stages, a developing industrial sector usually has the advantage of large labor reserves and low-cost labor, which may give a competitive advantage to products in the export market. Neither of these condi-tions exists in the Territory. There is no labor reserve as all willing to be employed have been able to find work within Israel. Wage rates in Israel were considerably higher than existed in the Territory, and so wages have risen rapidly within the Territory. In 1972, shortages of labor were already evident particularly in the construction sector in the West Bank. There is neither a large reserve of labor nor low-cost labor available.

Growth of the industrial sector will depend upon the amount of capital that can be attracted and upon continued trading relations with Israel and with Arab countries. If more industries can be established or expanded to serve as subcontractors for Israeli firms, then trade relations with the Arab world will be a precondition for development.

The West Bank Territory appears to be caught in the pre-take-off stage and unless there are massive capital inflows, it appears to remain destined to stay in that stage—that is, providing labor for industrial development and construction in other areas.

Notes

1. *Economic Development of Jordan,* published by the International Bank for Reconstruction and Development (Baltimore: Johns Hopkins Press, 1957), p. 19.
2. Ibid., p. 227.
3. *When Arab and Jew Meet* (New York: Israel Information Services, 1968), p. 6.
4. Ibid.
5. *The Israel Economist,* Vol. XXVI, No. 8–9 (1970), Vol. XXVIII, No. 8–10 (1972), and miscellaneous short articles from various issues; and *The Economy of the Administered Areas 1969;... 1970;... 1971; and ... 1972* (Jerusalem: Bank of Israel, 1970–1974).
6. "Business Notes: Administered Areas," *The Israel Economist,* Vol. XXVI, No. 8–9 (August–September 1970), p. 187.
7. *The Economy of the Administered Areas 1970,* p. 21.
8. *The Economy of the Administered Areas 1971,* p. 24.
9. *The Israel Economist,* Vol. XXVIII, No. 6 (June 1972), p. 162.
10. *The Economy of the Administered Areas 1972,* pp. 21–22.
11. *The Economy of the Administered Areas 1971,* p. 26.
12. *The Economy of the Administered Areas 1972,* p. 22.
13. "Five Years Israel Administration in Judea and Samaria," *The Israel Economist,* Vol. XXVIII, No. 9–10 (September–October, 1972), p. 243.
14. "News Briefs–Areas," *The Israel Economist,* Vol. XXVIII, No. 6 (June 1972), p. 167.
15. "Two Approaches to the Administered Areas," *The Israel Economist,* Vol. XXVIII, No. 8 (August 1972), p. 205.
16. Ibid.
17. Ibid., p. 206.
18. *The Economy of the Administered Areas 1971,* p. 27.
19. "Administered Areas Peaceful Revolutionary Development." *The Israel Economist,* Vol. XXIX, No. 1 (January 1973), p. 14.
20. Ibid.
21. *Economic Development of Jordan,* p. 227.

6

Human Resources and the Labor Force

Human Resources

Studies undertaken during the past two decades have highlighted the importance of qualitative deficiencies in human resources. Specifically, these studies stress shortages of educated, trained, and skilled personnel as a factor limiting the capacity of developing nations to absorb new investment. Human capital investment in the form of knowledge, skills, capacities, and attitudes are now considered to be as important for development as the provision of physical capital. This concern for human resource development has been voiced increasingly at the international level and in the context of development theory.

Human resource development is achieved mainly through education, both of a formal and informal nature. Education must be a major vehicle for developing a well-motivated and productivity-oriented labor force, for the quality of the labor force means more than simply acquiring technical skills. It includes the "will to economize," interest in output for the sake of output, pride of workmanship, the spirit of teamwork and other more elusive noneconomic qualities.[1] Also, it is not sufficient to recruit a large industrial labor force and induce it to accept the values of an industrial society. The requirements of development involve needs for foremen, technicians, supervisors, maintenance and production mechanics, and engineers. The majority of employees in the United States are interested in productivity, and their early training, formal and informal, is machine-, production-, and team-directed. In developing nations, it is necessary to motivate and "upgrade" the existing labor force and to provide all levels of labor and management for industrialization.

Accelerated development and rapid economic and social change create new demands on the governments and people concerned. These demands include the adoption of new values and ways of thinking as well as the emergence of new institutions, skills, ways of production, and habits of consumption. In most developing countries, these new demands meet with resistance stemming from the persistence of old traditions. As mentioned above, those of particular relevance are prevalent traditions that stand in the way of personnel development; specifically, the traditions related to occupational choice and to the status and role of women in society.

Bias against manual labor and industrial occupations is still quite strong in the Arab world. Office work, preferably in the government or in supervisory positions, is greatly favored by educated young. The desire and hope for clerical occupations have accelerated the migration of young and unskilled workers from rural areas to the cities, where such occupations are more readily available. The lessening of interest in traditional agriculture, the disappearance of marginal farms (see Chapter 4) and the disappearing tradition of hereditary occupations have increased the demand for urban white-collar jobs.

In spite of rapid changes occurring in the Arab world with respect to the status and role of women, strong traditional pressures still exist against their full participation in national life. Jordan has been one of the leading countries in providing opportunities for educating women, and while increasing numbers of women are entering the labor force in such occupations as clerks, teachers, nurses, and social workers, there is still a strong bias against their participation in the industrial work force. The tradition of early marriage for women often deprives these occupational fields of a high proportion of potential recruits.

Several measures have been found effective in counteracting these traditions: extension of education for girls (the expanded educational system now reaches most rural villages, and all girls have the opportunity for some education); greater investment in vocational education and training; social welfare services for out-of-school girls and women; and improvement of the pattern of incentives and wages. The process of urbanization and the progress of information media have also robbed tradition of its inviolability.[2]

The remuneration and incentive schemes generally are biased against manual or "blue-collar" workers and in favor of "white-collar" workers. Observers are particularly concerned about the unsatisfactory levels of remuneration for middle-level and auxiliary workers, who are vital in the development of such programs as health services, community development, cooperative agricultural extensions, and social welfare. This situation stems from, and results in, the fact that a higher value is placed on the attainment of academic degrees than on the possession of badly needed skills.[3] This attitude must stem directly from the understanding of the preferred position of the *ulama* within the Muslim society (see Chapter 2).

In Jordan, teachers receive somewhat higher salaries in relation to per capita income than in developed countries. Likewise, professionally trained persons in government service, such as physicians, nurses, and engineers, receive higher per capita incomes than in developed countries, but there is still a shortage of most professionals, because the demand from the private sectors is so great that it is usually more economically beneficial for trained professionals to work independently rather than in government service. This differential was reversed during the period 1967 to 1971, for during this time, government workers who received their wages from Jordan, as well as from the Israeli Military Government obtained double wages for their efforts. About 5,000 workers still receive salary payments from Jordan.

In the Middle East, there has been a movement of skilled personnel in two directions:

1. Within the Middle East region, to the oil-producing countries (mainly Kuwait, Libya and Saudi Arabia);
2. Outside the Middle East regions, to the industrial countries of western Europe and North and South America.

In Kuwait and Saudi Arabia, over 90 percent and 65 percent, respectively, of all teachers are expatriates, mostly from neighboring countries. Equally impressive ratios prevail in the health and social welfare fields, and in the civil services generally. The fact that Jordan is the largest contributor to this movement[4] relates directly to our earlier discussion of educated Arabs from the West Bank who were in need of monetary income. Unable to find work within the country, they were thus forced to seek work in another country. Such migration, however, does benefit the exporting country as it results in remittances that account for sizable foreign exchange inflows to the home countries. The inter-Arab migration tends to be temporary whereas the migration to Europe and North America tends to be more permanent, which thus results in a net loss to the home nations. Until recent years, many of these Arabs would return to Jordan, for instance, to retire. One had only to watch the mail in the villages surrounding Ramallah to appreciate how many families were living on U.S. social security payments. With the rising cost of living, however, this area may no longer be such a desirable place for retirement.

Jordan, and particularly the West Bank Territory, in spite of its modest natural resources, is relatively rich in human resources compared to other Middle Eastern countries, with the exception of Israel. There were certain shortages of skilled personnel, but Jordan educated and trained people who found less employment opportunities at home than in neighboring Arab countries or elsewhere in the world.

It is commonly agreed that the general educational system provides the key to solving the problem of personnel both quantitatively and qualitatively. This requires, however, a shift in emphasis to reorient general education more directly towards the objectives of national and social development and away from the development of an educated elite class. An attempt is being made in the primary and secondary schools to shift emphasis from the acquisition of knowledge to the development of skills, such as problem-solving skills.

Several special training schools have been set up by various international agencies, not only in conjunction with agricultural development (see Chapter 4), but also for the acquisition of other skills. In Ramallah, the United Nations and other agencies have established 22 training schools for a variety of skills and educational levels—from teacher training schools down to training centers that specialize in the revitalization of cottage craft industries. In the West Bank, there are two institutions of higher learning. Beir Zeit College is a two-year school, modelled after a community college, that offers either a pre-university curriculum or a program involving some academic and some skill training. Beir Zeit is currently expanding to include a complete four-year degree-granting program. In

1973, another private institution, the University of Bethlehem, was opened. It will eventually offer a full four-year curriculum although it will continue to emphasize special training in such areas as hotel management.

In summary, the quality of labor is as important as the quantity of labor. Investment in human capital, so-called by T.W. Schultz,[5] can take many forms: formal education, on-the-job training, specialized training institutes, and also expanded efforts in health and in job market information. It is often difficult to separate the elements of consumption from investment and the public good from the private, but the emphasis in developing nations must be upon improving the quality of labor and thus may have to be provided for initially by public expenditures.

Population[6]

The Six Day War seriously disrupted the manpower and employment situation in the West Bank Territory. Judea and Samaria were abruptly cut off from their eastern markets, at least temporarily. Jobs with the Jordanian administration, the army, and the U.N. Emergency Force came to an end. Construction work and other investments were virtually at a standstill. Immediately after the war, there was large-scale unemployment. The Israeli administration took immediate steps to restore life to normal, as quickly as possible. Large numbers of civil servants were re-employed; the schools were reopened in the fall (not without some difficulties); the Jordan River bridges were reopened to permit the movement of goods from Judea and Samaria to their traditional markets; and perhaps of greatest importance, the rapid growth of the Israeli economy from the second half of 1967 onward generated a demand for the goods and services— particularly labor—of the administered areas. Increasing numbers of unskilled laborers were hired in Israel and usually at a higher wage than was available within the Territory. By 1969, the level of employment was above its prewar level, and the labor market tightened, as reflected in the labor force participation rate, the total number of employed, and above all, the decreased rate of unemployment. As a matter of fact, the employment situation in 1969 was better in the Territory than in either the Jewish or non-Jewish sectors of Israel.

Several developments in the immediate postwar period changed the structure of the labor force considerably. Some 250,000 persons left the administered area during and after the war. Many of the emigrants were refugees or were supported by persons outside of Jordan; others who left were employees of the previous administration and the army or were professional people. Since many of the refugees had been unemployed, their departure raised the labor force participation rate of the remaining population. East Jerusalem (including the Old City) was annexed by Israel. The emigration of civil servants and the loss of Jerusalem reduced the share of service workers in Judea and Samaria, but there was a corresponding rise in the share of agricultural workers as it seems that relatively few farmers left their lands.

There is one very interesting demographic development: after the large-scale emigration during and shortly after the war, the population started growing. This represents a reversal of a trend that dates back to the early 1950s. In Judea and Samaria, the population had been practically stable with a high natural increase offset by a similarly high emigration to the East Bank, the Arab oil countries, and overseas. This emigration has almost ceased because of several factors:

1. Those who had suffered the most as a result of the war had emigrated during the months immediately following June 1967. Included in this group were not only the refugees and dependents of foreign residents, but governmental employees and large numbers of professional people, including doctors, lawyers, judges, and others.
2. Some Arab states restricted the entry of inhabitants of the areas. This was particularly true for the Gaza residents, but it may also have applied to West Bank residents.
3. The postwar economic prosperity in Israel and eventually in the Territory improved the employment opportunities and the standard of living so as to discourage emigration.

As a result of the slowing down of this emigration, 1969 was the first year since about 1950 when a real population increase was recorded.[7]

As stated above, about 250,000 persons left the administered areas during and immediately after the war. In the second half of 1968, the population of the Territory began to increase and in 1969 a growth of 2.5 percent was recorded (see Table 6-1). By the end of 1969, the population of Judea and Samaria was 601,000 of whom 45,000 were refugees. The working-age population averaged 313,700 or about 53 percent of the total population; the comparable figure for the Jewish population in Israel was 69 percent. The relatively low percentage for the Territory was due to a high birth rate, a relatively high mortality rate among adults, and the large-scale emigration of working-age groups during and immediately after the war.

The average population in the West Bank Territory in 1970 was 605,500. At the end of the year the population was 610,300, an increase of 1.8 percent over the end of 1969. The rate of natural increase was 2.6 percent with the difference in total growth due to emigration. For some reason, visitors going abroad are deducted from the population figures, so the growth rate of the population is biased downward. The working-age population was 322,900 or about 53 percent of the total population. In 1970, when data became available on women in the

Table 6-1
Population and the Labor Force, 1968–1972

	(thousands)					Average Annual Change (percent)			
	1968[a]	1969	1970	1971	1972	1968-69	1969-70	1970-71	1971-72
1. Mean Population	579.1	594.6	605.5	619.0	633.9	2.7	1.8	2.2	2.4
2. Working-Age Population	308.6	313.7	322.9	330.0	336.5	1.6	2.9	2.2	2.0
3. Belonging to the Labor Force	93.0	114.6	118.4	119.7	126.5	23.2	3.3	1.1	5.6
4. 3 ÷ 1 (percent)	16.0	19.3	19.6	19.3	20.0	—	—	—	—
5. 3 ÷ 2 (percent)	30.1	36.5	36.7	36.3	37.6	—	—	—	—
6. Participation Rate of Men (percent)[b]	56.0	62.2	61.4	62.0	66.5	—	—	—	—
7. Participation Rate of Women (percent)[c]	—	—	14.2	12.7	11.0	—	—	—	—
8. Employed in the Territory	77.9	100.9	99.9	91.2	90.3	29.5	-1.0	-8.7	-1.0
9. Area Residents Employed in Israel	5.0	9.0	14.7	25.6	34.9	80.0	63.3	74.1	36.3
10. Total Employed Persons (8 + 9)	82.9	109.9	114.6	116.8	125.2	32.5	4.3	1.9	7.2
11. Unemployed Job Seekers	10.1	4.7	3.8	2.9	(1.4)[d]	-53.5	-19.1	-23.7	-(51.7)[d]
12. Rate of Unemployed (11 ÷ 3)	10.8	4.1	3.3	2.4	(1.1)[d]	—	—	—	—

[a]In 1967, mean population was 595,900; the rate of unemployment was 7.6 percent.
[b]Ratio between men belonging to the labor force and all men aged 14 and over.
[c]Ratio between women belonging to the labor force and all women aged 14 and over; data not available prior to 1970.
[d]Figures in parentheses are not statistically significant.

Source: *Administered Areas Bulletin*, no. 8 (Jerusalem: Israel Central Bureau of Statistics, 1972); *Survey of Families in the Administered Areas* (Jerusalem: Israel Central Bureau of Statistics, 1971); and *The Economy of the Administered Areas 1971 and 1972* (Jerusalem: Bank of Israel, 1972 and 1974).

population it was found that women constituted 53 percent of the working-age population in the West Bank, although their participation rate was very low (14.2 percent).

In 1971, the mean population of Judea and Samaria had risen to 619,000; in 1972, the mean population was 633,900. The entire population growth stemmed from natural increase, and the 2.4 percent rate of growth, which was achieved between 1970 and 1971, was maintained in the 1971–72 period. During these periods, net emigration declined, which can probably be attributed to the more stable security situation, better employment opportunities, and to improved standards of living.

The natural increase in the Territory is on the rise, due both to a rising birth rate and a declining death rate. The birth rate is similar to that of the non-Jewish population in Israel, but the death rate is much higher than in Israel; the death rate is, however, declining due to improved health services and medical facilities sponsored by various international organizations and supported by Israel.

Employment

The 1967 population census and the *Family Surveys* conducted by the Central Bureau of Statistics show a continuing increase in employment; however, after 1969, there tended to be a fairly stable participation rate of men of about 62 percent. In 1972, the participation rate for men rose, while the rate for women continued to fall. Unemployment continued to decline through 1972.

The Labor Force Participation Rate

The participation rate leveled off in 1970 and 1971 and seemed to reflect the exhaustion of the area's manpower reserves. Directly after the war, there was widespread unemployment in the area, and shortly thereafter, when life returned to normal, residents found employment in Israel in large numbers. This was reflected in a rising participation rate. By 1970, most of the manpower reserves had been utilized. The participation rate is still below that of Israel and the reasons for this may be found in the age distribution and in social factors. The working-age population included all persons 14 years of age and older. There is a large percentage of the population in the 14 to 17 year age group, and most of these are attending school. It is interesting to note that there is a higher percentage of the working population in the 55+ year age group than there is in Israel, apparently because of the absence of retirement, pension, and other social security provisions. However, in 1972, the participation rate of men climbed to 66.5 percent. Perhaps the higher cost of living has attracted more into the labor force, as the rise in employment was accounted for entirely by an increase of employment in Israel.

Most of the increase in the civilian labor force in Judea and Samaria was in the rural areas, for in the towns the labor force remained relatively unchanged. In the refugee camps, the labor force grew only slightly, apparently because of the continuation of welfare grants.

From 1970 to 1972, the participation rate of women fell. Considering the economic developments in the Territory and the Israeli economy, one would have expected a more rapid increase in both participation rates. The Research Department of the Bank of Israel offers the following possible explanations:

> a. There is a relatively large sampling error in small populations such as persons belonging to the labor force.
> b. Part of the decline in the participation rate can be explained by the changes in the population's age distribution. The share of the 18–24 age groups, with low participation rates (relative to the 25–54 age group), grew. . . .
> c. There has been an increase in school attendance rates in the 14–17 age group, so that the participation rate of this group naturally declined.
> d. Finally . . . between 1969 and 1970 political stabilization and economic improvements encouraged the entrance of marginal groups such as women, youngsters, and elderly persons in to the labor force. In 1971, however, with the sizable increase in the income of families in the administered areas, consumption may have lagged behind incomes, and led the same marginal groups to leave the labor force.[8]

These are hypotheses; however, there are no data to support or reject them. It is also probable that as men are recruited into the Israeli labor force and the labor force within the agricultural sector has declined, more women have remained at home to tend the fields and crops. The women who are employed on their own farms are not properly represented in the data for the labor force.

From the 1967 census it appears that in Judea and Samaria the participation rate before the war was approximately 65 percent. The 1961 Jordanian census reported a participation rate of 68 percent. The decline to the present rate may be attributed to increased emigration among the working-age population and perhaps to some of the above factors.

Employment

The number of employed persons has continued to rise, though more slowly. Most of the increase is derived from a decline in unemployment as the number of persons belonging to the labor force did not rise significantly. Unemployment continued to decrease and reached 2.4 percent of the population in 1971. The slowdown in growth stems from the achievement of virtual full employment and from a decline in the participation rate. The entire increase in employment was a result of increased employment in Israel since the number of persons employed in the Territory itself actually declined.

There are several things to be noted regarding the occupational composition of employed persons (see Table 6-2). The percentage of persons employed in agriculture has continued to decline, even in the absolute number of persons employed in this branch, including persons engaged in agriculture in Israel. This is the trend that is predicted by development theory. However, the number of persons employed in industry, and in construction and public works, has also continued to decline, and the latter, at an accelerated rate in the 1970-71 period. Construction has declined in the Territory while at the same time the number of construction workers from the Territory working in Israel has increased. The wage differentials are probably the major contributing factor to the increased population commuting to Israel for employment.

Employment in Israel

There has been a significant increase in the number of residents from Judea and Samaria who are employed in Israel. In 1969, approximately 9,000 were so employed, and by 1972, the number had increased to 34,900, which is an in-

Table 6-2
Industrial Distribution of Employed Persons, 1969–1971 (percent)

	1969	1970	1971
Agriculture, Afforestation, and Fishing	43	37.1	31.3
Industry (Mining and Manufacturing)	12	12.8	11.5
Construction and Public Works	8	7.3	4.8
Trade and Catering	–	10.7	11.0
Trade, Storage, and Communications	29	3.9	3.4
Public Services	–	12.2	12.4
Financial Services, Electricity, Water and Other Personal Services	–	3.2	3.7
Employed in Israel	7	12.8	21.9
Total	100.0	100.0	100.0
Total (thousands)	109.9	114.6	116.8

Note: Branch classification according to distribution of employed persons by branches in administered areas proper; area residents employed in Israel are a separate branch.

Source: *Surveys of Families in the Administered Areas* (Jerusalem: Israel Central Bureau of Statistics, 1971).

crease of over 280 percent. It must be recognized that this figure is probably biased downwards as it reflects somewhat warped data taken from the *Family Surveys* of the Central Bureau of Statistics. A sample of the Territory's population is asked, among other things, about their place of work and where the rest of the family works. By definition, these data included both organized and unorganized labor, but frequently respondents are unwilling to report employment in Israel, especially if it is not obtained through the Labor Exchange. The Labor Exchange publishes data on the number of area residents employed in Israel through the efforts of the organization, but these data are also deficient in that not all people seek employment through the Labor Exchange. The Ministry of Labor published some preliminary figures on salaries paid through the labor exchange offices, and these data indicated that only 15 days per month had been worked in 1971, whereas the *Family Surveys* indicate 22 days per month worked. The discrepancy can be understood if, for example, the employee worked for more than one employer (especially if one job were not through the Labor Exchange) or worked some days in the Territory. Many workers prefer to find employment outside of the Labor Exchanges because both the employer and employee benefit on wages. The net wage received by the employee is about only 58 percent of the employer's labor costs, the balance being accounted for by various deductions such as income tax, transportation, accident insurance, social payments to special funds designed to finance various welfare projects in the territories and miscellaneous items. By circumventing the Labor Exchange, the employee can receive a higher than average wage, while the employer must pay out a lower than average wage. These workers would not appear on the rolls of residents employed in Israel. The Central Bureau of Statistics also conducts transit surveys that enumerate the number of persons crossing at the main transit points to work in Israel; these data would not include workers, especially those living along the previous borders, who cross over to neighboring villages to work or those who do not return to the Territory at night. For all these reasons, it is likely that the number of residents employed in Israel is understated.

The upper constraint on the number of residents employed in Israel appears to be on the supply side. Once the rate of participation failed to rise, it became possible to raise the number of persons employed in Israel only at the expense of those already employed in the Territory proper. And the number of persons employed in the Territory has indeed declined. Residents have left their places in the Territory to seek work in Israel. This has caused the wage in the area to rise more quickly than in Israel and the difference between the wage rates to be decreased.

In both 1970 and 1971, about half the residents working in Israel were construction workers (see Table 6–3). The share of workers in industry rose and that of agricultural workers declined. Most of this rise seems to have coincided with a decrease in workers in the Territory in agriculture and construction.

Table 6-3

Occupational Distribution of West Bank Territory Residents Employed in Israel, 1970 and 1971 (percent)

	1970	1971
Agriculture, Afforestation and Fishing	17.7	12.9
Industry (Mining and Manufacturing)	(12.9)	16.8
Construction and Public Works	57.1	57.0
Other Branches	(12.3)	13.3
Total	100.0	100.0
Total (thousands)	14.7	25.6

Note: Figures in parentheses (less than two thousand) are not statistically significant.

Source: *Surveys of Families in the Administered Areas* (Jerusalem: Israel Central Bureau of Statistics, 1971).

The distribution of residents employed in Israel depends both upon the demand for labor and upon the occupational composition of the workers. On the supply side, most of the workers are unskilled, highly mobile, and, as stated above, employed in construction and agriculture. In Israel, there has been a growing shortage of labor as well as extensive underemployment, particularly within the unskilled occupations. More recently, the demand for skilled Arab laborers has increased. But the Arabs are raising concern that they are being molded into the lowest working class and that there is very little upward mobility for them—the skilled and better paying jobs are filled by Israelis rather than by promoting from within the Arab labor force. In response to this concern, as well as in response to an increasing demand for skilled labor in Israel, the Military Government in cooperation with the Ministry of Labor has instituted additional vocational training programs. There have recently been increasing numbers of workers from the Territory finding work in industry in Israel. The upper limit to mobility again becomes education, and the government has responded to this need by establishing training centers.

Wages

In 1969, according to the *Family Surveys,* the average daily wage was IL 6.9 in the West Bank. This figure included the net wages of workers in Israel.

In 1970, the average daily wage had risen by 18 percent and had reached IL 7.9. Average daily wages earned in the Territory were IL 6.9 whereas net wages of residents employed in Israel were IL 11.8, which is an increase of 16 percent. Wages earned in Israel by West Bank residents were about 70 percent above those in the administered areas.[9]

In 1971, the average daily wage was IL 8.6 while net wages earned in Israel were IL 13.0, which is an increase of 14 percent. Labor shortages began to occur in the Territory, particularly in the construction and agricultural sectors, as workers crossed the "green line" in order to earn higher wages; this forced the employers in the Territory to increase their wage rates in order to attract necessary employees. The removal of administrative obstacles, which had prevented the free movement of labor between the administered areas and Israel, and the decreasing supply of labor are expected to continue to reduce the difference in wage rates between Israel and the West Bank Territory. A free labor market is another example of the economic integration that is taking place between Israel and the administered areas.

In 1972, the average daily wage was IL 11.5 and net wages earned in Israel were IL 17.2. The large increase in the administered area wages slowed the movement of area workers into Israel. The Israeli labor market could only attract more workers by offering significant wage increases. In 1971, area residents received wage increases amounting to 13.6 percent whereas Israeli laborers received increases of 16.4 percent. In 1972, however, residents received increases of 28.4 percent as compared with 14.4 percent increases for Israeli laborers.

Residents from the administered areas working in Israel earn about half the average wage in Israel. Only a small part of the difference is accounted for by branch composition. The Research Department of the Bank of Israel discusses this problem:

> There must therefore be other reasons, such as the lower skill level of workers from the administered areas in most branches. In the long run, economic forces will tend to equalize the wages earned by employers from the administered areas either in Israel or in the areas themselves, with those earned by Israelis of the same skill level. Official government policy is aimed at encouraging this process. We have no evidence on this point, but the overall impression is that the 'equality' principle has not yet been put into effect, either in the organized framework of the labor exchange in Israel and certainly not for unorganized employees from the administered areas whose numbers seem to be increasing in view of the freeze placed on the quota of organized laborers engaged through the labor exchange (at 40,000).[10]

Improvement of Human Resources

In Judea and Samaria, the school system is based on the Jordanian educational law of 1964, which provides for free compulsory education for six years in primary school and three years in preparatory school as well as free education for three years in secondary school. Under the Israeli occupation, a Bureau for Educational Affairs has assumed responsibility for the school system, and funds are provided by the Military Government. In 1970, there were 4,704 teachers in the system, and by 1972, the number had increased to about 6,000.

All refugee children seeking secondary education and other children in the compulsory age groups where United Nations Relief Works Agency (UNRWA) does not provide schools attend government schools.

In 1970, there were 681 government schools, 81 UNRWA schools, and 119 private schools. In July of that year, the Military Government approved a budget of IL 2.5 million for the construction of 218 new classrooms under a three-year building plan for the region. Municipalities and the local education committees were to contribute an additional IL 1.5 million for school extension and renovation over the three year period. At this time, about one-third of the inhabitants of the region were attending school; this, of course, is an additional reason for the low participation rate among the working-age population.

Matriculation examinations are conducted by the regional education committees who then send the results to the Jordanian government. Matriculation certificates are sent from Amman to the successful candidates. Between 1968 and 1970, some 10,000 certificates were so issued. Upon satisfactory completion of the secondary schools, students may proceed to Arab states for further education.

The Labor Exchange

Prior to 1967, there were no active labor exchanges, no employment services, only three vocational training centers, no social security, no system of collective work agreements, and considerable unemployment. All of these problems are now under the aegis of the Ministry of Labor whose staff works with the military command in the Territory. The Ministry operates in the fields of Employment Service, Vocational Training, Supervision of Labor and Cooperatives, and Trade Unions.

Labor exchanges were opened at the end of 1968 to cope with the unruly labor market and to provide an office to which workers could turn for assistance in labor-related problems. In order to reduce unemployment, relief work for 18,000 laborers was provided on a daily basis. Work was carried out on the roads, and in afforestation and public works projects. A few workers were sent to Israel, but there was still considerable unemployment. By 1972, the picture was quite different: near full employment had been achieved, and a shortage of labor was developing. Twenty-three labor exchanges had been set up in the West Bank in regional areas and populated villages.

By 1972, nearly 35,000 people were registered with the exchange, with some 25,000 renewing their permits on a regular basis. This represents only about 36 percent of the working population aged 14 and over. As stated above, this is probably accounted for by the low participation rate among women, the desire to complete the free education that is available to the age of 18, and the traditional attitude of an educated person towards manual or technical labor.

One of the main principles guiding the Ministry of Labor is the provision of equal wages and social benefits to the Arab workers employed in Israel and eventually an increase in the standard of living of the Arabs inthe Territory to that level of the Arabs living in Israel. An equal net wage for all workers in Israel would assure the non-discrimination and non-exploitation of the Arabs from the administered areas in comparison with their Israeli co-workers. Originally, the Arab workers would accept a wage considerably below the general Israeli standard as this wage was still considerably higher than that wage rate prevailing in the areas.

The Israeli Employment Service operates a Payments Center that handles wages and social benefits received from employers and transfers them to workers and various social funds maintained by the Treasury. In the early periods, prior to the extension of social benefits to the Arab workers, the deductions made by the employers were deposited in a Special Fund. It was government policy that no benefits could be paid unless all the Israeli laws were operative in the Territory. In the period of economic integration that followed, this resistance was weakened, and now benefits are available to the Arab workers. The Payments Center is responsible for ensuring that employees receive their rights regarding pensions, work accident insurance, employees' children allowances, holiday pay, sick pay, increment for a wife, and severance pay. On occasion, the Center will act as mediator between employer and employee on wage or social benefits or as an agent to ensure that rights are provided.

On March 1, 1973, a health insurance plan was instituted in the West Bank for about a quarter of the population (mainly civil servants and those working in Israel). For a monthly payment of Il 6, workers will be provided with all health services free, and family members will be eligible for a 50 percent reduction on medical fees. Temporary and seasonal workers can also obtain coverage if they register and pay the premiums. Arabs working in the Territory are free to join the plan.

In 1971, it was estimated that about 15,000 workers crossed over to work in Israel without going through the Labor Exchange. Some workers crossed individually, but others were organized through local bosses who pocketed the difference between official wage rates and the higher sums offered by employers to avoid paying the social benefits, which vary between 25 and 48 percent of the wages, as explained above. Israel is trying to eliminate this market, as the workers so employed are not eligible for social benefits. The exchanges in Israel send out teams of inspectors to prevent employers from breaking the law, and those who do are subject to heavy fines. Also, the Arab workers are now more cognizant of the benefits that are lost by their not participating within the Labor Exchange.

The impact of this labor market—Arab workers crossing into Israel—can be appreciated by the following example:

Nablus with its 70,000 population has a labor force of 20,000. About
4,000 Nablusis, mostly skilled workers, as the town is the center of
skilled labor in Samaria, work in Israel. Even taking IL 600 net as the
average monthly income of these workers and this is a conservative
estimate, because certain skilled men in building earn IL 50 and up to
IL 80 daily, then the sum flowing into Nablus from these workers is
IL 2.5 million monthly or IL 30 million annually. These 4,000 workers
on an average live in families of four or five persons, which means that
20,000 people are living from their earnings and the money they spend
locally is helping to provide work for another 25,000 people or so.[11]

Vocational Training

One of the most outstanding successes of the policy of the Ministry of
Labor has been in the field of vocational training. Prior to 1967, there were
three training centers in Judea and Samaria. Since 1968, some 20 centers have
been established, and it is estimated that about 6 percent of the total labor force
has participated in these schools. The training centers were originally designed
for senior workers who needed new skills and for school dropouts, and the
training was mainly in building crafts, metal working, and carpentry because of
the unprofessional natural, low educational level requirements, and lack of an
employment traditionamong the trainees in these fields. By 1970, the employment outlook had changed as unemployment continued to decline and a demand
for skilled labor developed. High school graduates and dropouts began to show
an interest in skilled, vocational training to qualify as electricity fitters, turners,
and mechanics.

The trainees receive a daily allowance, and their workday lasts from 8:00
a.m. to 2:30 p.m. Centers for various needs have been established: embroidery
and sewing for girls; academic studies on a one day per week basis for youth
aged 13 to 16 who work in factories; and special courses for building, draughts-
manship, accounting, agricultural mechanization, and employment in hotels and
restaurants (all of which attract secondary school pupils). There is also a special
school in Hebron that teaches skills related to the building industry—that is,
students are trained in cutting stone, erecting scaffolding, tiling, and plastering.

At the conclusion of the training period, the graduates are certified in both
Arabic and Hebrew and are free to work wherever they wish: within the Territory, in Israel, or in neighboring Arab states, many of which have come to recognize the high quality of the training that the students are given.

The program has been particularly successful in helping to reorient the
desires of women regarding work and in training them in some skills. In Samaria,
the number of women employed in sewing has risen from 100 in 1967 to just
over 3,000 in 1972. Many employers are willing to sign contracts with the girls

prior to the completion of their training period. Other Arab women are employed by the packing and canning factories in jobs which were formerly held by men. Though the participation rate is still low, there are indications that the trend may be established towards greater participation.

There has also been interest in re-establishing the cooperative. At the outbreak of the 1967 war, there were some 700 cooperative societies comprising 45,000 shareholders. They were principally savings societies concerned with agricultural loans, school savings, and similar projects. A smaller number of cooperatives engaged in public transport, artisanship, and agricultural marketing, as well as a sick-fund savings scheme. Most of the co-ops were mainly engaged in financial activity and when the June war froze all accounts held in Amman, most of these activities declined. In 1971, there were 202 active associations with an aggregate of approximately 15,000 members in workshops, agricultural production and marketing, women's handicrafts, transport and consumer cooperatives. About half are producing societies, some of which were established in 1967. The size of the societies ranges from a membership of seven (artisans, for example) to 300 (olive presses, bus cooperatives). The Israeli authorities are interested in transforming existing societies from consumer to producer cooperatives. The Israeli Cooperative Union and Hamashbir Hamercazi have expressed an interest in assisting the associations in reorganization activities that would enable them to provide better services.

Prospects for the Future

Many of the required steps are being taken to achieve greater development of the human resources of the West Bank Territory. Knowledge, skills, capacities, and attitudes are all undergoing change. The formal education system is adjusting to new demands for problem-solving and a work-oriented educated class. Some evidence of a change in attitudes can be found in increased numbers of secondary school students enrolling in training programs. The bias against manual labor and industrial occupations appears to be lessening. More women are entering training programs, and jobs formerly held by men but readily undertaken by women, such as work in packing and canning factories, are now available for women. Greater investments in vocational education and training are being undertaken, and the programs are geared to the needs of the market. Social welfare programs are being instituted, and workers now have available an increasing number of medical and health benefit schemes, as well as various social benefits, similar to those offered in more developed areas. The Labor Exchange has facilitated mobility of labor and has also offered protection and counseling to the employee.

The potential expansion of the labor force seems to be reaching a limit. Unemployment has fallen to 2 percent. It is possible that within the refugee

camps, more workers will be available, particularly because the welfare grants
to the refugees are not scaled to the cost of living, and as costs continue to rise,
additional income will be necessary to maintain a minimum standard of living.
As attitudes change and more training facilities are available for women, it is
possible that their participation rate will increase, particularly among those
girls currently in the secondary schools.

Israel will continue to demand labor. In the Five Year Plan, presented
in 1971, it was predicted that the Israeli labor force will grow to 1,760,000
persons in 1975, whereas the demand for labor is anticipated to be above
1,200,000. "The gap is to be filled by Arab labor from the West Bank and Gaza.
The report states specifically that it assumes the continuation of economic links
with those areas."[12] Thus, the input that Israel has invested in the improvement
of human resources and the labor force as well as the merging of the labor market are additional steps in the process of economic integration between Israel
and the West Bank Territory.

Growth in the labor force will depend upon various factors. Through education and training as well as through a reorientation of priorities, more women
will have to be encouraged to participate in the work force. Efforts will have to
be made to reduce the bias against women's participation in the industrial work
force. At the same time, more women can be trained to enter the labor force in
such occupations as clerks, teachers, nurses and social workers—areas where the
traditional bias is not so strong. Men will be released from these positions to
work in the industrial work force.

As the cost of living continues to rise, it is likely that more refugees will be
actively seeking work. Although their job skills will probably be at a low level,
with retraining they may be able to add to the effective labor force.

Additional members of the work force will become available as students
complete their education. If jobs cannot be found, however, many of these students may leave the Territory to seek employment elsewhere, which would thus
create a loss in human capital for the area.

Though there are and will be an increasing number of people who will be
able to join the labor force, whether or not they will become effective members
of this force may well depend on a re-emphasis in the educational system of the
"work ethic." Education is available for all young people, but there will not be
white-collar jobs available for all those completing their studies. The educational
system must place a new emphasis upon the skills and trades so that these too
will be considered of importance by the young people This will involve a longer
term re-orientation of the educational system, as well as a retraining of the current work force.

Though natural resources are limited and the possibility for significant industrial development appears to be unlikely, a commodity that the West Bank
Territory might develop is a well-educated, highly trained labor force. With
limited employment opportunities available in the Territory, these workers

could become available for employment under contract in neighboring states. Over time, with emphasis on developing and improving job skills, these workers could create a meaningful contribution to gross national product. This would depend in the short-run, upon a political settlement that would involve freedom of movement of the labor force.

Notes

1. Charles P. Kindleberger, *Economic Development*, 2nd edition (New York: McGraw-Hill Book Co., 1965), p. 105.
2. *Studies in Selected Development Problems in Various Countries in the Middle East* (New York: United Nations Press, 1968), p. 40.
3. Ibid.
4. Ibid., p. 41.
5. T.W. Schultz, "Investment in Human Capital," *American Economic Review*, Vol. 51, No. 1 (March 1961).
6. Data for the following analyses come from a variety of sources: various publications of the Research Department of the Bank of Israel, published and unpublished material from the Central Bureau of Statistics, National Employment Service data and the Labor Exchange, *The Israel Economist*, and *The Jerusalem Post*.
7. *The Economy of the Administered Areas 1969* (Jerusalem: Bank of Israel, 1970), p. 31.
8. *The Economy of the Administered Areas 1970* (Jerusalem: Bank of Israel, 1971), p. 39.
9. Ibid., p. 42.
10. *The Economy of the Administered Areas 1971* (Jerusalem: Bank of Israel, 1972), p. 44. Note: in 1974, this figure of 40,000 was exceeded from the West Bank alone.
11. "The Activities of the Ministry of Labor in Judea, Samaria, the Gaza Strip and Sinai—A Progress Report," *The Israel Economist*, Vol. XXIX, No. 3 (March 1973), p. 84.
12. "Five Year Plan Predictions," *The Israel Economist*, Vol. XXVII, No. 6 (July 1971), p. 202.

7

Some Sociopolitical Problems of the West Bank Territory

No consideration of independence and economic viability for the West Bank Territory would be complete without at least referring to three major problems that require intensive negotiation and concessions on the part of all countries and peoples involved. These three problems concern Jerusalem, the refugees, and Israeli settlements along the Jordan Valley.

Both Israel and Jordan have declared Jerusalem to be non-negotiable, and neither has shown interest in various plans of internationalization. Prior to 1967, Jerusalem served not only as a religious center for the Arab world, but it was also the market center for the Territory. Israel annexed East Jerusalem in June 1967 after the Six Day War, and although the annexation was not recognized by any other state or the United Nations, East Jerusalem was cut off from her traditional position within the West Bank Territory. Discussion of the future of Jerusalem will be an integral part of any political settlement. Concessions on the part of both Israel and the Arabs might allow the internationalization of Jerusalem to serve as a compromise solution to the problem.

The refugee problem has usually been in the forefront of any consideration of political settlement, and any likely solution to it would involve resettlement arrangements, as well as some form of compensation, for the refugees. Allowing the refugees to become integrated within society and to become economically productive would alleviate the potentially explosive political aspects of the problem, and integration of the refugee population would also expand the labor force. There would be positive response from the international community towards any such settlement of the refugee problem, for it seems that the question has been kept active for political considerations rather than for humanitarian considerations.

Israel has established a series of paramilitary kibbutzim along a north–south line, which runs some ten miles inland from the Jordan River. These kibbutzim have been established for defense purposes, but they have also virtually cut off from Arab farmers some of the most potentially productive agricultural area, the lands along the Jordan River. The climate is particularly well suited to two or three crop seasons per year, if adequate water can be provided. It has been suggested by Israeli politicians that return of this land is also not negotiable. With the loss of East Jerusalem, and the area in the Jordan Valley, the size of the Territory is considerably diminished; the Territory loses its natural capital and market center and also loses the last of the potentially productive agricultural lands. Let us consider each of these problems in detail.

127

Jerusalem

Jerusalem is a city that is unique in the world for it is a spiritual center of the three great monotheistic faiths: Christianity, Islam, and Judaism. This holy character of Jerusalem constitutes the basis for much of the political controversy over that city. One needs only to study a map of Jerusalem, or to spend some time wandering about the city, to realize that the places of interest of the three religions are intermingled in Jerusalem in such a way as to make their physical separation almost an impossibility. It is this characteristic of the Holy Land that has led to the rivalry and conflicts that have been prevalent for so many centuries. Now we have the additional problem that for the last fifty years or so, the religious beliefs and practices have become a prime factor in the growth of militant nationalism in this part of the world.[1] One could cite many instances from both the near and distant past when each of the religious groups suffered at the hand of another, either by insult, injustice, or worse. At any particular time in history, one faith appeared to have the upper hand, and the other two suffered because of this. The problem of Jerusalem is not a local problem, it is an international problem that transcends purely local issues, and therefore, since 1947, the solution to the problem has seemed to lie in the direction of some form of internationalization of the area.

Let us examine the history of internationalization of Jerusalem, as well as possible considerations for a current plan of internationalization. It should be remembered, however, that the government of Israel has declared the problem of Jerusalem is not negotiable; that the Arabs have taken a similar attitude; and that both parties concerned have in the past shown no interest in any internationalization schemes.

In the spring of 1947, after Britain declared that she wanted no further responsibility for Palestine and would refer the question of Palestine to the United Nations, a United Nation Special Committee on Palestine (UNSCOP) was established to report at the next regular session of the General Assembly. The Committee was instructed "to give most careful consideration to the religious interests in Palestine of Islam, Judaism, and Christianity."[2]

On November 29, 1947, the General Assembly recommended the partition of Palestine as suggested by the majority report of UNSCOP. Concerning Jerusalem, the resolution read:

> The City of Jerusalem shall be established as a *corpus separatum* under a special international regime and shall be administered by the United Nations. The Trusteeship Council shall be designated to discharge the responsibilities of the Administering Authority on behalf of the United Nations.[3]

The boundaries of Jerusalem were to include the municipality plus the surrounding villages and towns, including Abu Dis to the east, Bethlehem to the south,

Ein Karim and Motsa to the west, and Shu'fat to the north (see Figure 7-1). This area comprised about 100 square miles and a population of over 200,000 people. The Trusteeship Council was to draw up a detailed statute for the administration of the city within five months. This, of course, was never put into effect, for by that time there had been considerable fighting in Jerusalem, and the city had already been divided.

In December 1948, the General Assembly passed a resolution setting up a Palestine Conciliation Commission (PCC), which was directed to prepare a plan for a permanent international regime—with maximum autonomy—for Jerusalem. In the fall of 1949, when the plan was presented, it failed to pass, for there was developing a significant difference of opinion in the interpretation of internationalization: should it be territorial or functional internationalization?

Territorial internationalization referred to the placing of a specific area under international administration, as envisaged in the 1947 resolution—that is, a *corpus separatum*. Functional internationalization referred to the development of some form of international area. The former concept, territorial internationalization, was supported at the time by the Vatican, and hence by most Roman

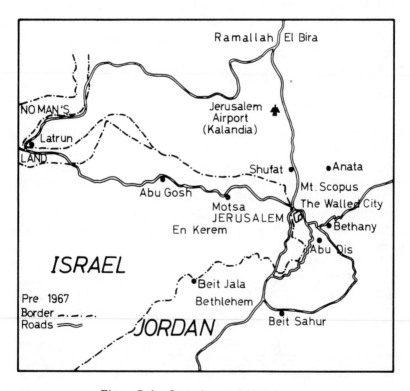

Figure 7-1. Jerusalem and Vicinity.

Catholic states, and by the Arab states with the exception of Jordan, which
wanted no international regime for Jerusalem. Functional internationalization
was supported by most of the Protestant states and, at least in the beginning, by
Israel.[4]

The PCC plan was neither fully territorial nor fully functional in scope,
and it was not approved by the Assembly, nor was a plan for functional internationalization as proposed by the Netherlands and Sweden. The Assembly
reaffirmed its support for full territorial internationalization and again instructed
the Trusteeship Council to prepare a plan for the city.

This plan was completed, but when it was presented to Jordan and Israel,
neither country would accept it. The Council therefore reported to the General
Assembly that it was taking no further action. In December 1950, a Belgian plan
calling for territorial internationalization failed to pass, and a subsequent Swedish
resolution for functional internationalization never came up for a vote. For the
next 17 years the question of Jerusalem lay dormant.

In the meantime, a partition of Jerusalem had been completed, as a result of
the Arab–Israel war of 1948–49. The fight for Jerusalem had begun within days
after the partition resolution had been passed. The battle line, with few exceptions, followed closely the communal division of the city, and on November 30,
1948, a cease fire in the Jerusalem area was completed. It found the Arab Legion
in control of the Old City of Jerusalem as well as those areas designated in the
original *corpus separatum* plan to the east, south, and north of the city. Jews
were denied access to their holy sites within the territory. And so conditions
remained until June 7, 1967.

The de facto partition of Jerusalem lasted some 19 years. The line of partition, although technically only a cease fire line, was a solution to a complex
political, economic, and sociological problem. During the 19 years that Jerusalem
was divided, the factors that had originally divided these peoples became even
more pronounced. It is difficult to imagine any single municipal charter that
could bridge the cultural, economic, and ideological gap between the Israeli of
West Jerusalem and the Arab of East Jerusalem but at the same time allow each
individual to maintain some evidence of self-identity.

The partition of Jerusalem reflected the diverse economic orientations of
East and West Jerusalem. East Jerusalem served as a market center of the West
Bank Territory, and the commercial, communication, and transportation links of
the areas of Judea and Samaria focused on the city. It was a vital part of the
economic structure of the West Bank prior to 1967. However, West Jerusalem
was not in ecological relationship with the rest of Israel. It developed into an
urban complex with the administrative offices of the government of Israel,
Hebrew University, and various administrative branches of world Jewry located
in the city by choice, not by economic necessity.

Ideologically, the gap between the residents of East and West Jerusalem
seemed irreconcilable. The Arab of East Jerusalem derived his entire identity

from his "Arabism." No matter how violent the character of inter-Arab difficulties, it was still to Arab nationalism that the East Jerusalemite turned for a definition of the situation. The Jew of West Jerusalem was a part of a political movement that was more than just Israel; it was a movement that was in constant and significant relationship with all of world Jewry. The Jew of West Jerusalem looked westward; the Arab of East Jerusalem looked east to other parts of the Arab world. In a real sense, the two parts of Jerusalem stood back to back ideologically. The partition line affirmed a division which had existed in the Holy City for half a century.[5]

In June 1967, after three days of heavy fighting in which both sides suffered considerable losses, East Jerusalem fell to the Israeli army. On the very day that the Jordanian sector of Jerusalem was brought under Israeli military control, Mayor Teddy Kollek of West Jerusalem put forward a plan to extend Israeli municipal services to the captured area.[6] On the following day, the Jerusalem Municipal Council approved a $5,000,000 Jerusalem Fund for the restoration of the Wailing Wall and other religious sites in the Jordanian sector. The Jerusalem Master Plan was expanded to include East Jerusalem. On June 8, the water system of West Jerusalem was connected with that of East Jerusalem, then shortly thereafter the sanitation, telephone, and electrical systems of the two sectors were united. The Egged bus service was extended to East Jerusalem although the Arab bus lines were not allowed to operate in West Jerusalem. The barriers separating Jerusalem were removed and extensive plans were undertaken for repaving roads, joining major highways, and designing parks in the vicinity of the walls of the Old City.[7]

Efforts toward political unification were also swift. On June 15, the Israeli Cabinet met to study a bill that would allow Israel to annex East Jerusalem. On June 27, the Knesset approved a series of enabling laws for the "fusion" of Jerusalem. On June 27, the Law and Administration Ordinance was passed that gave the State of Israel the right to extend to any area so designated by the Israeli government, the law, jurisdiction, and administration of the State of Israel. On June 28, 1967, Israeli law and administration were applied to an expanded East Jerusalem that included the walled city, Sur Bahir, Sheikh Jarrah, Kalandia Airport, Mount Scopus, and the vicinity of Shufat.[8] At later times, the area was expanded to extend to the borders of Bethlehem. Thus "unified" Jerusalem covered over 100 square kilometers and included a population of at least 260,000 people, some 70,000 of whom were Arabs.[9]

Within a week after the capture of Jerusalem, Israel razed some 100 homes in the vicinity of the Wailing Wall.[10] In the following month, 100 more homes were destroyed in the same area.[11] In 1968, the government expropriated land and buildings within the walled city that included more than 700 buildings, about 50 acres of land, 437 shops and 1,084 apartments housing more than 5,000 Arabs.[12] The Arabs were becoming increasingly concerned that Israel intended to alter the demographic character of East Jerusalem to make all of

Jerusalem a Jewish city. However, most of the expropriation has been confined to that sector of the Old City, known as the Jewish quarter.

On June 13, 1967, the question of Jerusalem once again came up at the United Nations, at an emergency special session of the General Assembly called to debate the Middle East Crisis. After extensive debate, the Assembly approved the following resolution:

The General Assembly
Deeply concerned at the situation prevailing in Jerusalem as a result of the measures taken by Israel to change the status of the City,

1.   Considers that these measures are invalid;
2.   Calls upon Israel to rescind all measures already taken and to desist forthwith from taking any action which would alter the status of Jerusalem;
3.   Requests the Secretary-General to report to the General Assembly and the Security Council on the situation and on the implementation of the present resolution not later than one week from its adoption.[13]

In the following months, additional calls were made upon Israel to refrain from integrating East Jerusalem. No national state in the world supported Israel's actions, but nevertheless, efforts towards integration went forward.

Early reports on conditions in Jerusalem expressed continued concern that the identity of the Arab would be lost in the integration process. In February 1968, Teddy Kollek complained that "efforts to integrate the two sectors of Jerusalem 'had been a total failure' because Israel had failed to recognize the cultural and psychological patterns of the Arabs and that the Israeli government '. . . cannot automatically impose on [the Arabs] the approach and procedures used in Tel Aviv.'"[14] For a period of time, Arab resistance to Israeli occupation was expressed in individual and group attacks on Israeli civilian and military targets, but over the longer period, an attitude of accommodation has developed, and in some areas, the Arabs, while continuing to resent the occupation, their loss of self-determination, and the higher taxes, have been able to prosper in the Old City. The Arabs are allowed to vote in municipal elections and had participated in increasing numbers until the election in December 1973, when only a small percentage of the electorate voted.

But what of the future of Jerusalem? As stated earlier, both Israel and Jordan have claimed that Jerusalem is not negotiable. In March 1972, while King Hussein was visiting the United States, he did propose a joint rule shared by Jordan and Israel over the administration of Jerusalem, as

. . . a unified, open city—a meeting place for the three great religions of the world. In the context of peace, Jerusalem could become an open city. It could be the capital of Israel and the capital of the Palestinian portion of Jordan. There is no reason why they cannot exist together.[15]

Any agreement would have to be based on Israel's recognition of sovereignty over the eastern portion of the city. Hussein rejected a return to a divided city as well as internationalization of the city. The king also noted in the interview that he had tested the Israeli reaction to his proposal on Jerusalem, and found it "violently negative."[16]

Of all the alternative plans proposed for the internationalization of Jerusalem perhaps the most promising is that of Evan M. Wilson, former U.S. Minister Consul General at Jerusalem. Wilson proposes a partial Territorial Internationalization of an area smaller than the *corpus separatum* of the 1947 plan, with Israel and Jordan controlling the remainder of the territory.[17] Any proposal should cover the Walled City, which is a finite area that can be identified readily and more easily administered than a larger area. The Old City also contains the most important shrines: notably the Church of the Holy Sepulchre, the Wailing Wall, and the Haram al-Sharif with the Dome of the Rock. There are a number of shrines that lie outside of the walls but nearby: the Mount of Olives (sacred to Muslims and Christians), the Garden of Gethsemane (Christian), and the Jewish tombs, which lie between the Old City and the Mount of Olives. Wilson also proposes that Mount Zion (sacred to all three faiths) be included in the international sector. These areas were in control of Jordan and Israel, respectively, prior to 1967, so counterbalancing concessions by each side would be involved.

Wilson also suggests that Government House (headquarters of the United Nations Truce Supervision Organization) and its surrounding U.N. enclave be included in the international zone, with a connecting corridor to the Walled City. However, since Government House is about one and a half miles from the Walled City, some topographical problems might be involved. Wilson also proposes that supreme authority for the international sector would rest with the United Nations, which would appoint a Special Representative to embody its presence in the city. A City Council, elected by the residents of the sector, would handle day-to-day administration of the municipal services. Some arrangements would be made to allow both Israel and Jordan to benefit from the revenues from tourism in the sector, and an agreement with respect to customs and currency matters and to citizenship of the residents would have to be established.

Access to all Holy Places would be guaranteed for all people, for even today Arab Muslims and Christians from other Arab countries do not have full access to Jerusalem. Protection of the Holy Places would be the responsibility of the Special Representative, but the maintenance and care of them would be the responsibility of the different religious communities.

Israel would be allowed to retain no-man's land, which it occupied in 1967, and with the exception of Mount Zion, she would be asked to give up no territory formerly in the Israeli sector. The New City would continue to be the capital of Israel. Israel would stand to gain respect in the international community that has opposed her annexation of Jerusalem, and she could anticipate the elimination of a serious source of friction with Christian and Muslim opinion.

In his report, Wilson concludes:

How and when such a proposal would be put forward and how to bring
in the various interested parties (not Jordan and Israel alone, but the
wider interests, Christians, Jewish and Muslim and the United Nations
itself) would have to be determined. But it seems clear that the two
countries most immediately affected are going to need some outside
assistance, and even outside pressure, if they are going to come to a
solution regarding Jerusalem.[18]

The Refugees

In 1967, after Israel had occupied the West Bank, a controversy arose with
the United Nations Relief Works Agency with regard to the number of refugees
living within the West Bank Territory. Part of the problem lay in the definition of
"refugee," for Israel counts only those who lived in Israel before June 1949. In
1970, according to UNRWA there were 1,425,000 refugees (in all countries) of
whom those aged 19 or more—that is, those who lived in Israel before June
1949—totalled about 580,000. Israel estimated that the total number of refugees
numbered between 1,050,000 and 1,100,000.[19] Of the total number on
UNRWA's lists, about 560,000 lived in refugee camps and of these 440,000 were
1949 refugees and 120,000 were refugees since 1967. On the West Bank, Israel
lists 57,800 "original" refugees whereas the UNRWA total is 73,100.[20] United
Nations sources, when discussing refugees, talk in terms of 272,692 living in the
West Bank Territory.[21]

There are few data available on the status of the refugees. One has only to
visit the various camps in the Territory to appreciate that there are perhaps half
as many living in the camps as in the pre-1967 period. The largest camp in Jericho
is almost completely deserted. The refugees on the West Bank fared much better
than those in the Gaza Strip, for instance, for the former were granted Jordanian
citizenship, and many were already being integrated into the productive sectors
of the economy. More efforts were expended to improve the camps and to
provide services, including educational outlets in addition to those provided by
UNRWA, and also some efforts were made to incorporate the younger men into
the labor force. The refugees in the Gaza Strip were not given Egyptian citizenship but only identity cards, were not offered opportunities for improvement,
and were thus on a much lower standard of living than those in the Territory.

Moshe Dayan's policy towards the refugees, a policy which has been carried
out de facto, appears to be directed towards a gradual blurring over of the status
of the 1948 refugees by finding employment for the inhabitants of the areas
and thus turning them into productive workers. Dayan has encouraged the municipalities to include the refugee camps in their tax systems and then to provide
services to the camps in return.[22]

In January 1968, Don Peretz published an article evaluating "Israel's Admin-istration and Arab Refugees."[23] In any discussion of the refugee problem, it is necessary to attempt to consider both the economic and social implications of resettlement. Israel argued for integration and rehabilitation of the refugee popu-lation and estimated the cost of the program at approximately $100 million. Israel hoped that the U.S. government would provide a substantial part and suggested that the United States shift contributions from UNRWA to Israel to assist in their program.[24]

Peretz discussed another plan, called "Model A," that envisioned resettling 2,000 Palestinian families by placing two-thirds in farming and one-third in other rural services. It was proposed that former Jordanian state lands would be utilized and technological improvements in agriculture would be introduced to enable profitable resettlement. Peretz indicated that details as to the number of land parcels per family, types of irrigation and crops, probable crop yields, and income and productivity estimates were projected.[25] This plan was apparently never implemented as no further information regarding it is available. In all the planning that was carried on regarding resettlement, Peretz reports that a "bewil-dering number and variety of committees were set up" involving ministers, directors-general of ministries, university professors, and specialists such as agronomists, urban planners, statisticians, demographers, agriculturalists, hydrolo-gists, and engineers, but no Arabs were included in the discussions.[26]

In June 1970, A Trust Fund Committee for the economic development and rehabilitation of refugees was appointed by the Israel government.[27] The func-tion of the committee was to raise the living standards of refugees by programs of economic development. Vocational training and industrial development were considered areas of vital importance, but the committee was also to concern itself with the necessary investments in infrastructure, such as road, water, and sewage systems. *The Israel Economist* commented:

> Since the committee is headed by Mr. Zandberg, who apart from his function as Chairman of the Industrial Development Bank enjoys spe-cial confidence of the Minister of Finance, Mr. Pinhas Sapir, the possibilities of inter-departmental friction that might have hamstrung its work have been reduced to a minimum.[28]

It appears that in the West Bank Territory little has been accomplished. In the Gaza Strip, there have been some accomplishments in resettling of refugee fami-lies in apartment complexes, and the introduction of some light industry.

In an address delivered at a special session of the Council of the David Horowitz Institute for Research on Developing Nations, in December 1971, Mr. Moshe Sanbar, Governor of the Bank of Israel, discussed "Peace and the Solu-tion of the Refugee Problem."[29] In any consideration of the refugee problem, it would be necessary to first discuss the problem of compensation. Should com-pensation be made on a personal or a "global" basis—that is, individual payment to each refugee based on the value of the property abandoned, or an overall payment based on the total number of refugees. If the latter, to whom would the payment be made? The problem would be to determine the level of compensation and to whom it was due. Israel always discusses compensation in terms of the value of the property in 1948, not at current values. This is one of the main stumbling blocks to negotiations regarding compensation. Sanbar stresses the importance of concentrating efforts on the resettlement as well as economic and social rehabilitation of the refugees, and he argues that the refugee problem within the areas must be solved within the framework of a comprehensive development program. There are two approaches: one would be to establish special settlements in which to absorb the refugees; the other, based on the extensive experience that Israel has had in absorbing refugees and immigrants, would be to raise the standard of living of the refugees and to integrate them into the existing population both socially and economically.[30] Local economies would have to be supported in order for them to supply employment and thus contribute to a balanced and complete absorption. Sanbar concludes:

> This cannot, of course, be implemented without a comprehensive financing scheme. Israel alone cannot shoulder the burden; the scheme would have to be based on international institutions, on the great powers, on the Arab countries and on Israel. Israel's participation would have to be limited to the amount of net compensation it would have to pay, allowing for the sums due to Jews who immigrated to Israel from Arab countries. I hope that an international fund would be able to raise the very substantial amounts required for implementing the development program and also examine the plans to be submitted by Arab countries for the development of particular areas.[31]

In February of 1972, *The Jerusalem Post* reported that Moshe Sanbar had proposed setting up an International Fund for Arab Refugees to Robert McNamara, president of the World Bank.[32] The fund would finance industrial and agricultural development in Arab areas and employ workers from those areas, including refugees. As proposed, the fund would also compensate the refugees for their displacement and supply housing and social services. The proposal received strong support from Israeli officials, including Finance Minister Pinhas Sapir, who continually expressed concern about the long-run implications of Arab employment in the Israeli economy. (See Chapter 5, The Industrial Sector.) No fund has yet been established.

In the meantime, economic accommodation appears to be taking place. The camps appear to be in better condition, with more public utilities available. The number of people who have left each camp has alleviated the extensive overcrowding, and those people who have remained in the camps appear to have been involved in the integration process. Many of the men have apparently joined the labor force and are employed within Israel. No distinction in the data regarding the labor force is made for refugees and non-refugees. So while plans and proposals are discussed, economic integration goes forward.

Jordan Valley Settlements

Although it was generally acknowledged that Israel was establishing settlements in the administered areas, little information regarding this activity was available in the press, with the exception of an occasional brief note listing the name and location of a recent settlement. However, early in 1973, the full significance of these settlements was made known. On February 7, 1973, it was reported:

> Defense Minister Moshe Dayan said tonight that any peace agreement Israel concluded with Jordan should include the right of Israelis to settle, anywhere on the West Bank of the Jordan River. The West Bank—I prefer to call it Judea and Shomron—is part of our homeland. Being our homeland, we should have the right to settle everywhere without visas or passports from anyone else. The Israeli Government should make sure that any peace agreement it signs included that right.[33]

The New York Times article indicated that Dayan felt, regardless of the cost, Israel would have to settle the areas at a faster pace than she had during the previous year. By February 1973, 49 military, paramilitary and agricultural settlements had been established in the administered areas; by 1975, there were 60 settlements.

Later in February 1973, another article in *The New York Times* reported that in November, Israel had begun work on a ten-mile section of a new highway along the occupied West Bank that could ultimately link Jerusalem with the upper Jordan Valley.[34] No word concerning the construction of the highway was released in the Israeli press. Terence Smith, a most highly respected correspondent for the *Times,* reported that the Israeli foreman at the site said that when completed the road would be wide enough to accommodate three lanes of traffic in each direction. When a spokesman was queried as to why a six-lane highway would be necessary to connect two small and isolated settlements (Gitit and Mechora), he responded that this was the new standard for "regional roads." The only other six-lane highways in Israel at present are portions of roads connecting Tel Aviv to Haifa and to Jerusalem.

If this ten-mile section of highway were extended along its present course, the new road would divide the West Bank roughly along the line proposed by Yigal Allon in his plan that envisioned an Israeli paramilitary "security belt" composed of settlements along the length of the Jordan River Valley from Beisan (in Israel) to Jericho. Allon had proposed that Israel retain such a strip while returning the more populated hilly regions of the West Bank to Jordan. Although an official map of this security belt was never released, it is assumed that it would correspond roughly to the ten-mile-wide area between the proposed new road and the Jordan River to the east (see Figure 7–2).[35]

In the February 1973 edition of *The Israel Economist,* a brief article appeared in the "Business Notes" under the heading "Agriculture," a category which followed several articles on the "Administered Areas."[36] Mr. Zvi Weininger of the Settlement Department of the World Zionist Organization reported that "the Jordan Valley crops have virtually escaped the ravages of the recent frost

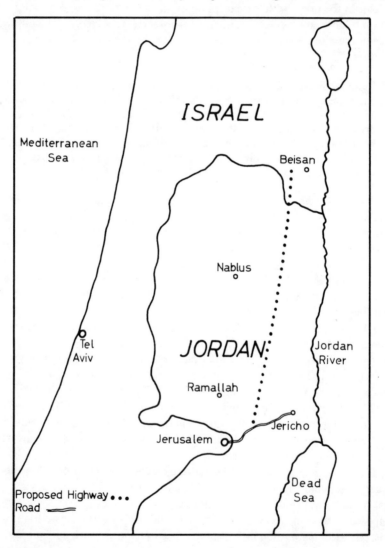

Figure 7–2. Proposed Highway Linking Kibbutzim in the Jordan Valley.

wave confirming the assumption of planners that the valley can eventually become 'the Hothouse of Europe.'"[37] The article went on to discuss the various settlements, both Nahal (paramilitary settlements engaged in agriculture) and Moshavim and the agricultural experiments that were being conducted. It reported that members of Gittit and Moshav Phasael had moved into permanent dwellings and that Gilgal would eventually become a regional center, according to the Israeli spatial plan. A request had been submitted to the government to build an airstrip in the Valley to fly winter produce directly to Europe. Mr. Weininger added:

> We know very little about agriculture in the Valley and we spend much money on experiments. We have introduced Californian palms, which thrive on salty water, while the Kalia settlement is planning to establish a dairy with cows from Arizona, which are believed to be able to stand the climate well.[38]

It was also reported that fish ponds were being established (a profitable industry in the pre-1967 period), and experimentation with papaya trees, vineyards, and gladioli nurseries were being undertaken. All this activity would seem to confirm the attitudes as expressed by Dayan that these settlements were viewed by the government as permanent establishments, for why else would so much be invested in the Valley? The produce from these settlements is not included in the agricultural data of the Territory and must be counted as a part of Israeli agricultural produce.

Prospects for the Future

The difficulty in evaluating the above-mentioned problems is that they are more of a sociopolitical nature than of an economic nature. The two major problems that would have to be considered in any planning for the establishment of a nation are a territorial problem and the refugee settlement problem. It is most unlikely that the area of Jerusalem will be easily given up by Israel, and it seems apparent that she intends to settle and hold the "security belt" along the length of the Jordan Valley. We originally defined the West Bank Territory as extending from the Jordan River west to the cease fire lines established in 1948, which comprises, roughly, historical Judea and Samaria. If the land area of greater Jerusalem is not negotiable, then the newly defined Territory would be stripped of its natural market center and capital, as well as of its main center of tourism, which industry could generate considerable foreign exchange reserves. Many of the well-educated Arabs live in Jerusalem, as well as many who were formerly highly placed in government and judicial positions. Unless these people were willing to move, their services, abilities, and training would be lost to the new state.

The area from the Jordan River west in the "security belt," some ten miles into the Territory, includes some of the most potentially productive agricultural land available. The climate in the area would favor year-round cultivation and to develop this land, it is only necessary to provide a supply of water. Israel has already established permanent settlements in the area and has begun to develop the agricultural potential of the land. Capital investment includes housing, irrigation systems, farm buildings, roads, and a proposed air strip to facilitate export of produce to Europe. Were this area from the "belt" to the River, from Jericho north to Beisan, to be also excluded from the Territory, then the last possible area of agricultural expansion would be lost to the new state. As in many developing areas, and particularly in the Middle East, agriculture is a major sector of the economic structure of the Territory. Short-term improvement programs are operating successfully in the sector, and any long-term improvement will be dependent upon capital investment in developing water sources and irrigation systems and in developing potentially productive areas not previously cultivated. If the area in the Jordan Valley is lost to the Territory, the last most potentially productive agricultural area will be lost.

And finally, if the plan of integrating the refugee population into the economy continues to progress as it appears to be, then before long the refugee "problem" may be alleviated. If the refugees are removed from the lists of the various international organizations, then there will be a substantial decrease in the amount of aid and support that the inhabitants will receive from UNRWA and other organizations. Negotiations would have to include some consideration of compensation for the properties lost by the refugees in 1948. One of the problems arising is that Israel proposed compensation based upon land values in 1948, and few Arabs have been willing to forego their claim to property based on such a compensation plan. The Territory could benefit greatly from the experience that Israel has had in the integration of people into a country, but this would be a long-term process and would probably be successful only if there were continued cooperation with international organizations.

How can these problems be overcome? It is difficult to imagine any solution for Jerusalem, for it is more of a religious problem than either a political or economic problem. Internationalization might be a consideration, but as discussed above, none of the immediately affected parties favors internationalization. Israel might be willing to negotiate the Jordan Valley settlements, but only in exchange for some type of defense agreements, for Israel feels that maintaining a position in the valley is essential for the defense of her eastern borders. It is difficult to imagine how the West Bank Territory as a new Palestine would be able to guarantee security along Israel's borders, unless in the settlement with Jordan some accommodations were made. If the Territory were stripped of the Valley areas, any significant development of agricultural potential would be severely limited.

It would be highly desirable to integrate the refugees into the economy and allow them to become a productive element in the new society. The Territory could benefit greatly from the vast experience that Israel has in relation to absorbing segments of the population, be they immigrants or refugees. It is probable that the international organizations would continue their support until the refugees were able to be absorbed into the economy.

Notes

1. Evan M. Wilson, "The Internationalization of Jerusalem," *Middle East Journal,* Vol. 23, No. 1 (Winter 1969), p. 1–2.
2. United Nations, Special Committee on Palestine, *Report to the General Assembly,* Vol. I, Doc. A/364 (1947), p. 27.
3. United Nations General Assembly Resolution 18 (II), Doc. A/519 (1947).
4. Wilson, "The Internationalization of Jerusalem."
5. Richard H. Pfaff, *Jerusalem: Keystone of an Arab–Israeli Settlement* (Washington, D.C.: American Enterprise Institute, 1969), pp. 33–34.
6. *The Jerusalem Post,* June 8, 1967.
7. United Nations, Security Council, *Official Records, Supplement for July, August and September, 1967,* Document S/8146.
8. Ibid.
9. Ibid.
10. *The New York Times,* June 19, 1967.
11. *The New Outlook,* September 1968, p. 39.
12. United Nations, Document A/7107 (S/8634).
13. United Nations, General Assembly, *Official Record, 5th Emergency Special Session,* Supplement 1, p. 4.
14. Pfaff, *Jerusalem: Keystone of an Arab–Israeli Settlement,* p. 42.
15. *The New York Times,* March 30, 1972. © 1972 by the New York Times Company. Reprinted by permission.
16. Ibid.
17. Wilson, "The Internationalization of Jerusalem," p. 9.
18. Ibid., p. 12.
19. Moshe Sanbar, "Peace and the Solution of the Refugee Problem," *Economic Review, Bank of Israel,* Vol. 39 (August 1972), pp. 128–9.
20. Ibid.
21. *The New York Times,* September 27, 1970.
22. "Two Approaches to the Administered Areas," *The Israel Economist,* Vol. XXVIII, No. 8 (August 1972), p. 205.
23. Don Peretz, "Israel's Administration and Arab Refugees," *Foreign Affairs,* Vol. 46, No. 2 (January 1968), pp. 336–47.
24. Ibid., p. 346.
25. Ibid., p. 347.
26. Ibid., p. 344.
27. "Refugee Turning Point," *The Israel Economist,* Vol. XXVI, No. 6 (June 1970), p. 129.

28. Ibid.
29. Moshe Sanbar, "Peace and the Solution of the Refugee Problem."
30. Ibid., p. 128.
31. Ibid.
32. *The Jerusalem Post,* February 28, 1972.
33. *The New York Times,* February 8, 1973. © 1973 by the New York Times Company. Reprinted by permission.
34. *The New York Times,* February 20, 1973.
35. Ibid.
36. *The Israel Economist,* Vol. XXIX, No. 2 (February 1973), p. 54.
37. Ibid.
38. Ibid.

8 Conclusions

Consider the definition of viability as it was developed in Chapter 1: a country will be regarded as economically viable if its economic characteristics permit it to experience sustained economic growth and rising welfare per capita. After having examined in detail the economic sectors of the West Bank Territory, it is now necessary to evaluate its potential for economic viability.

Throughout the analysis of the sectoral development, we have stressed the sociopolitical and religious determinants as they affect development in the West Bank Territory. It is sometimes claimed that such constraints, which are difficult to assess and almost impossible to quantify, are rather rigid. Perhaps their strength has been overestimated, for it appears that man and religion are more adaptable than many had believed, at least within the frame of reference of this study. This finding is supported by the research of the Inter-university Study.[1] In the short run, the effectiveness of these constraints is very important. In the long run, however, adaptation to change occurs, as is evidenced in all areas of the economy of the West Bank Territory.

But there is one very important constraint that must be taken into consideration explicitly when discussing the potential of the West Bank Territory—that is, the political relationship of the Territory with its neighbors. Though we do not know the precise political settlement that will eventuate in the Middle East, let us examine three major possible solutions and evaluate the potential economic prospects of the Territory within each of these. As a means of testing the viability concept, these possibilities will be considered: (1) the West Bank Territory in some close relationship or federation with Israel; (2) the Territory in federation with Jordan; (3) the Territory as a "Palestinian region." There are other alternatives, such as the establishment of the Territory as an independent state, but the problems of staffing a government, establishing a banking system, creating international contacts for both diplomatic and trading purposes, and so forth would so overwhelm the Territory's capabilities, economic as well as administrative, as to make complete independence impractical in the short run. The Israeli Military Government has already set up an administrative structure that did not exist in the Territory prior to 1967. The currency problem could be solved through expanded use of the dinar (see below). But for the sake of testing the viability definition, let us concentrate on the above proposals.

In Chapter 1 we discussed various developmental conditions with regard to labor force characteristics, entrepreneurship, capital and social overhead requirements, and so forth. Further on, it was concluded that another prerequisite for development is an extensive market. There are several potential markets for the West Bank Territory, but the full development of these markets will depend upon political considerations—that is, on the Territory's integration with and access to other markets in the region. Let us then examine the realization opportunities for developmental conditions as they would exist under each of the proposals for political settlement.

Federation with Israel

The quality and position of West Bank labor have been greatly improved since 1967, and some credit for these changes must go to the Israeli government. Great investments in vocational education and training are being undertaken and the programs are geared to the needs of the market. Israel has had extensive experience in retraining and integrating labor into its economy, and it has directed similar efforts at improving the quality of the Territory's work force. Israel has instituted social welfare programs, and workers now have available an increasing number of medical and health benefit schemes as well as various social benefits similar to those offered in more developed areas. The Labor Exchanges have facilitated mobility of labor and have also offered protection and counseling to the employees. Though these Exchanges are now geared primarily to the requirements of the Israeli labor market, with some modifications they could also serve the Territory's local market.

Knowledge, skills, capacities, and attitudes are all undergoing change. There is beginning to be a shift in emphasis in the formal education system as it adjusts to new demands for a problem-solving and work-oriented educated class. As full employment is achieved, future sources of labor will depend upon fuller employment of members of the Palestinian refugee population, and the increased entrance of women into the work force. Here Israel is also well prepared to serve the needs of the growing labor force. A major source of job opportunities for the population of the Territory is employment in Israel, and this source would be maintained in the federation. This may become an efficient and quantitatively important method through which Israeli entrepreneurship and capital can be combined with excess labor in the Territory. The Rand Study on the *Economic Structure and Development Prospects of the West Bank and the Gaza Strip*[2] estimates that by 1978, Israel will be able to absorb up to 75,000 workers from the administered areas (the West Bank and the Gaza Strip).[3] In the long run, it would of course be undesirable if the population of the West Bank would depend on employment opportunities in Israel. Employment opportunities within the Territory would open up in tandem with industrial development. To these possibilities we turn next.

The Rand Study estimated the expected rate of endogenous industrial growth in the West Bank Territory to be almost 5 percent per year.[4] This estimate conforms to the expected growth of domestic demand for industrial products. The study emphasized that Israel could assist by relaxing some existing constraints on output and by increasing the potential demand for West Bank industrial products. The relaxation of effective constraints would require provision of

1. Technical assistance to overcome some of the needs for skilled labor;
2. Managerial know-how, either in the form of technical assistance or by joint ventures;
3. Entrepreneurship, both public and private;
4. Marketing facilities and know-how to promote exports.[5]

One must be cautioned not to overestimate the likely effectiveness of Israel's assistance, however, since Israel's own industry is lagging because of a severe scarcity of some of the above prerequisites. Israel can become a source for additional stimulation to the West Bank's industrial growth by purchasing industrial products, and some of this is being done through subcontracting arrangements between Israeli firms and local firms within the Territory. With the effect of this Israeli aid and trade, the basic rate of growth of industrial production might increase from 5 percent to 10 percent per annum.[6]

Israel has already attempted to provide the West Bank Territory with some of the necessary technical infrastructure. Extensive road building has been undertaken, and the roads are well maintained. There has been some expansion of the electrical systems to tie in areas not previously electrified as well as to improve service in existing systems. Some areas have been allowed to import generating equipment while other areas have been tied into the Israeli electrical grids. Further improvement of the infrastructure will depend upon the amount of available capital. Israel is hard pressed to provide much of this, for the needs of her own country are extensive. However, the Territory will benefit from the technological know-how of Israel.

Israel has provided the Territory with an extensive market and has also allowed the Territory's agricultural sector to participate in Israel's export trade. As the agricultural sectors have become integrated, the interdependence of the Territory and Israel has increased. Some products in which the Territory was formerly self-sufficient are now imported from Israel. The Territory has greatly benefited from expert Israeli advice on planning, producing, and marketing within the agricultural sector.

Although the Territory would gain much from federation with Israel, there are important constraints to consider. The Palestinians would probably find themselves severed from the rest of the Arab world. This would not only interfere with traditional family ties, but would also limit the available market for both agricultural and industrial commodites. This federation would also create a bi-national state, and bi-national states have never functioned successfully.

There is no reason to assume that this arrangement would be an exception. Israel would be financially burdened to take on such a responsibility as well, for the various benefits that now are available only to those Arabs working in Israel would have to be extended to the total West Bank population.

In federation with Israel, the West Bank Territory would benefit from an integrated, but limited, agricultural sector and an integrated labor market. But it is unlikely that much additional investment would be directed to the Territory, for Israel has great investment needs of her own to fulfill. Arabs who might be potential investors would be cut off from the Territory or might be unwilling to invest in the Territory. The West Bank Territory would lose her contact with the Arab world, and this would include a diminution of the size of her potential markets. Israel would again be in a position in which she is cut off from trade with her immediate neighbors. Under these circumstances, it is unlikely that the Territory could achieve a rate of growth much beyond 6 percent per annum, which would not allow her to participate fully in the growth and welfare prevailing in the region. While such a rate might be compatible with the economic aspects of the viability definition, the political aspects are not likely to be met.

Federation with Jordan

Another possibility for the West Bank would be for the Territory to rejoin Jordan in a new affiliation, as proposed by King Hussein. The return to Hashemite rule, even under a federation arrangement, is not appealing to the West Bank residents nor to the Palestinians abroad. Although the Palestinians are more culturally advanced and better educated than the Jordanians, the Jordanians have become more politically cohesive as a result of their interaction with a "center," in this case, a kingdom. The Palestinians always have lacked a center and thus are fragmented politically. It is reasonable to assume that even in a federation the difficult relationships between the Jordanians and the Palestinians in the pre-1967 period would reassert themselves.

What of the economic conditions of development under such circumstances? Prior to 1967, little effort was directed at vocational training, except by some international agencies. There remains an unemployment problem on the East Bank, and it is reasonable to assume that the East Bankers would be given preference in employment in filling available vacancies. If the labor market in Israel were closed to the residents of the Territory, as it well might be in a new Jordanian federation, there would be an immediate dislocation of some 40,000 laborers with varying degrees of skills. Some of these could be absorbed within the local economy, but the majority would become unemployed. In the past, Palestinians emigrated to various Arab countries to find employment, but they were usually the better-educated, better-trained workers, and professional people. There has been little Arabic foreign demand for the unskilled and semi-skilled workers, since the surrounding countries have an abundance of these workers in their own economies. There would thus probably be widespread unemployment in the Territory.

Jordan would have little to offer the West Bank Territory in either entrepreneurial or managerial skills. Traditionally the Palestinians have been the suppliers of these skills to the Jordanians, but as we have seen, the Territory itself is now in need of trained people to provide these functions. It is unlikely that these talents can now be found anywhere in the Arab world on the scale they would be available in Israel. This is particularly true in view of the new oil wealth and the improved growth prospects of the Arab states.

In the pre-1967 period, Jordan expended little effort towards industrial development of the West Bank Territory. Whatever capital was available was used in the East Bank areas, particularly to expand the industrial area around Amman. As long as political control lies in the hands of the East Bankers, it is reasonable to assume that the same situation would exist within a new federation. It is probable, however, that the Territory would benefit from investment by the various oil-rich countries who are directing some of their new financial efforts towards development of the Arab world.

Since 1967, there have been structural changes in various sectors, particularly in the agricultural sector. The Territory had formerly exported melons to the East Bank and on to other Arab countries, as discussed above. The land on which the melons were grown has now been planted in commodities that are exported, via Agrexco, to Europe. In case of federation with Jordan, it would be necessary for the Territory to establish new trading relations with countries outside the Arab world to obtain maximum benefit from her crop specialization programs. It is questionable how well Jordan would be able to assist her in these efforts.

In the pre-1967 period, many Arab tourists traveled to the West Bank as religious pilgrims or for recreational purposes. This tourism provided an important source of revenue for the Territory. Much of this tourism, with the exception of family visits, was stopped after the Six Day War, but federation with Jordan would once again allow for the free flow of Arab tourism to the West Bank. This would provide employment as well as foreign exchange.

In comparison with the first solution and with present conditions, federation between the West Bank Territory and Jordan would restrict, rather than encourage, development of the Territory. It is unlikely that the Territory would benefit from capital inflows because of the traditional preference given to the development of the East Bank. Although the Territory would benefit from an expanded Arab market, at least as long as there is some political stability in the area and the conditions of 1970-71 did not reoccur,[7] it is impossible to conceive of a rate of growth in excess of 3 to 4 percent per annum under these conditions of a federation with Jordan. The level of social welfare and the standards of living might very well decline. The Territory could not achieve economic viability as defined for our purposes.

A Palestinian Region

The final alternative is the possibility of a "Palestinian region" that could arise in cooperation with Israel, in cooperation with Jordan, or more probably through a settlement with both of them.[8] The region might be restricted to the present Territory, or it might include the Gaza Strip and other areas. The disposition of the Jerusalem problem will have to be an integral part of the solution. The regional solution need not involve statehood of an area but could specify a semi-independent status. This type of political arrangement is not new, but it would have to be adapted to specific requirements of the Territory and its neighbors. The regional solution could arise from the practical relations with Israel, based on economic necessities and strategic requirements, as a result of a political settlement between Jordan and Israel. The longer the current association of the West Bank with Israel, the more marked will be Israel's effects on the economic and social development of the West Bank and perhaps the dependency of the West Bank on Israel. There are definite economic advantages to be gained within the region. In addition to these benefits, a Palestinian region may not be the realization of full justice, but at least it might be a step forward toward "practical justice."[9]

All of the benefits to be gained from federation with either Israel or Jordan individually might be had with the development of a Palestinian region supported by both: an extensive, well-developed labor market, with the continuing development of vocational and training programs, and a labor exchange; availability of entrepreneurial and managerial skills; interest in and deveolpment of a technological infrastructure; and extensive potential markets for a great variety of agricultural and industrial products. It is also reasonable to assume that with some political stability in the area, there would be more interest in investing by Arabs as well as by international institutions. Oil-rich Arab countries might also be prepared to participate in joint ventures requiring capital and technology inflows. An important advantage to be gained from good relations with the Arab world involves access to markets for both agricultural and industrial output of the Territory, and the benefits from specialization that this entails. It also would tend to increase the stability of the market (and thus, the economy) by diversifying across sources of demand and reducing the dependence upon any one source, such as Agrexco. Finally, this solution would imply a political stability that is not as likely to exist in previously discussed scenarios.

The Rand Study, in evaluating the potential of the Territory, estimated that agricultural production will increase on the average during 1973-78 at a rate of

about 6 percent.[10] This estimate is based on a variety of assumptions with respect to the period 1973–78:

1. A lower increase in local consumption resulting from a somewhat smaller
    rate of increase of population and of per capita consumption. A working
    assumption is an expansion of 4 percent.
2. Export to Europe will continue to increase at lower rates . . . . Export will
    constitute a significant proportion of the off-season market in Europe, but
    it will become increasingly difficult to expand it further.
3. Export to the EB (East Bank–Jordan) may continue to expand at a rate of
    3 percent.
4. Trade with Israel will be under the previous assumption of free trade, but
    expansion will be at a lower rate . . . .
5. Productivity will continue to increase at similar rates.[11]

A growth rate of 6 percent would not be as impressive as the rate of growth
in the period immediately following the Six Day War, but that rate was a short-
term achievement, as idle resources were re-employed and agricultural methods
were upgraded in a once-and-for-all way. But a rate of 6 percent would be
achieved only if free trade with all neighbors—that is, *all* regional markets—were
maintained. If there were relative political stability and if efforts towards regional development were fostered, it is reasonable to assume that there would
then be greater inflows of capital available for the development of water supplies. The growth rate would of course be higher with an increase in the water
supply. The Rand Study estimates that an addition of 200 million cubic meters
of water in the 1973–78 period would increase the average rate of economic
growth for that period to 9.4 percent.[12]

Likewise, within the context of regional development, it would be possible
for the endogenous expected rate of industrial growth in the West Bank Territory to be greater than the originally estimated rate of 5 percent,[13] which
conforms only to the expected growth of domestic demand for industrial
products. A greater rate of growth (8 percent) was estimated when free trade
with the neighboring Arab countries was considered possible.[14] The Rand Study
emphasized that Israel could assist by helping to overcome the existing constraints on output and by increasing the potential demand for West Bank
industrial products. This might allow the expected rate of industrial growth to
reach 10 percent per annum in the period 1973–78.

The labor force in the Territory has continued to grow and develop as a
result of an integrated labor market between the Territory and Israel. If there
were free mobility of labor within the region, the Arab states would also benefit
for they too would have access to a trained and skilled labor source. Perhaps, of
greater importance, if capital inflow occurs and if broadly based development
could proceed relatively securely and without interruption, there might be a
return of the Palestinian diaspora—those Arabs of the entrepreneurial and pro-

fessional classes who originally left the Territory for lack of job opportunities. This, of course, raises the problem of the absorption capacity of the Territory— that is, how many returnees can be integrated into the economy—but this must await further analysis.

There is yet another sector in which the West Bank Territory would benefit as a result of regional development: tourism. In the pre-1967 period, tourists were mainly European and American pilgrims and those from Arab countries coming for religious and recreational purposes. The lack of peaceful relations with Israel, difficulties in transportation between the West Bank and Israel, re- striction on travel, and prohibition of the travel of Jews in Arab countries prevented the full development of tourism in the Territory for foreign tourists. The free flow of tourists between the West Bank, Israel, and neighboring Arab states would increase the attractiveness of all areas.

Since 1967, Israeli facilities for tourists, which are mostly superior to those of the West Bank, have attracted the majority of tourists. The West Bank has had some benefits from tourist purchases of souvenirs and food during excur- sions in the Territory. The main source of tourism for the West Bank could be tourists from Arab countries. As discussed above, Arab tourism provided an im- portant source of revenue for the Territory and development of a Palestinian region would allow for the freer flow of Arab tourism to the West Bank. Reve- nues from tourism would provide the Territory with foreign currencies that could be used for development purposes. These revenues would also help to improve the balance of payments.

The regional solution opens the possibility for more rapid agricultural development, enhancement of industrial growth, and the revival of tourism. This would permit a less extreme form of "unbalanced growth" and would improve the conditions for the economic viability of the region. The West Bank Territory should continue along a path of unbalanced growth. Any investment funds available should be directed towards improvement in the agricultural sector, particularly towards the development of water supplies. Improved methods of production and marketing will make possible a greater export trade with Europe and other non-Arab countries, as well as with regional trading partners. The industrial sector is so poorly developed and would need such massive inflows of capital and technology to accomplish development that rapid development is literally impossible.

Additional funds available should be directed towards the continuing improvement of the labor force. More vocational and skill training centers should be established and greater efforts exerted towards training and re- training all potential members of the work force. This will also involve the development of an improved attitude towards the work ethic.

Few countries have been able to become viable when dependent upon agriculture alone. The West Bank would have a comparative advantage, for with a regional development plan she could specialize in agriculture. Continued development of the labor force through training and skill development would provide another source of growth for the Territory, particularly if there were free mobility of labor within the region. The Territory also would benefit greatly from increased tourism.

The development of a Palestinian region might also help to alleviate socio-political problems discussed earlier. There are certain actions by the Israel government that have not aided the economic condition of the Territory, and these have to do with decisions regarding territorial claims. The annexation of East Jerusalem has removed from the Territory the natural capital and market center. But of even greater importance, the religious center and one of the three most important sites of Islam has been lost to the Arabs. If agreement cannot be reached on internationalization of that part of Jerusalem known as the Old City, then the control of the city by Israel will have long-term adverse political implications for cooperation between Arabs and Jews. Furthermore, the settlement of the land in the Jordan Valley and the establishment of paramilitary kibbutzim have deprived the Territory of the last potentially productive, but undeveloped agricultural areas available. These territorial claims, in addition to reducing the size of the Territory, are serious sources of tension and unrest.

Also, some settlement of the refugee problem will be necessary in order to achieve a degree of peace. The refugees must be incorporated into society for they not only can serve as a source of labor, but the existence of the camps constitutes a destabilizing center of discontent.

All of these problems might be somewhat alleviated under the terms of a Palestinian region. If there were freedom of tourism, the religious center of Jerusalem would be available to all. Regional development might allow some of the area in the Jordan Valley to be developed for the benefit of the Arabs, as well as for the kibbutzim residents, particularly with reference to water sources. Any regional development plan would have to incorporate the refugees into the general population and labor force, and the resources available for improved housing, education, and training would be greater than under any plan of federation.

Only under regional development might adequate monetary arrangements be established. The regional integration outlined above, with the West Bank serving as a politically acceptable economic intermediary between Israel, Jordan, and other Arab states, might, in economic terms, indicate an optimum currency area. Yet the history of the different monetary systems of the various countries (with Jordan being a member of the sterling area and having a convertible currency, and the Israeli lire being inconvertible), together with the political constraints on a Palestinian region, will inevitably mean the continuance of two currencies in the region. The lire—as the currency received both from exports to Israel and as wage payments as the currency in use at higher levels of integration of government budgetary expenditures—will account for a growing share of total receipts by West Bank residents. The convertibility of the two currencies will be dependent upon the foreign exchange policies of Israel. On the other hand, a federation of the West Bank with either Jordan or Israel would, almost by definition, dictate a financial system dominated by and integrated with that system of the partner in the federation.

In summary, federation with Israel may work economically, but it will not work politically. Federation with Jordan may work politically, but it will not work economically. Neither solution meets our viability criterion. Of the three possible settlements, there is, in my opinion, only one that can be considered both economically and politically feasible: a Palestinian region. Assuming the Territory has economic and political relations with both Israel and the Arab world, one can estimate an overall growth of 8 percent per annum for the West Bank Territory, which rate is significantly greater than that estimated under either of the two federation proposals. This would be similar to the rate achieved by Israel in recent years. It may still be several years before the West Bank Territory can experience sustained economic growth, but economic viability will be approached in a shorter period under conditions of regional development than under any other possible plan. Social and political stability will surely be enhanced if regional partners can cooperate in economic endeavors. A Palestinian region could serve as an intermediary between Israel and the Arab world.

The hope for the future of the Middle East lies in the establishment of peaceful regional development. A Palestinian region might be the first building block in such a scheme. Economic necessities might create political realities.

Notes

1. Clark Kerr, John T. Dunlop, Frederick H. Harbison, and Charles A. Myers, *Industrialism and Industrial Man* (Cambridge, Mass.: Harvard University Press, 1960).
2. Haim Ben Shahar, Eitan Berglas, Yair Mundlak and Ezra Sadan, *Economic Structure and Development Prospects of the West Bank and the Gaza Strip* (Santa Monica, Calif.: The Rand Corporation, R839FF Sept. 1971).
3. Ibid., p. 126.
4. Ibid., p. 102.
5. Ibid., p. 103. Reprinted with permission.
6. Ibid., p. 104.
7. During this period Jordan's borders with Arab states were closed and Jordan severely restricted agricultural imports from the West Bank. See Chapter 4.
8. This idea has also been proposed by Yehoshafat Harkabi in *The Problem of the Palestinians* (Jerusalem: Israel Academic Committee on the Middle East, 1973).

9. Ibid., p. 9.
10. Ben Shahar et al., *Economic Structure* . . ., p. 95.
11. Ibid., p. 94. Reprinted with permission.
12. Ibid., p. 96.
13. Ibid., p. 102.
14. Ibid.

Bibliography

Books

Abidi, Aquil Hyder Hasan, *Jordan, a Political Study 1948–57*. New York: Asia Publishing House, Inc., 1965.

Abu-Lughod, Ibrahim, ed. *The Arab–Israeli Confrontation of June 1967: An Arab Perspective*. Evanston, Ill.: Northwestern University Press, 1970.

Agarwala, A.N. and S.P. Singh, eds. *The Economics of Underdevelopment*. London: Oxford University Press, 1958.

A.I.D. Economic Data Book Near East and South Asia. Washington, D.C.: Agency for International Development, 1971.

Alray, Gil Carl. *Attitudes Toward Jewish Statehood in the Arab World*. Jerusalem: Middle East Information Series, n.d.

Antonius, George. *The Arab Awakening*. New York: J.B. Lippincott Co., 1939.

The Arabs Under Israeli Occupation. Beirut: Institute for Palestine Studies, 1970.

Arnoni, M.S. *Rights and Wrongs in the Arab Israeli Conflict*. Passaic, N.J.: Minority of One Press, 1968.

Asher, Robert E. et al. *Development of the Emerging Countries*. Washington, D.C.: The Brookings Institution, 1962.

Avineri, S. ed. *Israel and the Palestinians*. New York: St. Martins Press, Inc., 1971.

Avnery, U. *Israel Without Zionists: A Plea for Peace in the Middle East*. New York: The Macmillan Publishing Company, Inc., 1968.

de Azcarati, Pablo. *Mission in Palestine 1948–52*. Washington, D.C.: The Middle East Institute, 1966.

Baer, Gabriel. *Population and Society in the Arab East*. Translated from the Hebrew, 1960. New York: Frederick A. Praeger, Inc., 1964.

Baber, A. *The Other Israel: The Radical Case Against Zionism*. New York: Doubleday and Company, Inc., 1972.

Baldwin, R.E. *Economic Development and Growth*. New York: John Wiley & Sons, Inc., 1966.

Basch, A. *Financing Economic Development*. New York: The Macmillan Publishing Company, Inc., 1964.

Bauer, P.T. *Economic Analysis and Policy in Underdeveloped Countries*. Durham, N.C.: Duke University Press, 1957.

Beling, W.A. and G.O. Totten, eds. *Developing Nations: Quest for a Model*. New York: Van Nostrand Reinhold Co., 1970.

Ben-Porath, Yoram. *The Arab Labor Force in Israel*. Jerusalem: Falk Institute for Economic Research, 1966.

155

Bentwich, Norman DeMattas. *Israel: Two Fateful Years 1967–69*. New York: Drake Publishers, 1972.

Ben Shahar, Haim, Eitan Berglas, Yair Mundlak, and Ezra Sadan. *Economic Structure and Development Prospects of the West Bank and The Gaza Strip.* Santa Monica, Calif.: The Rand Corporation, 1971.

Ben Shemich, A. *Taxation in Islam.* Baltimore: Johns Hopkins University, 1964.

Berger, M. *The Arab World Today.* New York: Doubleday-Anchor, 1964.

Bhagwati, Jagdish. *The Economics of Underdeveloped Countries.* London: World University Library, 1966.

Blanchard, R. and M. Du Buit. *The Promised Land.* New York: Hawthorn Books, Inc., 1966.

Bonne, A. *State and Economics in the Middle East.* London: Routledge and Kegan Paul Ltd., 1948.

Bovis, H.E. *The Jerusalem Question 1917–1968.* Stanford, Calif.: Hoover Institution Press, 1970.

Burns, E.L.M. *Between Arab and Israeli.* New York: I. Obolensky, 1963.

Caincross, A.K. *Factors in Economic Development.* London: Allen & Unwin, 1962.

Clark, C. and M.R. Haswell. *The Economics of Subsistence Agriculture.* 3rd. ed. New York: St. Martin's Press Inc., 1968.

Clawson, M., H.H. Landsberg, and L.T. Alexander. *The Agriculture Potential of the Middle East.* New York: American Elsevier Publishing Co., Inc., 1971.

Cohen, Abner. *Arab Border Villages in Israel.* Manchester: Manchester University Press, 1965.

Cohen, Aharon. *Israel and the Arab World.* New York: Funk & Wagnalls Publishing Co., 1970.

Cook, H.V. *Israel: A Blessing and a Curse.* London: Stevens & Sons, Ltd., 1960.

Cook, M.A., ed. *Studies in the Economic History of the Middle East.* London: Oxford University Press, 1970.

DeGregori, T.R. and O. Pi-Sunyer. *Economic Development.* New York: John Wiley & Sons, Inc., 1969.

Demas, W.G. *The Economics of Development in Small Countries with Special Reference to the Caribbean.* Montreal: McGill University Press, 1965.

Dodd, P. and H. Barakat. *River Without Bridges: A Study of the Exodus of 1967 Palestinian Arab Refugees.* Beirut: Institute for Palestine Studies, 1968.

Douglas-Home, C. *The Arabs and Israel.* London: The Bodley Head, 1968.

Draper, T. *Israel and World Politics.* New York: The Viking Press, 1968.

Economic Development of Jordan. Published by International Bank for Reconstruction and Development. Baltimore: Johns Hopkins Press, 1957.

Eisenstadt, S.N. *Essays on the Sociological Aspects of Political and Economic Development.* The Hague: Mouton, 1961.

Encyclopedia Britannica, 14 ed. Chicago: William Benton, 1972.

FAO Mediterranean Development Project Jordan Country Report. Rome: F.A.O., 1967.

The First Census of Population and Housing. Amman: The Government Press, 1961.

Fisher, E.M. and M. Cherif Bassiouni. *Storm Over the Arab World.* Chicago: Fallett Publishing Co., 1971.

Fisher, R. *Dear Israelis, Dear Arabs—A Working Approach to Peace.* New York: Harper & Row, Publishers, 1972.

Frankel, S.H. *The Economic Impact on Underveloped Societies.* Oxford: Blackwell Press, 1953.

Gabrieli, F. *The Arab Revival.* New York: Random House, Inc., 1961.

Gerschenkron, A. *Economic Backwardness in Historical Perspective.* Cambridge, Mass.: Harvard University Press, 1962.

Gibb, H.A.R. "The Reaction in the Middle East Against Western Culture." In *Studies on the Civilization of Islam,* edited by Stanford J. Shaw and William R. Polk. Boston: Beacon Press, 1962.

Glubb, Sir John Bagot. *A Soldier With the Arabs.* New York: Harper and Brothers, 1957.

Gray, C.S. *Resource Flows to Less-Developed Countries.* New York: Frederick A. Praeger, Inc., 1969.

Grunwald, K. and J.O. Ronall. *Industrialization in the Middle East.* New York: Council for Middle Eastern Affairs Press, 1960.

Hadawi, Sami. *The Arab Israeli Conflict (Cause and Effect).* Beirut: Institute for Palestine Studies, 1967.

——. *Palestine in Focus.* Beirut: Institute for Palestine Studies, 1968.

Hagen, E.E. *On the Theory of Social Change: How Economic Growth Begins.* Homewood, Ill.: Dorsey Press, Inc., 1962.

Halevi, N. and R. Klinov-Malul, *The Economic Development of Israel.* New York: Frederick A. Praeger, Inc., 1968.

Halpern, M. *The Politics of Social Change in the Middle East and North Africa.* Santa Monica, Calif.: The Rand Corp., 1963.

Harari, M. *Government and Politics of the Middle East.* Englewood Cliffs, N.J.: Prentice-Hall Inc., 1962.

Harbison, F.H. and C.A. Myers. *Education, Manpower and Economic Growth Strategies of Human Resource Development.* New York: McGraw-Hill Book Company, Inc., 1964.

Harris, G.L., ed. *Jordan: Its People, Its Society, Its Culture.* New Haven, Conn.: Human Relations Area Press, 1958.

Higgins, R. *United Nations Peacekeeping 1946-1967 Documents and Commentary.* London: Oxford University Press, 1969.

Hirschman, A.O. *The Strategy of Economic Development.* New Haven, Conn,: Yale University Press, 1958.

Hitti, P.K. *History of the Arabs.* London: Macmillan Publishing Company, Inc., 1970.

Hurewitz, J.C., ed. *Diplomacy in the Near and Middle East.* Princeton, N.J.: D. Van Nostrand Company, Inc., 1956.

——. *The Struggle for Palestine.* New York: W.W. Norton Co., 1950.

Industrial Estates in Europe and the Middle East. Published by U.N. Industrial Development Organization. New York: United Nations Press, 1968.

The Israel Year Book. Annual issues, 1967-1972. Jerusalem: Israel Yearbook Publishers, Ltd., 1969-73.

Jaguaribe, H. *Economics and Political Development—A Theoretical Approach and a Brazilian Case Study.* Cambridge, Mass.: Harvard University Press, 1968.

Jerusalem. Jerusalem: Keter Publishing House, Ltd., 1973.

Johnson, E.A.J. *The Organization of Space in Developing Countries.* Cambridge, Mass.: Harvard University Press, 1970.

Jordan Census of Housing. Amman: Department of Statistics Press, 1952.

Jordan. First Census of Population and Housing 1961. Amman: Department of Statistics Press, 1961.

Jordan 1965. Statistical Guide to Jordan. Amman: Department of Statistics Press, 1965.

Jurji, E.J. *The Middle East: Its Religion and Culture.* Philadelphia: Westminister Press, 1956.

Kanovsky, E. *The Economic Impact of the Six Day War.* New York: Frederick A. Praeger, Inc., 1970.

Kerr, C., J.T. Dunlap, F.H. Harbison, and C.A. Myers. *Industrialism and Industrial Man.* Cambridge, Mass.: Harvard University Press, 1960.

Khadduri, M.D. *The Arab–Israeli Impasse.* Washington, D.C.: Robert B. Luce, Inc., 1968.

Khadduri, M. and J.H. Lieberny. *Law in the Middle East.* Washington, D.C.: The Middle East Institute, 1955.

Khalaf, N.G. *Economic Implications of the Size of Nations: With Special Reference to Lebanon.* Leiden: E.J. Brill, 1971.

Khan, Tawfiq M., ed. *Middle Eastern Studies in Income and Wealth.* London: Bowes & Bowes, 1965.

Khouri, Fred J. *The Arab–Israeli Dilemma.* Syracuse, N.Y.: Syracuse University Press, 1968.

Kindelberger, C.P. *Economic Development.* New York: McGraw-Hill Book Company, Inc., 1958.

Kirk, George E. *Contemporary Arab Politics: a Concise History.* New York: Frederick A. Praeger, Inc., 1961.

Kraines, O. *Government and Politics in Israel.* London: Allen & Unwin, 1969.

Kuznets, S. *Economic Growth and Structure.* London: Heineman Educational Books Ltd., 1965.

———. *Economic Growth of Nations.* Cambridge, Mass.: Belknap Press of Harvard, 1971.

———. "Notes on the Take-Off." In *The Economics of Take-Off into Sustained Growth,* edited by W.W. Rostow. New York: St. Martin's Press, Inc., 1963.

Lall, A. *The U.N. and the Middle East Crisis 1967.* New York: Columbia University Press, 1968.

Landau, J.M. *The Arabs in Israel.* London: Oxford University Press, 1969.

Laquer, Walter Ze'ev, ed. *The Israel–Arab Reader.* London: Harmondsworth-Penquin Books, Inc., 1970.

———. *The Middle East in Transition.* New York: Frederick A. Praeger, Inc., 1958.

Laufer, L. *Israel and the Developing Countries: New Approaches to Cooperation.* New York: The Twentieth Century Fund, Inc., 1967.

Lenczowski, G. *The Middle East in World Affairs.* Ithaca, N.Y.: Cornell University Press, 1962.

———. *United States Interests in the Middle East.* Washington, D.C.: American Enterprise Institute for Public Policy Research, 1968.

Lerner, D. *The Passing of Traditional Society: Modernizing the Middle East.* New York: The Free Press, 1958.

Lewis, W.A. *The Theory of Economic Growth.* London: Allen & Unwin, 1959.

Longrigg, S.H. *The Middle East: A Social Geography.* Chicago: Aldine Publishing Co., 1964.

Lösch, A. *The Economics of Location*, 2nd rev. ed. Translated by Wolfgang F. Stolper. New Haven, Conn.: Yale University Press, 1954.

Magnus, R.H., ed. *Documents on the Middle East.* Washington, D.C.: American Enterprise Institute, 1969.

Manual on Economic Development Projects. New York: United Nations Press, 1958.

Marcy, G. "How Far Can Foreign Trade and Customs Agreements Confer Upon Small Nations the Advantages of Large Nations?" In *Economic Consequences of the Size of Nations,* edited by E.A.G. Robinson. New York: St. Martin's Press, Inc., 1960.

Meade, J.E. *The Economic and Social Structure of Mauritius.* London: Methuen Press, 1961.

Measures for the Economic Development of Underdeveloped Countries. Published by U.N. Secretariat, Department of Economic Affairs. New York: United Nations Press, 1951.

Mehdi, M.T. *Peace in the Middle East.* New York: New World Press, 1967.

Meier, G.M. *International Trade and Development.* New York: Harper & Row Publishers, 1963.

Meier, G.M. and R.E. Baldwin. *Economic Development.* New York: John Wiley & Sons, Inc., 1957.

Methods of Financing Economic Development in Underdeveloped Countries. Published by U.N. Secretariat, Department of Economic Affairs. New York: United Nations Press, 1949.

Meyer, A.J. *Middle Eastern Capitalism.* Cambridge, Mass., Harvard University Press, 1959.

Mezerik, A.G., ed. *The Arab Israeli Conflict and the United Nations.* New York: International Review Service, 1969.

The Middle East and North Africa. London: Oxford University Press, 1960.

Mikes, G. *Coat of Many Colors: Israel.* Boston: Gambit Inc., 1969.

——. *The Prophet Motive: Israel Today and Tomorrow.* London: Deutsch Press, 1969.

Mountjoy, A.B. *Industrialization and Under-developed Countries.* Chicago: Aldine Publishing Co., 1967.

Mundell, R.A. *International Economics.* New York: The Macmillan Company, 1968.

Musrey, A.G. *An Arab Common Market—A Study in Inter-Arab Relations, 1920-67.* New York: Frederick A. Praeger, Inc., 1969.

Myint, H. *The Economics of the Developing Countries,* 3rd. ed. London: Hutchinson University Press, 1967.

Myrdal, G. *Asian Drama, An Inquiry into the Poverty of Nations.* New York: Twentieth Century Fund, 1968.

Nolte, R.H. *The Modern Middle East.* New York: Atherton Press, Inc., 1963.

Nurske, R. *Patterns of Trade and Development*. New York: Oxford University Press, 1961.
——. *Problems of Capital Formation in Underdeveloped Countries*. Oxford: Blackwell Press, 1953.
Pack, H. *Structural Change and Economic Policy in Israel*. New Haven, Conn.: Yale University Press, 1971.
Patai, Raphael, ed. *Jordan*. New Haven, Conn.: Human Relations Area Files, 1957.
——. *The Kingdom of Jordan*. Princeton, N.J.: Princeton University Press, 1958.
Pearson, L.B. *Partners in Development*. New York: Frederick A. Praeger, Inc., 1969.
Peres, S. "Industrial Development in the Occupied Territories." In *Seminar*, published by Israel Academic Committee on the Middle East. Jerusalem: Ahva Press, 1971.
Peretz, D., E.M. Wilson, and R.J. Ward. *A Palestine Entity?* Washington, D.C.: Middle East Institute, 1970.
Peretz, D. *Israel and the Palestine Arabs*. Washington, D.C.: Middle East Institute, 1958.
Pincus, J.A. *Reshaping the World Economy*. Englewood Cliffs, N.J.: Prentice-Hall, Inc., 1968.
Polk, W.R. *Developmental Revolution North Africa, Middle East, South Asia*. Washington, D.C.: Middle East Institute, 1963.
Processes and Problems of Industrialization of Underdeveloped Countries. New York, United Nations Press, 1955.
Reese, H.C. et al. *Area Handbook for the Hashemite Kingdom of Jordan 1969*. Washington, D.C.: Government Printing Office, 1969.
Reisman, M. *The Promised Land*. Princeton, N.J.: Princeton University Press, 1970.
Report to the General Assembly. Prepared by United Nations Special Committee on Palestine. Vol. I, Doc. A/364. New York: United Nations Press, 1947.
Resistance of the West Bank Arabs to Israeli Occupation. New York: New World Press, 1967.
Rivlin, B. and J. Szyliowicz. *The Contemporary Middle East*. New York: Random House, Inc., 1965.
Robinson, E.A.G., ed. *Economic Consequences of the Size of Nations*. New York: St. Martin's Press, Inc., 1960.
——. *Problems in Economic Development*. New York: Macmillan Publishing Company, Inc., 1965.
Romdat, P. *The Changing Patterns of the Middle East*. New York: Frederick A. Praeger, Inc., 1961.
Rostow, W.W. *The Stages of Economic Growth*. Cambridge, England: Cambridge University Press, 1960.
Roth, G. and C. Wittich, eds. *Economy and Society*. 3 vols. New York: Bedminster Press, 1968.

Sachar, H.M. *Europe Leaves the Middle East, 1936–54.* New York: Alfred A. Knopf, 1972.

Scitovsky, T. "International Trade and Economic Integration as a Means of Overcoming the Disadvantages of a Small Nation." In *Economic Consequences of the Size of Nations,* edited by E.A.G. Robinson. New York: St. Martin's Press, Inc., 1960.

Search for Peace in the Middle East. Philadelphia: American Friends Service Committee, 1970.

Shair, K.A. *Planning for a Middle Eastern Economy.* London: Chapman & Hall, 1965.

Sharabi, H. *Palestine and Israel–The Lethal Dilemma.* New York: Pegasus, 1969.

Shonfeld, A. *The Attack on World Poverty.* London: Oxford University Press, 1960.

Shwadian, B. *Jordan, A State of Tension.* New York: Council for Middle Eastern Affairs Press, 1959.

Smith, H.H. et al. *Area Handbook for Israel.* Washington, D.C.: Government Printing Office, 1970.

Sparrow, G. *Modern Jordan.* London: Allen & Unwin, 1961.

Stetler, R. ed. *Palestine–the Arab–Israeli Conflict.* San Francisco: Ramparts Press, Inc., 1972.

Stevens, G.C., *Jordan River Partition.* Stanford, Calif.: Stanford University Press, 1965.

———, ed. *The United States and the Middle East.* Englewood Cliffs, N.J.: Prentice-Hall, Inc., 1964.

Studies on Selected Development Problems in Various Countries in the Middle East. New York: United Nations Press, 1968.

Tatah, K.A. *Dynamite in the Middle East.* New York: Philosophical Library, Inc., 1955.

Taylor, A.R. and R.N. Setlie. *Palestine: A Search for Peace.* Washington, D.C.: Public Affairs Press, 1970.

Teveth, S. *The Cursed Blessing: The Story of Israel's Occupation of the West Bank.* New York: Random House, Inc., 1971.

Tinbergen, J. *Lessons from the Past.* Amsterdam: Elsevier Publishing Co., 1963.

———. *Shaping the World Economy.* New York: Twentieth Century Fund, Inc., 1962.

Triffin, R. "The Size of the Nation and Its Vulnerability to Economic Nationalism." In *Economic Consequences of the Size of Nations,* edited by E.A.G. Robinson. New York: St. Martin's Press, Inc., 1960.

Warriner, D. *Land Reform and Development in the Middle East,* 2nd ed. London: Oxford University Press, 1962.

Weber, M. *Economy and Society,* edited by Guenther Rath and Claus Wittich. New York: Bedminster Press, 1968.

Wilson, E.M. *Jerusalem, Key to Peace.* Washington, D.C.: Middle East Institute, 1970.

Wolf, L. *The Passion of Israel.* Boston: Little, Brown & Co., 1970.

Articles in Periodicals

"The Activities of the Ministry of Labor in Judea, Samaria, the Gaza Strip and
   Sinai—A Progress Report." *The Israel Economist,* Vol. XXIX, No. 3 (March
   1973).
"Administered Areas Peaceful Revolutionary Development. *The Israel Econo-
   mist,* Vol. XXIX, No. 1 (January 1973).
Becker, G.S. "Investment in Human Capital: a Theoretical Analysis." *Journal of
   Political Economy,* Vol. 70, No. 5 (October 1962), supplement.
Bingman, B.K. and J. Clark, "Labor in Israeli-Occupied Arab Territories." *Labor
   Development Abroad,* Vol. 15, No. 1 (January 1970).
"Business Notes: Administered Areas." *The Israel Economist,* Vol. XXVI, No.
   8–9 (August–September 1970).
Chenery, H. "The Role of Industrialization in Development Programs." *American
   Economic Review Proceedings,* Vol. 45, No. 2 (May 1955).
Chenery, H. and A. Strout. "Foreign Assistance and Economic Development."
   American Economic Review, Vol. 56, No. 4 (September 1966).
Cunningham, N.J. "Public Funds for Private Enterprise: The International
   Finance Corporation." *The Journal of Development Studies,* Vol. 2, No. 3
   (April 1966).
Dawson, R.H. "Where is the Middle East?" *Foreign Affairs,* Vol. 38, No. 3
   (March 1960).
Dominguez, L.M. "Economic Growth and Import Requirements." *The Journal
   of Development Studies,* Vol. 6, No. 3 (April 1970).
Eayrs, J. and R. Spencer, ed. "Middle Eastern Reverberations." *International
   Journal,* Vol. XXIII (Winter 1967–68), special issue.
Eisenman, R. "How the West Bank Views Terrorism." *Bulletin of the American
   Academic Association for Peace in the Middle East,* No. 1 (October 1972).
Feron, J. "Time Stands Still in an Israeli-Occupied Town." *The New York Times
   Magazine,* May 17, 1970, p. 30.
"Five Year Plan Predictions." *The Israel Economist,* Vol. XXVII, No. 6 (July
   1971).
"Five Years Israel Administration in Judea and Samaria." *The Israel Economist,*
   Vol. XXVIII, No. 9–10 (September–October 1972).
Harkabi, Y. "The Position of the Palestinians in the Israeli–Arab Conflict and
   Their National Covenant (1968)." *New York University Journal of Inter-
   national Law and Politics,* Vol. 3, No. 1 (Spring 1970).
Hudson, M. "The Palestinian Arab Resistance Movement: Its Significance in the
   Middle East Crisis." *Middle East Journal,* Vol. 23, No. 3 (Summer 1969).
"Israel Guarantees Loans in Administered Areas." *The Israel Economist,* Vol.
   XXIX, No. 1 (January 1973).
Issawi, C. "Growth and Structural Change in the Middle East." *Middle East Jour-
   nal,* Vol. 25, No. 3 (Summer 1971).
Kanovsky, E. "Arab Economic Unity." *Middle East Journal,* Vol. 21, No. 2
   (Spring 1967).
Kleiman, E. "The Place of Manufacturing in the Growth of the Israeli Economy."
   Journal of Developmental Studies, Vol. 3, No. 3 (April 1967).

Lewis, B. "The Arab–Israeli War—The Consequences of Defeat." *Foreign Affairs,* Vol. 46, No. 2 (January 1968).

"More Fruit to Come from Judea & Samaria." *The Jerusalem Post,* July 28, 1971.

"News Briefs—Areas." *The Israel Economist,* Vol. XXVIII, No. 6 (June 1972).

Peretz, D. "Israel's Administration and Arab Refugees." *Foreign Affairs,* Vol. 46, No. 2 (January 1968).

———. "Israel's New Arab Dilemma." *Middle East Journal,* Vol. 22, No. 1 (Winter 1968).

Raphaeli, N. "Military Government in the Occupied Territories: An Israeli View." *Middle East Journal,* Vol. 23, No. 2 (Spring 1969).

"Refugee Turning Point." *The Israel Economist,* Vol. XXVI, No. 6 (June 1970).

Rosenstein-Rodan, P.N. "Problems of Industrialization of Eastern and Southeastern Europe." *The Economic Journal* (June–September 1943).

Rubenstein, A. "A Sort of Social Revolution." *The New York Times Magazine,* May 6, 1973, p. 34.

Sanbar, M. "Peace and the Solution of the Refugee Problem." *Economic Review, The Bank of Israel,* Vol. 39 (August 1972).

Schatz, S.P. "The Role of Capital Accumulation in Economic Development." *Journal of Developmental Studies,* Vol. 5, No. 1 (October 1968).

Schultz, T.W. "Investment in Human Capital." *American Economic Review,* Vol. 51, No. 1 (March 1961).

Tuma, E.H., "Agrarian Reform and Urbanization in the Middle East." *Middle East Journal,* Vol. 24, No. 2 (Spring 1970).

"Two Approaches to the Administered Areas." *The Israel Economist,* Vol. XXVIII, No. 8 (August 1972).

Ward, R. "The Long Run Employment Prospects for Middle East Labor." *Middle East Journal,* Vol. 24, No. 2 (Spring 1970).

"West Bank Farm Output Doubles in Four Years." *The Israel Economist,* Vol. XXIX, No. 2 (February 1973).

"The West Bank's Agricultural Revolution." *The Jerusalem Post Magazine,* June 2, 1972.

Wilson, E.M. "The Internationalization of Jerusalem." *Middle East Journal,* Vol. 23, No. 1 (Winter 1969).

Wykstra, R.A. "Economic Development and Human Capital Formation." *Journal of Developing Areas,* Vol. 3, No. 4 (July 1969).

Yost, C.W. "The Arab–Israeli War—How It Began." *Foreign Affairs,* Vol. 46, No. 2 (January 1968).

Miscellaneous

A Helping Hand. (The Activities of the Ministry of Social Welfare in Judaea and Samaria.) Jerusalem: *The Israel Economist,* 1970.

The Administered Areas: Aspects of Israeli Policy. Jerusalem: Ministry of Foreign Affairs, 1973.

Administered Areas Bulletin, no. 8. Jerusalem: Israel Central Bureau of Statistics, 1971.

The Administered Territories. (Additional Data from the Sample Enumeration.) Jerusalem: Israel Central Bureau of Statistics, 1970.

L'Administration Israelienne en Judee-Samaire et à Guza, Progrès et Réalisations. Tel Aviv: Ministère de la Défense, 1969.

Alon, Dafna. *Arab Racialism.* Jerusalem: *The Israel Economist,* 1969.

American Interests in the Middle East. Washington, D.C.: Middle East Institute, 1969.

The Arab Israeli Conflict Before 1967 and Since. Jerusalem: Israel Information Center, 1973.

The Arabian Peninsula and Jordan. Economist Intelligence Unit, *Quarterly Economic Review.* London: Spencer House, 1970.

Aumann, Moshe. *Land Ownership in Palestine 1880–1948.* Jerusalem: Israel Academic Committee in the Middle East, n.d.

Bank Leumi–Economic Review. Various annual issues. Jerusalem, 1967–72.

Bavly, Dan and David Farhi. *Israel and the Palestinians.* Pamphlet No. 29. London: Anglo-Israel Association, 1971.

Census of Population, 1967. Publication No. 12. Jerusalem: Israel Central Bureau of Statistics, 1970.

Demographic Characteristics of the Population in the Administered Areas. (Data from Sample Enumeration.) Jerusalem: Israel Central Bureau of Statistics, 1968.

Economic Survey of the West Bank. (Summary.) Jerusalem: Prime Minister's Office–Economic Planning Authority, 1967.

The Economy of the Administered Areas. Various annual issues. Jerusalem: Bank of Israel, 1970, 1971, 1972, 1974.

Harkabi, Y. *The Problem of the Palestinians.* Jerusalem: Israel Academic Committee on the Middle East, 1973.

Housing Conditions, Household Equipment, Welfare Assistance and Farming in the Administered Areas. Jerusalem: Israel Central Bureau of Statistics, 1968.

Industrial Development in the Arab Countries. New York: United Nations Publication, 1967.

The International Herald Tribune. Various issues.

The Israel Economist. (Monthly periodical, published in English, in Jerusalem.) Various issues.

Jerusalem: Issues and Perspectives. Jerusalem: Hamakor Press Ltd., 1973.

The Jerusalem Post. (English daily newspaper published in Jerusalem.) Various issues.

Labour Force. Jerusalem: Israel Central Bureau of Statistics, 1968.

Monthly Statistics of the Administered Areas. Jerusalem: Israel Central Bureau of Statistics, 1971–72.

The New Outlook. (News magazine published in Israel.) Various issues.

The New York Times. Various issues.

Palestine Refugees–Aid With Justice. Geneva: World Council of Churches, 1970.

Pfaff, Richard H. *Jerusalem: Keystone of an Arab-Israel Settlement*. Washington, D.C.: American Enterprise Institute for Public Policy Research, 1969.

Quarterly Statistics of the Administered Areas, 1973. Jerusalem: Israel Central Bureau of Statistics, 1973.

Secure and Recognized Boundaries. Jerusalem: Carta, 1971.

Stendel, Ari. *Arab Villages in Israel and Judea-Samaria—a Comparison in Social Development*. Jerusalem: *The Israel Economist*, 1969.

Survey of Families in the Administered Areas. Jerusalem: Israel Central Bureau of Statistics, 1971.

United Nations, Document A/7107 (S/8634).

——, General Assembly, Resolution 18 (II), Document A/519 (1947).

——, General Assembly, *Official Record, 5th Emergency Session*, Supplement 1.

——, Security Council, *Official Records, Supplement for July, August and September, 1967*, Document S/8146.

West Bank of the Jordan, Gaza Strip and Northern Sinai, Golan Heights. (Data from full enumeration.) Jerusalem: Israel Central Bureau of Statistics, 1967.

When Arab and Jew Meet: Life in the Israel Administered Areas. New York: Israel Information Services, 1968.

Index

Abdullah, Emir, 19–20, 22
Agrexco, 77, 89
agriculture: budget allocations, 79; comparative advantage in, 150–151; constraints upon, 88–89; crop improvement program, 73; development programs, 25, 70–71; five-year plan, 75; labor, 64, 74–75, 84; limited capital, 70–71; natural resources, 64–65; new markets, 76–77; of Jordan Valley settlements, 139; output, pre-June, 1967, 67; policy, 76–77; post-1967 objectives, 72; potential, 148–149; products for industry, 96; purchased inputs, 84; role in development, 63; size of farms, 66; trading, 70; trade with Israel, 58; trade with Jordan, 51, 53, 59; water development, 67, 79. *See also* field crops; fruit; livestock; olives; productivity; vegetables
Agricultural Credit Corporation (Jordan), 71
Allon, Yigal, 138
Amiad, Ariel, 25
Arab Conquest, 18
Asefa, al-, 22

balance of payments, 47, 55
Balfour Declaration, 19
Bank of Israel, 14, 96
banks, 59–61; revised loan regulations, 79
barter, 1–2
Bedouin, 18
Beir Zeit College, 111
Bhagwati, J., 12
bi-national state, 33–34, 145–146
border adjustments, 1920–1967, 21f, 24f
British Mandate, 19–22, 128

capital investment: requirements for industrialization, 6–7, 93, 104; sources of, 102–103
Central Bureau of Statistics (Israel), 13, 65
Clawson, M. (Clawson-Landsberg-Alexander study), 85
construction, 49; 1967–1972, 98–100; workers in Israel, 118. *See also* labor
Consumer Price Index, 43f

consumption, 46–47; effect on imports, 53
cooperative societies, 124
credit: "directed," 79; extended by banks, 60; farm, pre-1967, 71
customs duties, 51, 53, 59, 102

Dayan, Moshe, 71; on settlements, 137, 139; policy re areas, 100–103; policy re refugees, 135
Demas, William G., 9
devaluation, August, 1971, 42
development, conditions of: capital requirements, 4; labor force characteristics, 3–4; social aspects of, 8–9. *See also* industry
domestic product, 49

East Bank. *See* Transjordan; Hashemite Kingdom of Jordan
econometric models, for area, 14
economic integration: in agriculture, 81, 89; of refugees, 137; towards freer trade, 11; with Israel, 51, 56; with Israel and Gaza, 41, 43–44
economic viability, 12–13, 143
economies of scale. *See* nations, size of
Economy of the Administered Areas, 14
education, 111, 120–121, 144; higher education, 112–112; vocational training, 111, 123–124
Egypt, 22, 26–27
emigration, 37, 40, 113, 115
employment, 37–44, 112, 115–120; in Israel, 117–119; occupational composition, 117; participation rate, 115–116
entrepreneurial ability; from diaspora, 149–150; need for, 3, 6–7
Eretz Israel, 33
exports, 42

Family Surveys, 118, 119
FAO Mediterranean Development Project-Jordan, 13
farms, type of, 65. *See also* agriculture
Fatah, al-, 22
federation with Israel, 114–146; constraints, 145–146; estimated growth, 146

167

About the Author

Vivian A. Bull is professor of economics at Drew University. She received the B.A. from Albion College, Michigan, and the Ph.D. from New York University Graduate School of Business Administration. Additional experience has included studies at the University of Oslo, Norway, and the London School of Economics, and resident director of the Drew University Semester on the European Community, Brussels (Fall 1974). Dr. Bull's first trip to the Middle East was in 1957 and since then she has made ten more trips for study, research and archaeological work.